Extending
Children's Mathematics

Fractions and Decimals

Extending
Children's Mathematics

Fractions and Decimals

SUSAN B. EMPSON

LINDA LEVI

Foreword by Thomas P. Carpenter

HEINEMANN
Portsmouth, NH

Heinemann

361 Hanover Street

Portsmouth, NH 03801–3912

www.heinemann.com

Offices and agents throughout the world

The authors and publisher wish to thank those who have generously given permission to reprint borrowed material:

Figure 1–17: "Equal Sharing and the Roots of Fraction Equivalence" by Susan B. Empson from *Teaching Children Mathematics*, 2001, Volume 7, pages 421–425. Copyright 2001 by the National Council of Teachers of Mathematics. All rights reserved. Reprinted by permission of the publisher.

Figures 1–10 and 1–13: "Fractions as the Coordination of Multiplicatively Related Quantities: A Cross-Sectional Study of Children's Thinking," by Susan B. Empson from *Educational Studies in Mathematics*, January 1, 2005, Volume 63, Issue 1, pages 1–28. Published by Springer Science and Business Media. Reprinted by permission of the publisher.

Excerpt adapted from "Equal Sharing and Shared Meaning: The Development of Fraction Concepts in a First-Grade Classroom" by Susan B. Empson from *Cognition and Instruction*, January 9, 1999, Volume 17, Issue 3, pages 283–342. Published by Taylor and Francis Group, http://www.informaworld.com. Reprinted by permission of the publisher.

Introduction, Chapter 4, and Figure 7–1 photos courtesy of Lynne Nielsen; Chapter 1, Chapter 2, Figure 4–6, Figure 5–5, Chapter 8, Figure 8–1, and Figure 9–1 photos courtesy of Linda Levi; Figure 2–7, Chapter 3, Figure 3–4, Chapter 5, Chapter 6, Figure 6–2, Figure 6–9, Chapter 7, and Chapter 9 photos courtesy of Susan Empson; Figure 6–1 photo courtesy of Julian Joseph.

The research and writing of this book was supported in part by grant number 0138877 from the National Science Foundation and a Faculty Research Award from The University of Texas at Austin.

For information regarding teacher professional development on the material presented in this book, please contact Linda Levi at linda.levi@teachersdg.org or 877-650-1914.

Library of Congress Cataloging-in-Publication Data

Empson, Susan B.

  Extending children's mathematics : fractions and decimals / Susan B. Empson and Linda Levi.

    p. cm.

  Includes bibliographical references and index.

  ISBN-13: 978-0-325-03053-1

  ISBN-10: 0-325-03053-7

  1. Fractions—Study and teaching (Elementary). 2. Decimal fractions—Study and teaching (Elementary). 3. Fractions—Study and teaching (Middle school). 4. Decimal fractions—Study and teaching (Middle school). I. Levi, Linda. II. Title.

  QA117.E47 2011

  372.7′2—dc22   2011001314

Editor: Victoria Merecki

Production editor: Sonja S. Chapman

Typesetter: Publishers' Design and Production Services, Inc.

Cover and interior designs: Bernadette Skok

Author photo of Linda Levi courtesy of Katrin Talbot

Author photo of Susan Empson courtesy of Robert Donald

Cover photo courtesy of Susan Empson

Manufacturing: Steve Bernier

Printed in the United States of America on acid-free paper

15 14 13 12 11 VP   2 3 4 5

To our children Eric and Nick (SBE), and Kevin and Eve (LL)

Our love for you inspires us to do our part to make schools better for all children.

Contents

ACKNOWLEDGMENTS

many people have contributed to our understanding of children's mathematical thinking and to the work that has resulted in this book. More than twenty years ago we were graduate students of Thomas P. Carpenter and Elizabeth Fennema. Through their example, we learned to listen to children and focus on their mathematical ideas. Without Tom and Eliz, this book would not have been possible.

This book is the result of our experiences in real classrooms and we are grateful to the teachers who opened their classrooms and shared their students with us. We know it wasn't always easy. We ask lots of questions and sometimes try things with students that don't work very well. The following teachers welcomed us into their classrooms and provided us with insights into children's thinking that could only be gained by teaching on a daily basis: Kerry Alexander, Vicki Barker, Susan Gehn, Tammy Hughes, Annie Keith, Therese Kolan, Carolyn Konkol, Jean Lee, Meghan Ling, Carla Nordness, Kathy Oker, Ellen Ranney, Kathy Statz, Lisa Stein, and Lesley Wagner. Sincere thanks as well to the following teachers who contributed in other valuable ways: Amy Warshauer, Laura Wieland, Diane Wu, and Sylla Zarov.

We are constantly growing in our understanding of children's thinking. We are grateful for colleagues who question our ideas, share their perspectives, and support us in advancing our thinking. Thanks especially to: Jae Baek, Dinah Brown, Joan Case, Theodore Chao, Higinio Dominguez, Linda Foreman, Vicki Jacobs, Linda Jaslow, Debra Junk, Laura Kent, Jennifer Knudsen, Chris Nugent, Lynne Nielsen, Luz Maldonado, Randolph Philipp, Margie Pligge, Jeremy Roschelle, Olof Steinthorsdottir, and Erin Turner.

We thank all of the teachers who have participated in our teacher professional development sessions and are reading this book. We learn something new every time we work with teachers. Teaching well is hard work and we are grateful that you are willing to do this work to make things better for all of our children.

Extra special thanks to Andy Levi, who falls into a category of his own.

We were fortunate to work again with Victoria Merecki as our editor and Sonja Chapman as our production editor. We thank them and everyone else at Heinemann who worked so hard to bring this book into your hands.

Finally, we would like to thank the children who have been so patient in helping us understand their thinking. Sometimes we don't understand and sometimes we ask the wrong questions but we are always amazed by their ideas. We went into teaching to help children learn, but we have learned more from children than they will ever learn from us.

FOREWORD

ver since publishing *Children's Mathematics: Cognitively Guided Instruction* (Carpenter et al. 1999), we frequently have been asked when we were going to do something about fractions. With the publication of *Extending Children's Mathematics: Fractions and Decimals*, we finally have an answer. With the collaboration of a number of dedicated teachers and their students, Susan Empson and Linda Levi have produced a volume that is faithful to the basic principles of Cognitively Guided Instruction (CGI) while at the same time covering new ground with insight and innovation.

In *Children's Mathematics*, we described how young children's intuitive strategies for solving whole-number word problems can provide a basis for learning arithmetic with understanding. Using this knowledge, primary-grade teachers have had remarkable success in helping their students learn basic whole-number concepts and operations. *Children's Mathematics* built on a long history of research that documented children's surprisingly sophisticated problem-solving strategies and rich informal knowledge of whole-number arithmetic. On the other hand, much of the research on fractions has documented students' misconceptions and computational errors. As a consequence, it has generally been assumed that children's natural insight into whole-number arithmetic does not carry over to fractions and decimals and that there are inherent difficulties in learning even basic fraction and decimal concepts and skills. In *Extending Children's Mathematics: Fractions and Decimals*, Empson and Levi challenge these assumptions and show how the same kinds of intuitive knowledge and sense making that provide the basis for children's learning of whole-number arithmetic can be extended to fractions and decimals. The book provides unique and often surprising insights into how children can learn about fractions and decimals with understanding in ways that provide a foundation for learning algebra and other advanced mathematics.

Two defining features of learning with understanding are that knowledge that is learned with understanding is rich in connections and it is generative. These general principles provide broad guidelines, but the devil is in the details. To develop learning with understanding for a given content area like fractions entails figuring out how to connect new knowledge with what students already know and which connections are most productive in supporting problem solving and future learning. Empson and Levi develop initial fraction concepts by connecting them to children's intuitive understanding of sharing and allowing children to construct their own representations of sharing situations. Rather than defining fractions using physical or pictorial models showing a unit partitioned into equal parts, Empson and Levi introduce fraction notation as a way of representing partitioning situations that students are already familiar with. By holding back on the introduction of fraction symbols, instruction offers a chance for students to ground their experience with fraction symbols in conceptual knowledge and avoid the errors resulting from attending to superficial features of fraction notation.

At all stages of instruction, new fraction concepts and problem-solving skills are introduced as extensions of what students already understand. Because fractions are encountered as a natural outcome of whole-number division, children see fractions as quantities that follow the same basic principles as whole numbers. As a consequence, the fundamental properties of whole-number operations serve as the basis for learning to add, subtract, multiply, and divide fractions, and students generate insightful ways of solving fraction problems by applying these properties. Students essentially learn by problem solving, using basic number properties to transform problems into simpler problems that they have techniques for solving. Furthermore, the thinking that students employ in solving these problems not only helps them learn fraction concepts and skills, it also engages them in the kinds of thinking that they will need to be successful in learning algebra and other advanced mathematics. The properties that students use to extend their fraction knowledge are the foundation of algebra. Setting subgoals for solving complex problems rather than applying a prescribed sequence of calculations is fundamental for success in all advanced mathematics and many other related fields as well.

In reading the creative examples of children's thinking included in this book, it is easy to think: "That is great, but those are exceptional students. Not all students can do that. A lot of my students cannot do that." Perhaps not all students will exhibit the exact same strategies illustrated in this book, but all students come to class knowing a great deal of mathematics from experiences in and outside school and are capable of and benefit from the kinds of engagement described in this book. Virtually all students have knowledge of equal sharing that can serve as a basis for developing fraction concepts and notions of equivalent fractions. Given the opportunity, most students will show knowledge of properties of operations that can be extended to develop fraction procedures. In the long run, learning with understanding makes learning easier, more efficient, more adaptable, more readily retained, and generally better. Providing all students opportunity to learn with understanding is fundamentally an issue of equity. Failure to do so condemns some students to second-rate education and limits their opportunities. An argument is sometimes made that it is necessary to focus on skills for some students or classes of students because it is necessary to remediate their deficient skills before they can hope to learn concepts. We think a strong case can be made that the reverse is true. Students whose skills are perceived as deficient can actually be more successful extending the conceptual knowledge they do have than learning isolated skills.

As was the case with previous CGI books, this book does not provide a formula for teaching or a collection of curriculum materials. It takes seriously the thesis expressed in the title, *Extending Children's Mathematics*. This implies that instruction needs to be adapted to the backgrounds and experiences in and out of school of the students in each class. Although teachers' primary responsibility is not to demonstrate a prescribed sequence of procedures, teachers do play a critical role in their students' learning. This includes listening to children to figure out what they understand and selecting and adapting problems so that the problems connect to and extend the knowledge the children have already acquired, supporting children's learning by introducing appropriate symbols and ways of organizing and representing children's ideas, and providing a forum and active listening support for children to discuss alternative ways of thinking about problems and the concepts they embody.

While not offering prescriptions about how and what to teach, Empson and Levi provide a great deal of support to help teachers understand their students' thinking, select and sequence appropriate problems, introduce notation to represent students' strategies, and engage students in productive discussion.

Anyone reading this book will encounter remarkable examples of the kind of mathematical thinking students are capable of. But the book offers a great deal more. In the process of learning about children's insight and problem solving in learning about fractions, readers who may have struggled with mathematics themselves have the opportunity to learn a great deal about mathematics and how to think flexibly and creatively about solutions to mathematics problems. Anyone who takes the time to carefully work through the many intriguing examples of student work cannot help but enrich their own understanding. We constantly hear experienced CGI teachers talk about how much they learn from their students. This book offers a similar opportunity to readers to learn from the rich mathematical thinking generated by students.

Thomas P. Carpenter
Emeritus Professor
University of Wisconsin-Madison

Reference

Carpenter, T. P., E. Fennema, M. L. Franke, L. W. Levi, and S. B. Empson. 1999. *Children's Mathematics: Cognitively Guided Instruction*. Portsmouth, NH: Heinemann.

Introduction

Issues in Learning Fractions and Decimals: Rethinking Our Approach

a teacher drew a picture of a brownie that had been cut with a slice removed and asked a first grader and a third grader to decide how much had been eaten (Figure I–1). The first grader studied the picture for a moment and then said the missing piece was "half of a half." The third grader said it was an impossible amount, because the pieces were not all the same size and it therefore could not be "1 out of 3."

The teacher was surprised. What could have led the younger boy to see a mathematical relationship, and the older boy to say that this shaded amount—which could easily be cut out of a brownie—was no amount at all?

As we puzzled over this episode, we realized it touched on several issues involved in teaching fractions. The first grader's response suggests that children have some conceptually sound understanding of fractions, even before instruction. But the third grader's response suggests that children can learn to ignore

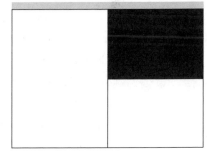

Figure I–1.
The darkened part shows what part of this brownie Jackie ate. How much of the brownie was eated?

Models

this understanding in favor of models introduced in school that portray fractions in narrow ways. If models do not draw on children's formative experiences of sharing and partitioning, then they are likely to prevent teachers from cultivating the natural insights about quantities that young children have.

We do not need to look far for evidence that U.S. students, in general, are not learning fractions very well. For example, on a recent international comparison test, only 25 percent of U.S. eighth graders correctly solved "Laura had $240. She spent $\frac{5}{8}$ of it. How much money did she have left?" A slightly higher percentage of U.S. students, 37 percent, correctly calculated $\frac{6}{55} \div \frac{3}{25} = $ ____ (Trends in International Mathematics and Science Study 2003). A recent report noted that difficulty learning fractions is "pervasive and is an obstacle to further progress in mathematics," particularly in algebra (United States Department of Education 2008, 28).

In this book, we share what we have learned about how children can learn fractions and decimals, thoroughly understand them, and become proficient mathematical thinkers who enjoy solving problems. What we know is drawn from many years of research and work with teachers and children. Our work extends prior research on children's thinking about addition, subtraction, multiplication, and division, presented in *Children's Mathematics: Cognitively Guided Instruction* (Carpenter et al. 1999), and prior research on children's algebraic thinking, presented in *Thinking Mathematically: Integrating Arithmetic and Algebra in Elementary School* (Carpenter et al. 2003). The emphasis in all of this work has been on what children can do when given the chance to reason things out for themselves and the kinds of mathematics understanding that emerges.

Children's learning in this book is framed in terms of problem types and children's strategies for solving these problems. These problems types and strategies extend the Cognitively Guided Instruction (CGI) problem types and strategies to reflect children's emerging understanding of fractions and decimals. We categorize the types of strategies that children use to solve these problems, describe how these strategies evolve, and provide teaching vignettes that show how you can direct discussions of students' strategies that make explicit the mathematics that students are to learn.

We focus in particular on the role that children's early understanding of algebraic relationships plays in the development of children's understanding of fractions and decimals. We build on the work presented in *Thinking Mathematically* to describe how you can use instruction in fractions to foster the development of students' intuitive use of algebraic relationships and how a focus on algebraic relationships helps students learn fractions with understanding. By focusing on relationships, children come to see fractions as connected to other things they know about number and operation. Learning fractions in this way builds students' understanding as an integrated whole and prepares them for future learning.

Three themes appear throughout the book: building meaning for fractions through solving and discussing word problems, the progression of children's strategies for solving fraction and decimal problems, and designing instruction that integrates algebra into teaching and learning fractions. We discuss these themes and then outline the chapters of the book for you.

Using Word Problems to Build Meaning for Fractions

Start with Equal Sharing

Four-year-old Emma had 7 cherries that she wanted to share with her aunt. She gave them out one by one to the two of them, saying to herself as she dealt, "1 for me, 1 for you. 1 for me, 1 for you. 1 for me, 1 for you. 1 for me." Emma saw when she was done that she had 4 cherries and her aunt only had 3. Her aunt protested, and Emma slid a cherry from her share over to her aunt. Emma was surprised when she saw that the division was still unequal—now Emma had 3 and her aunt had 4! She picked up the extra cherry, gave it to herself again, and then giggled as she realized that no matter who she gave it to, the shares would not be equal. And then she had a wonderful idea: "Let's cut it in 2!" Her aunt got a knife and cut the little cherry into 2 pieces. Satisfied with their equal shares, they ate their fruit.

Division into equal groups is a process that young children such as Emma understand intuitively. In this book, we show how children's early thinking about multiplication and division provide the foundation for learning fractions. Building this foundation can begin as early as kindergarten, when children are capable of solving simple equal grouping problems much the way Emma did, by drawing on their intuitive understanding of sharing, measuring, grouping, and distribution (Carpenter et al. 1993).

In a first-grade classroom, the teacher gave her students this division problem:

> 4 CHILDREN WANT TO SHARE 5 candy bars so that everyone gets the same amount. How much candy bar can each child have?

She encouraged the children to imagine themselves in this situation and to figure out the answer in a way that made sense to them. Almost all of the children drew pictures to help them think. Elliot decided to distribute 1 candy bar to each person, and then split the remaining candy bar into fourths (Figure I–2a), for a share of 1¼ candy bars each. Sofia decided to share each candy bar with all 4 children, for a share of ⁵⁄₄ each (Figure I–2b). They showed how much each person would get by marking 1 person's share. (Sofia also notated each person's share as "5 qutrs," for "five-quarters.")

imagine themselves & make sense on your own

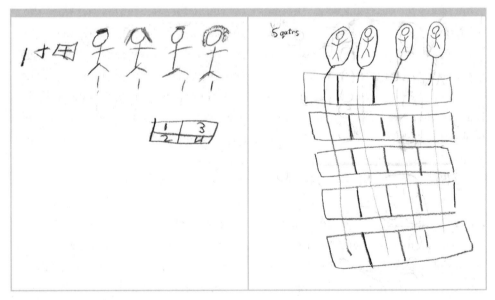

(a) Elliot's strategy   (b) Sofia's strategy

Figure I–2. *Two first graders' strategies for sharing 5 candy bars equally among 4 children*

The division story problem involves fractions in its solution and can be solved by children without direct instruction. Elliot's and Sofia's informal knowledge of equal distribution and repeated halving helped them construct valid solutions; and they did not need to know how to use fraction symbols or terminology to solve these problems or report their solutions.

Continue with Problems That Build on Children's Understanding

Solving and discussing Equal Sharing problems prepares children to learn from a variety of other problems involving fractions and decimals. We introduce and discuss several other types of problems to help you teach fraction equivalence and order and computation involving fractions and decimals. We recommend, in general, that instruction start with word problems and gradually incorporate equations. When problems are sequenced in ways that are sensitive to children's developing understanding, children can solve both word problems and equations without explicit instruction. Word problems help students connect their informal understanding of quantities and actions on quantities to new concepts of fractions and decimals. Equations help students make explicit their developing concepts of fractions and decimals and to become proficient in the use of number relationships and symbols.

Focus on the Progression of Meaning

Textbooks often start by introducing fraction symbols and then presenting a meaning for the symbol—usually, a part-whole or "*n* parts out of *m* equal parts" model (Fig. I–3). However, our research on how children's thinking develops has led us to conclude that the opposite approach is more productive in the long run. Equal Sharing situations such as the one above are especially rich with mathematical meaning to which symbols can be later attached. The idea that meaning can precede symbols, or vice versa, is simplistic, but illustrates the contrast between different approaches to instruction.

Furthermore, fractions do not have a single meaning, such as *n* parts out of *m* parts. They can stand for amounts

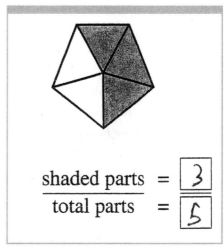

Figure I–3.
Exercise from textbook introduction to fractions as number of parts out of total number of equal parts

of stuff, such as ⅗ of a candy bar. They can stand for relationships between amounts, such as 3 candy bars for every 5 children, or processes involving amounts, such as 3 candy bars shared among 5 children. They can also of course be interpreted in terms of mathematical models, such as points on a number line or ordered pairs of numbers satisfying certain properties, as in the formal mathematical definition for rational numbers.

When children learn to think of fractions only, or mainly, as parts of wholes—as the third grader at the beginning of the chapter did—it is hard for them to grasp what really makes a fraction what it is: a number whose value is determined by the *multiplicative relationship* between the numerator and the denominator. A common interpretation of this relationship involves how a part is related to the whole. But there are other, more powerful, interpretations. For example, here is what two sixth graders said when they were asked to explain what ⅔ meant.

> **Daisy:** ⅔ is what you get if you take 2 things, split each into 3 equal pieces, and take 1 piece from each thing. Or you could take 2 pieces from 1 of the things. It doesn't matter.

> **Roberto:** ⅔ is like dividing 2 by 3. You can think of breaking 2 into 3 equal parts. Each part would be ⅔. Or you can think of how many threes fit into 2. You can't get a whole 3 into 2 but you can get ⅔ of a 3 into 2.

Daisy and Roberto both understand ⅔ in terms of a multiplicative relationship between 2 and 3. (Because multiplication and division are inverse operations, we refer to reasoning that includes either as *multiplicative*.)

Thinking of fractions in these ways may seem beyond the grasp of elementary students, but it is not. The important thing is to begin by building meaning, and not by introducing the symbol alone. Because children's experiences with slicing, splitting, distributing, measuring, and combining quantities are meaningful to them, problems that are based on these experiences are a rich source of meaning for fractions.

Use Fractions to Develop Algebraic Thinking

Many educators believe that proficiency with fractions is a necessary prerequisite to the study of high school algebra. The traditional argument is that if students are unable to compute with fractions quickly and accurately, they will be unable to solve algebraic equations. But this type of proficiency is only part of the picture. We view the study of fractions as foundational to the study of algebra in particular because it offers students the opportunity to grapple with the fundamental mathematical relationships that constitute the core of algebra. These relationships govern how addition, subtraction, multiplication, and division work in algebra as well as arithmetic; allowing students to grapple with them as they study fractions helps students to develop a tightly integrated understanding of number and operation that prepares them to understand algebra and, at the same time, develops computational fluency.

With encouragement, children routinely use algebraic relationships in their reasoning about fractions. For example, Kevin, a fourth grader, computed $12 \times 6\frac{3}{4}$ by reasoning, "12 times 6 is 72. I need to do 12 times $\frac{3}{4}$. One-fourth of 12 is 3; so $\frac{3}{4}$ of 12 would be 9. 72 plus 9 is 81 so 12 times $6\frac{3}{4}$ is 81." We call strategies such as this one *Relational Thinking* strategies because they are carried out on the basis of the child's understanding of fundamental mathematical relationships. One of the relationships embedded in Kevin's strategy is the distributive property of multiplication over addition. This equation represents how Kevin used the distributive property:

$$12 \times 6\tfrac{3}{4} = 12 \times (6 + \tfrac{3}{4}) = (12 \times 6) + (12 \times \tfrac{3}{4})$$

The distributive property is used extensively in algebra. For example, we use it to simplify algebraic expressions such as $8(a + b)$ and $(3x + 2)(x + 7)$. The mathematical relationships that students use in their Relational Thinking strategies are the same relationships that are used to solve algebraic equations.

How Do Decimals Fit In?

Like children's understanding of fractions, children's understanding of decimals often suffers from too little attention to building meaning for symbols. Decimals can be introduced as fractions whose denominators are powers of 10—10, 100, 1,000, and so on—written using a new notational convention. This convention extends our place value system to the right into units less than 1—tenths, hundredths, thousandths, and so on. Although we usually write a number like fifty-four and two-tenths as 54.2, there is no reason why we could not write this number as $54\frac{2}{10}$. In later chapters, we detail how the development of children's understanding of decimals

This Book and Curriculum Standards in Mathematics Education

In 2010, the Common Core Standards in Mathematics (CCSM) were published and adopted by many states in the United States. The material in this book can help you address the standards focused on fractions and decimals as well as some that involve algebra.

The CCSM recommend that fractions be taught by defining unit fractions first and then relating unit fractions to other fractions. For example, students would learn first what $\frac{1}{4}$ means, and then that $\frac{3}{4} = \frac{1}{4} + \frac{1}{4} + \frac{1}{4} = 3 \times \frac{1}{4}$. We describe, on the basis of empirical research, how children's understanding of fractions progressively develops following such a pathway. We detail the strategies that children use to solve a variety of problems including equal sharing and multiple groups word problems and open number sentences, and explain what these strategies indicate about children's understanding of fractions. By tracing the development of children's thinking, we unpack what it means for students to understand fractions as quantities with a referent and as numbers that could be represented by a point on a number line.

CCSM also recommend that students understand and use algebraic properties to make sense of computation. We describe how you can design instruction so that children engage naturally in reasoning with algebraic properties as they solve problems involving fraction and decimal operations and how you can draw out this structure in children's verbal explanations and written equations.

Finally, CCSM calls for the integration of mathematical content and practices. Throughout the book, we explicitly address this integration and provide concrete suggestions on how to accomplish it. Some of the most important mathematical practices recommended by CCSM on which we focus include:

- Making sense of problems and persevering in solving them
- Reasoning abstractly and quantitatively
- Using appropriate tools strategically
- Looking for and making use of structure

simultaneously draws on their understanding of fractions *and* our base-ten place value system. We describe in particular how children build meaning for decimal numbers based on relationships rather than concrete materials.

Looking Ahead: What You Can Expect from This Book

In this book, we describe how children's understanding of rational numbers[1] in the form of positive fractions and decimals grows as they solve and discuss a variety of types of problems in grades 1–6. We present a research-based framework to organize problem types and discuss children's strategies and their development over time, and we describe the teacher's role in supporting the development of children's understanding and confidence.

In Chapters 1, 2, and 3, we present the problem types you can use to introduce fractions and the strategies children use to solve them. These problems draw on children's informal knowledge of partitioning and grouping. Children's strategies provide teachers with important information about what children understand and

---

[1] A *rational number* is any number that can be expressed as $\frac{p}{q}$ where p and q are *integers* and $q \neq 0$. The integers include the positive and negative whole numbers and 0: $\{...-3, -2, -1, 0, 1, 2, 3, ...\}$.

how it is developing. Chapter 1 focuses on Equal Sharing problems. These problems allow children to create and manipulate fractional amounts and to reflect on the relationship between the numerator and denominator. In Chapter 2, we describe how two teachers began a unit of instruction on fractions with Equal Sharing. Chapter 3 focuses on Multiple Groups problems and represents a significant departure from typical curricular recommendations. These word problems involve a whole number of groups with a fractional amount in each group—such as 10 boxes with $\frac{1}{4}$ pound of fudge in each box—and help reinforce children's understanding of the relationships between whole units and the fractions into which they are subdivided. For example, to solve the fudge problem, a child needs to use knowledge of the relationship that $\frac{1}{4} + \frac{1}{4} + \frac{1}{4} + \frac{1}{4} = 1$.

As children's understanding of basic fraction relationships grows, they begin to use it to think relationally about operations involving fractions. The teacher plays a critical role in extending children's thinking. In Chapter 4, we introduce Relational Thinking and explain how it bridges arithmetic and algebra and embodies the core of what it means to understand fractions. In Chapter 5, we address the teacher's role in making explicit the Relational Thinking that children use in their strategies. Specifically, this role involves introducing equations to represent children's use of fundamental properties of operations—such as the distributive property—to justify the steps in a solution.

In Chapter 6, we describe how children's understanding of equivalent fractions and fraction comparisons develops and the types of problems you can use to promote this understanding. The problems include word problems as well as equations. We describe in particular how teachers can be alert to children's emerging ideas about equivalence and highlight these ideas for students using equations to depict these relationships. The types of recommendations that we offer differ from typical presentations of this content that focus on the use of physical models and manipulatives.

In Chapter 7, we show how instruction on decimal numbers helps students integrate their understanding of base-ten concepts with their understanding of fractions. We discuss the problems and types of interactions that support students in this integration and pay particular attention to how teachers can differentiate decimal instruction for students working from different levels of understanding in fractions and/or base-ten understanding.

In Chapter 8, we bring the conceptual strands developed in previous chapters together to show how students learn to add, subtract, multiply, and divide fractions and decimals. We detail the kinds of strategies that children use, discuss the development of proficiency and fluency in children's thinking, and present a unified framework to portray the nature of children's deep and lasting understanding of arithmetic.

Finally, we believe that listening to children is essential to effective teaching. We exemplify this view throughout the book and in Chapter 9 discuss what we know about teachers learning to listen to children in a more responsive manner and how teaching changes as a result. We call the chapter "The Long View" because developing the capacity to listen to children's thinking and act upon what you hear is an ongoing journey. It takes time to develop the knowledge, skills, and confidence to interact with children about their thinking. But the rewards can begin immediately, when you take the first step—whether it is asking a child to solve a problem and listening with an open mind to a report of her thinking or engaging in solving a problem in this book with a group of teachers and listening to each other.

As resources to support your teaching, at the end of each chapter in which we introduce new problems, we provide sets of sample problems that represent a variety of levels of sophistication. We also provide instructional guides organized by grade level to help you decide when to give each problem type, what numbers to use, and when to introduce and emphasize specific mathematics concepts and processes. Our goal when we work with teachers is to support them to take in the material in this book, adapt it to their own teaching practices, and make it their own. The instructional guides and problem sets at the end of each chapter provide a broad set of directions for how to teach fractions and decimals. We believe that you are in the best position to decide the focus and timing of instruction at the moment when it is needed—whether it is further probing of students' thinking to reveal details, asking new questions and posing new problems based upon a strategy a student just used, pushing students to use more sophisticated strategies, or showing them how to write equations to represent their mathematical ideas.

chapter 1

Equal Sharing Problems and Children's Strategies for Solving Them

Children learn mathematics by using what they know to make sense of new material. In this chapter, we describe how you can use *Equal Sharing* problems to help children use what they know about partitioning and division to learn fractions. We introduce Equal Sharing problems and present a framework to make sense of children's strategies. We suggest that instruction begin with mixed numbers, then move to proper and improper fractions, because this sequence fits more naturally with children's understanding of the counting numbers. We conclude by describing how to introduce fraction terminology and symbolism in ways that avoid some common misconceptions.

What Are Fractions?

Fractions are a way of writing numbers in the form a/b where b is not equal to 0. The fractions that we work with in elementary and middle school typically have integer values for *a* and *b*.[1]

The value of any fraction is determined by the multiplicative relationship between the numerator and denominator. However, thinking of a fraction as a number with a single value is a novel idea for many children. In their minds, fractions are something different—two numbers, a shape like a piece, or a way to cut things up—but not a number that can be used to name a precise magnitude or to identify a unique point on a number line.

Figure 1–1.
Child's representation of a fourth as "a little pie shape"

Sometimes the way children think about fractions is obvious, because they put it into words for you. For example, when asked, "What is ¼?" one child said that ¼ was a "little pie shape," which she carefully drew (Figure 1–1).

At other times, you have to listen carefully to infer a child's working definition of a fraction. Holly, a fifth grader who had been exposed to a typical amount of instruction in fractions, was asked to solve this problem (Empson, Levi, and Carpenter, in press):

JEREMY IS MAKING CUPCAKES. He wants to put ½ cup of frosting on each cupcake. If he makes 4 cupcakes for his birthday party, how much frosting will he use to frost all of the cupcakes?

She drew 4 circles, each split in half, to show 4 half cups of frosting (Figure 1–2), and decided that Jeremy needed "4 halves" to frost the cupcakes. This was true.

---

[1] It is appropriate to use the notation $^a/_b$ when *a* and *b* are not integers. For example,

$$\frac{\frac{3}{4}}{\frac{5}{3}}, \frac{5y}{9}, \frac{4}{7.8} \text{ and } \frac{\pi}{2}$$

are appropriate uses of fraction notation. However, numbers such as these are usually not studied in elementary school and so are not a focus of this book.

However, when the teacher asked her how much 4 halves would be altogether, she insisted it was "4 halves, and 4 halves only." Rather than thinking of a half as an amount, Holly thought of it as an image. Asking Holly how much 4 halves would make altogether was like asking her how much 4 cupcakes would be altogether—it's 4 cupcakes!

Figure 1–2.
Holly's representation of "4 halves"

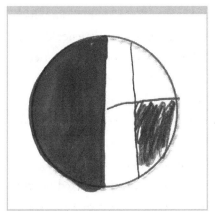

Figure 1–3.
Ernesto's representation of ¼ of a circle that is already partitioned into halves

When asked to represent ¼ of a cookie, Ernesto drew a circle partitioned into fourths. When shown a picture of a half of a cookie and asked, "The part of the cookie that isn't colored in is a half of a cookie; how could you show ¼ of the cookie?" he used the same partitioning gesture—a stroke down and then a stroke across—to show what he considered to be ¼ of the cookie on one side of the cookie (Figure 1–3). For him, "one-fourth" was the process of partitioning into 4 parts, rather than 1 part in a specific relationship to a whole.

Children who understand fractions in the ways that Holly, Ernesto, and the other children do have little foundation for understanding equivalent fractions or how to add, subtract, multiply, and divide fractions. Their weak understanding of fractions will prevent them from understanding these and other more advanced topics later.

As extreme as these cases are, they are not especially unusual. Teachers often do not devote enough time to helping children build meaning for fractions before moving on to equivalencies, comparisons, and operations involving fractions. These children's notions about the nature of fractions are evidence of this lack of attention.

Introducing Fractions Using Equal Sharing Problems

On the first day of instruction on fractions, a second-grade teacher gave this problem to her students:

> FOUR CHILDREN WANT TO SHARE 10 brownies so that everyone gets exactly the same amount. How much brownie can each child have?

This problem has three features that make it a good problem to introduce and develop fractions. The first is that it involves Equal Sharing, a situation about which children have strong intuitive understanding. Most children have experience sharing food and other things with siblings or friends and they can draw on that experience to solve this problem.

The second feature of this problem is that the solution is a mixed number, $2\frac{1}{2}$. Children are essentially creating a fractional quantity ($\frac{1}{2}$ brownie) in a context that allows them to relate it to a whole-number quantity (2 brownies). Introducing fractions through mixed numbers goes against the conventional practice of starting with fractions between 0 and 1 such as $\frac{1}{4}$, $\frac{1}{2}$, and $\frac{2}{3}$ and then introducing mixed numbers and improper fractions later. However, when children solve problems that involve a set of objects such as brownies that they can count *and* individually split into parts, it helps them understand that a countable set of objects can also include fractions of an object. Children learn from the beginning that fractions are a type of number that "fills in" the whole numbers, and they avoid the misconceptions that fractions are not numbers at all or appear only between 0 and 1. In later grades, children will be better prepared to understand that a fraction can be represented by a unique point on the number line.

Finally, the third notable feature of this problem is that the number of sharers (4) facilitates halving or repeated halving into fourths. Children do not need to be shown how to partition brownies to solve this problem because partitioning into halves comes so naturally to them.

Notice that the problem statement contains no fractions. It is the relationship between the number of items to be shared (10 brownies) and the number of people

good way to introduce fractions

sharing (4 children) that leads to the need for a fractional amount. Because the problem statement involves whole numbers, children do not need to be taught how to read or write fractions before solving it. They will be able to find a way to share the brownies by drawing on their understanding of whole-number quantities and informal partitioning strategies; most young children will draw rather than name fractional quantities in their solutions.

Other examples of number combinations that yield mixed numbers include 3 children sharing 7 brownies and 8 children sharing 30 brownies. Equal Sharing problems can also be written so that the answer is a fraction less than 1. For example, if 3 children share 2 brownies, each child gets less than a whole brownie. With problems such as these, fractions can be introduced in a mathematically rich context that allows children to extend what they understand about whole numbers and division and to integrate it with partitioning into parts and relating parts to wholes.

In contrast to Equal Sharing, problems that have children identify a fraction based on a given number of parts (e.g., Figure 1–4a) or divide a shape into a specified number of pieces (e.g., Figure 1–4b) offer few opportunities for children to make connections between fractions and whole numbers. Even though such problems are concrete in that children can see and maybe even manipulate the shapes, they are

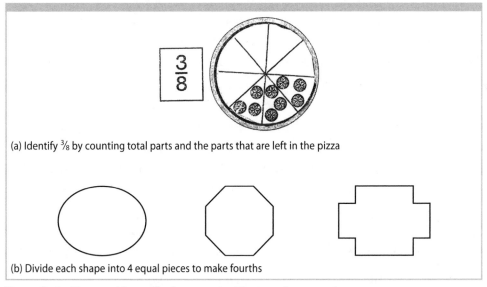

(a) Identify ⅜ by counting total parts and the parts that are left in the pizza

(b) Divide each shape into 4 equal pieces to make fourths

Figure 1–4. *These problems offer few opportunities to make connections*

not situated in any meaningful context—such as the process of sharing food with friends—that would allow children to use their understanding of number to create and make sense of the resulting parts as quantities. Instead, partitioning a variety of shapes outside of a context such as Equal Sharing requires knowledge of geometry—such as where exactly to place a cut to partition a circle into 4 equal parts—but not necessarily number. Because many children do not realize that fractions are numbers, devoting a great deal of time to solving and discussing such tasks, especially at the outset of instruction, does little to increase children's understanding of fractions. These tasks may also contribute to misconceptions such as Holly's that a fraction is a certain type of picture.

The Structure of Equal Sharing Problems

The essential structure of Equal Sharing word problems involves a total number of items to be distributed to a given number of groups, usually people. This type of problem requires that children give each person the same-sized share and use up (or exhaust) all of the sharing material. The brownie problem above is an example of Equal Sharing.

Before instruction in fractions, children—even children in kindergarten, first, and second grades[2]—need experience with multiplication and division story problems with whole numbers (Figure 1–5). These problems include Multiplication, Measurement Division, and Partitive Division.[3] Before you read on, we invite you to study these problems to see what the differences are between them—in particular, between the two different types of division.

These problems all involve the same equal-groups context: 5 packets of gum, 3 pieces of gum in each packet, and 15 total pieces of gum. The problem type is determined by which quantity is unknown. If the total number of pieces is unknown, then the problem is Multiplication. If the number of packets is unknown, then the problem is Measurement Division.[4] And finally, if the number in each packet is

---

[2] See Carpenter et al. (1993) for a report of the kinds of story problems that kindergartners can solve and how they solve them. The problems include multiplication and division story problems and multistep problems.

[3] See Chapter 4 in *Children's Mathematics: Cognitively Guided Instruction.*

[4] Sometimes this type of division is called quotative.

Problem Type	Number of Groups	Amount per Group	Total	Equation
Multiplication. *Eric has 5 packets of gum. Each packet has 3 pieces of gum in it. How many pieces of gum does Eric have all together?*	5	3	Unknown	$5 \times 3 = c$
Measurement Division. *Eric has 15 pieces of gum. He wants to put 3 pieces of gum in each packet. How many packets can he fill?*	Unknown	3	15	$a \times 3 = 15$
Partitive Division. *Eric has 15 pieces of gum. He put the gum into 5 packets, with the same number in each packet. How many pieces of gum are in each packet?*	5	Unknown	15	$5 \times b = 15$

Figure 1–5. *Multiplication, Measurement Division, and Partitive Division problems*

unknown, the problem is Partitive Division. Although adults typically view the two different division problems as similar, until the middle grades, children usually view these problems as distinct from each other.

Children's experiences solving these types of whole-number multiplication and division problems prepare them to solve Equal Sharing problems. Equal Sharing is a type of Partitive Division, because the number of groups (sharers) is known and the amount in each group (size of each person's share) is unknown. These experiences also help children begin to develop conceptions of a group as a flexible type of unit—namely, that a group can be counted as a single unit and it can be partitioned into smaller units. The idea that a collection can be counted as a single unit plays a central role in the development of children's understanding of base-ten concepts and decimals. For example, 10 can be thought of 1 ten or 10 ones; similarly, 1 can be thought of as 1 group of 10 one-tenths each or 10 groups of one-tenth each. (We discuss this idea further in Chapter 7.)

Fractions can be introduced through Equal Sharing problems that use countable quantities that can be cut, split, or divided, such candy bars, pancakes, bottles of water, sticks of clay, jars of paint, bags of sand, and so on. These quantities can be shared by people or distributed into other groupings, such as onto plates or into packages. Figure 1–6 includes examples of Equal Sharing problems that yield mixed numbers (or improper fractions) and fractions less than 1 (that is, proper fractions).

Equal Sharing

(answer is more than 1)	*4 children want to share 10 candy bars so that everyone gets the same amount. How much candy bar can each child have?*
(answer is less than 1)	*4 children want to share 3 blueberry pancakes so that everyone gets the same amount. How much pancake can each child have?*

Figure 1–6. *Equal Sharing problems*

Equal Sharing problems where the answer is greater than 1 are easier for young children to solve and help bridge children's understanding of whole numbers and fractions. These problems involve items that are easily drawn and divided. Later, you can use problems that involve more abstract quantities that children cannot point to or draw as easily, such as yards of material, liters of liquid, miles, pounds, and so on.

Equal Sharing problems help children establish rich mental models for fractions. Children can use these models later to make sense of problems that are not situated in sharing contexts, such as computation problems and problems set in other kinds of contexts.

The teacher is critical in supporting the development of children's thinking about fractions. The basic teaching practices that support children to draw on what they understand to make sense of new content include:

- posing problems to children without first presenting a strategy for solving the problems
- choosing problems that allow children to craft a solution on their own
- facilitating group discussions of children's strategies

Because a variety of strategies is necessary for rich mathematical discussions, teachers need to establish and reinforce routines to help students realize they are expected to solve problems in their own ways rather than by applying teacher-demonstrated strategies.[5]

---

[5] To read more about how to set up a classroom where children solve and discuss problems, see *Making Sense*, by Hiebert et al. (1997); *Teaching Problems and the Problems of Teaching*, by Lampert (2002); and *Elementary and Middle School Mathematics: Teaching Developmentally*, by Van de Walle et al. (2009). We discuss teaching in more depth in Chapters 5, 6, and 7.

The framework that follows outlines the kinds of strategies you can expect students to use to solve Equal Sharing problems. This framework can help you choose problems that are at an appropriate level of difficulty for your students and to understand what each student's strategy tells you about his or her understanding. It can also help you prompt students to make connections between strategies, the problem situation, and mathematical concepts and processes when students present their strategies to the group.

Children's Strategies for Equal Sharing Problems

The evolution of children's strategies for Equal Sharing problems follows a predictable pattern. The most important feature of this pattern involves how children relate the two quantities in the problem—the people sharing and the things to be shared—to make equal shares. Coordinating the partitions of shared items with the number of sharers is critical because it results in an equal and exhaustive partition and it is the basis for children's developing understanding of the multiplicative relationship between the numerator and denominator in a fraction.

▶ How to Begin

We suggest that you try some of the problems with your students as you read each chapter. There is no need to finish the book before getting started. Choose a problem that you think will challenge your students but not be too difficult. (There is a list of Equal Sharing problems at the end of the chapter.) Make sure that the problem involves a context with which students are familiar. Do not worry about choosing the perfect problem type or number sizes. You may find it easier to start by working with only one student or a small group, but if you feel more comfortable working with your whole class, then by all means do so.

Next, pose this problem without providing instruction on how to solve it. If your students are not accustomed to solving problems without teacher input on what strategy to use, you may need to tell them that you are deliberately not going to show them how to solve the problem so that they can solve it using their own ways of thinking. As students work, observe their strategies and listen to their explanations. If students find the problem too difficult, give them an easier one. If students are not sure what to do, encourage them to imagine the situation the problem is about and then figure out the answer in a way that makes sense to them. If everyone uses the same strategy, such as a standard algorithm, ask for a second strategy. Have a few students share their strategies with the other students. Some students who did not solve the problem may gain some understanding by listening to how other students solved the problem. Do not worry if you forget some of these suggestions while you are working with your students; you can always try them out the next time you pose one of these problems.

No Coordination Between Sharers and Shares

When young children first solve Equal Sharing problems, they may not think about how the number of people is related to how to partition the things being shared. Either children create equal shares but do not use up everything to be shared, or more commonly, children use up everything to be shared but do not create equal shares. In both cases, as children are figuring out how to solve the problem, they are paying attention to only one requirement of the sharing situation—either the need for equal shares or the need to use up everything.

For example, consider the problem:

 3 CHILDREN WANT TO SHARE 5 candy bars so that each person gets the same amount. The candy bars are the same size. How much can each child have?

First-grader Michelle began her solution by drawing 5 candy bars and 3 people. She gave each person 1 candy bar (Figure 1–7a) and then paused when she realized that she did not have enough to give each person 1 more candy bar. She decided to split each candy bar in half. She gave each person a half candy bar and decided that she could not distribute any more candy bar to the sharers (Figure 1–7b). Although each person got an equal share, Michelle did not use up all of the candy bars and so her solution is incomplete. When the teacher asked her how the children could share the extra piece, she said that it would just be left over.

(a) Each person gets 1 candy bar

(b) Each person gets a half candy bar more, with a half leftover

Figure 1–7. *Michelle's incomplete strategy*

Michelle's classmate Miguel also began by drawing 5 candy bars and 3 people. In contrast, after he had given each person 1 candy bar, he decided to split the remaining 2 candy bars into a total of 3 pieces by leaving the fourth candy bar intact and splitting the last candy bar in half. He then distributed a whole candy bar to 1 of the sharers and a half candy bar to the remaining 2 sharers (Figure 1–8). He exhausted the sharing material but did not distribute equal shares and so his solution is also incomplete.

Michelle and Miguel were each paying attention to a different aspect of the Equal Sharing context. They were on the right track in their thinking but did not coordinate the number of people sharing with how they partitioned the candy bars. They each paid attention to only one of the two requirements of a sharing situation and did not think about how it was related to the other. Sometimes students like Michelle and Miguel arrive at a correct answer because halving leads them to share everything completely and equally. For example, if they solved a problem about 2 children sharing 3 candy bars, they would have likely gotten the correct answer.

Nonanticipatory Coordination Between Sharers and Shares

The most basic coordinating strategies for Equal Sharing are nonanticipatory, because students do not start out with a plan about how to share everything equally and completely. Instead, students work out as they go how to make sure everybody gets the same amount and everything is shared. These strategies involve either repeated halving or trial and error.

Repeated Halving with Coordination at the End.
A common, basic strategy for solving Equal Sharing problems is to begin by halving or repeated halving and to finish by coordinating the fractional partitions with the number of people sharing. This strategy is nonanticipatory because as children begin to solve the problem, they are not thinking about how their partitioning is related to the number of people sharing.

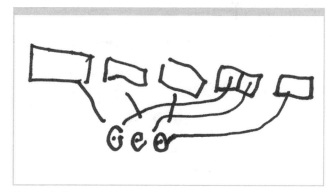

Figure 1–8.
Miguel's incomplete strategy

But when they reach a point where they are dealing with small pieces, they conceive of a partition other than repeated halving.

A fourth grader was given this problem:

 6 CHILDREN WANT TO SHARE 4 candy bars so that each gets the same amount. How much can each child have?

He began by drawing the 6 people as circles and the 4 candy bars as rectangles. He split the candy bars in half and gave everyone a half by redrawing the piece under each child (Figure 1–9). After distributing 6 of these halves, he split the last candy bar into eighths, and again distributed these parts by redrawing them. With 2 eighths pieces left over, he finally coordinated the partition of the candy bars with the number of people sharing by splitting the leftover fractional amount into 6 parts. Each share therefore consisted of 3 pieces: ½ of a candy bar, ⅛, and the difficult-to-name ⅙ of ⅔.

Teachers deal with these kinds of imprecise answers in a variety of ways. At the end of this chapter, we talk about how to draw students' attention to the sizes of the pieces they create and introduce fraction terminology to describe the pieces. Sometimes, you may want to just acknowledge that the child has used a valid strategy, even if it involves different-sized pieces that are hard to name or combine. At other times, you may ask the child to listen to other children share their strategies and focus the discussion on how to decide how big a part is.

Use of Trial and Error to Coordinate. As children learn to conceptualize partitions beyond halving and repeated halving, they develop a small repertoire of fractions to call upon in their solutions to Equal Sharing problems. Some children draw on this repertoire to use trial and error to

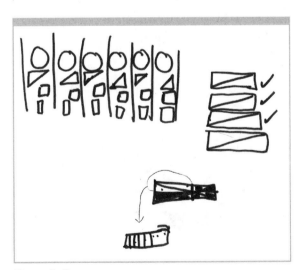

Figure 1–9.
Nonanticipatory Coordination: repeated halving

determine which fraction results in an equal and exhaustive partition of the shared material. For example, a third grader used trial and error to solve this problem:

THERE ARE 5 TORTILLAS FOR 3 CHILDREN who would like to share so that everyone gets the same amount. How much tortilla can one person have?

She drew 3 children and gave them each a tortilla. Then she drew the 2 remaining tortillas. She split them in fourths and wrote the initials of 3 friends ("J," "G," and "T") on 2 pieces each. She saw that there would be some pieces left over, so she redrew the remaining 2 tortillas and decided instead to split them into thirds (Figure 1–10). She concluded that each child would get one and two-thirds tortilla.

Figure 1–10.
Nonanticipatory Coordination: trial and error

Strategies such as these indicate that children are in the midst of learning how to coordinate the number of people sharing with the fractional partitions of the items to be shared. They realize at some level that to share everything equally and completely requires fractions that are related to the number of people sharing, but they are not able to use that knowledge to make sense of the problem in terms of a single all-encompassing relationship.

Coordinating Fractions with the Number of Sharers

Additive Coordination—One Item at a Time. The most straightforward anticipatory strategy used by children to solve Equal Sharing problems involves sharing one item at a time. Children using this strategy start by splitting the first item to be shared in exactly as many parts as there are people sharing. They then repeat the process for each item until everything is shared. This strategy always leads to an exhaustive and equal distribution of the items shared. It is a fairly common strategy. It is used by

I teach at a school where kids come from a variety of backgrounds, but they all have experiences with sharing things at home with their families. My kindergarteners solve Equal Sharing problems at least once a week. In these problems, the children are cutting or dividing or in some way changing a whole so that there are enough pieces for each person to get some. One idea that we work on is equality. Let's say we are solving a problem where 4 kids are sharing 2 cookies. At first, some children may just want to break off a piece and give it to a kid and then give the rest of the cookie to the other kid. The pieces may not be equal. The kids who have had experience sharing things at home help the rest of the kids. I ask questions like, "Would this be fair?" "Would all the people be happy?" We have many discussions about how to resolve unequal shares. By the end of the year, most kids have the idea of breaking up a whole into equal parts. At first, they don't name the pieces when they solve the problem. I just ask them to show me what each kid gets. Kids came up with their own ways to describe those parts and those amounts. Eventually I talk with kids about what we might call these pieces, but this isn't my focus in kindergarten.

In some curricula, they don't talk about pieces less than one until third grade. I see this as a big loss. Although most traditional fraction activities aren't appropriate for five- and six-year-olds, Equal Sharing problems are. Kids bring an understanding of sharing to school with them and we should build on that understanding. To be good problem solvers, kids need to know how to break up numbers and put them back together in different ways. We spend so much time helping kids understand how ones can be grouped to make a ten. We also need to spend time going in the opposite direction. Kids need to understand how a whole can be broken down in smaller parts and put back together to make a one.

Meghan Ling
Kindergarten Teacher, Capri School
Encinitas, CA

first graders who have some experience solving and discussing Equal Sharing problems and as an initial strategy by older children, including middle-grades students, who have had a minimal amount of exposure to Equal Sharing problems.

For example, a fourth-grade class was beginning a unit on fractions. The teacher gave the following problem:

8 KIDS WERE SHARING 10 small pizzas. How much pizza would each kid get if they shared the pizza equally?

James drew 10 rectangles to represent the pizzas. He partitioned each one into eighths and wrote a person's initial on each piece to show how much 1 person would get (Figure 1–11). He decided that each person would get $^{10}/_8$ pizza.

Children eventually realize that they do not need to partition every single item to figure out how much one person sharing will get. Breelyn, a fifth grader, solved this problem using a transitional strategy:

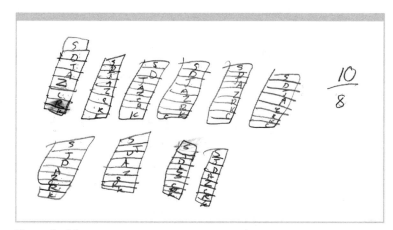

Figure 1–11.
Additive Coordination strategy, one item at a time

THERE ARE 12 CHILDREN who want to share 8 little pies so that everyone gets an equal share. How much pie can one child have?

She began by drawing 8 circles for the 8 pies and partitioned 1 of them in 12 parts so that each child could have 1 part. It was tedious to draw twelfths and so she decided to

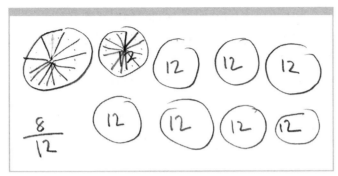

Figure 1–12.
Transitional strategy for solving 8 pies shared equally by 12 children

label the remaining circles with *12* to indicate similar partitions (Figure 1–12). She wrote that each person would get "⁸⁄₁₂."

Additive Coordination—Groups of Items. Children who are learning to reason about equal groups—such as by skip-counting groups or solving multiplication word problems—will often apply what they are learning in their solutions to Equal Sharing problems. They coordinate the number of parts they want to make with the number of items to be shared, usually by aiming to create a number of parts equal to the number of people sharing. The number of items they work with can be the entire set or a smaller subset.

For example, a fourth grader used his knowledge of number facts to decide into how many pieces to partition each candy bar to solve this problem:

LUZ HAS 9 CANDY BARS to share with her friends. Altogether, there are 12 children, including Luz. Everyone wants the same amount. How much candy bar can each child have?

He began by drawing the 12 children and 9 candy bars. His goal at each step was to create 12 pieces, 1 for each child. First he decided to split 6 candy bars in half, because 6×2 is 12. Each child got half of a candy bar, which he redrew under each child (Figure 1–13). Then he split the next 2 candy bars into sixths, because 2×6 is 12. He gave each child ⅙ more candy bar, which he redrew as a small piece under each child. Finally, there was 1 candy bar left. He split this candy bar into twelfths and distributed ¹⁄₁₂ of a candy bar to each person. His final answer was that each sharer got ½ + ⅙ + ¹⁄₁₂ of a candy bar.

These intermediate strategies are rich with possible connections to other content, such as multiplication of whole numbers, addition of fractions with like and unlike denominators, and equivalent fractions. We discuss some of these possible connections in Chapters 6 and 8.

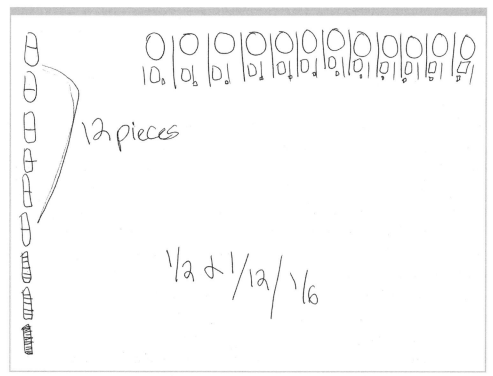

Figure 1–13. *Additive Coordination, working with groups*

Multiplicative Coordination: Fraction as Quotient. With experience solving and discussing Equal Sharing problems, children abbreviate the single-item strategy described above. The two processes that a child carries out separately in that strategy—partitioning each unit individually and then combining the fractional parts—are synthesized into a single, mental strategy in which the child coordinates the operation of division with its outcome, a fraction. This abbreviation is a significant advance in the development of their thinking about fractions.

For example, a sixth grader was solving a problem in which 8 children share 5 small pizzas (Figure 1–14). He wrote "$5 \div 8 = \frac{5}{8}$" for his entire solution and

Algebraic notation	Example	Natural language
$a \div b = \frac{a}{b}$	$5 \div 8 = \frac{5}{8}$	"5 divided into 8 equal parts is five-eighths"

Figure 1-14. *Multiplicative coordination: Fraction as quotient (b ≠ 0)*

explained, "⅝ is what you get when 8 people share 5 things. That's what ⅝ means." When pushed to elaborate he said, "You could think that it is like 5 groups of 1 divided by 8 but I do not think of that anymore. I just know it is ⅝." This way of thinking about fractions illustrates the key idea that the value of a fraction is determined by the division of the numerator by the denominator.

Coming to this understanding takes some time for children. Although this relationship could be learned rotely as a rule—much as learning that to multiply a number by 10, you "add" a 0 to the end of that number can be learned as a trick—students will have trouble remembering when and how to apply the rule if they do not understand it and cannot unpack it. For example, a fifth grader who had memorized $a \div b = {}^a\!/_b$ as a rule was given a problem in which 8 people shared 5 pizzas and said that each person would get ⅝. Then she was asked what would happen if there were 10 pizzas for 5 people and said that each person would get ⁵⁄₁₀. When she was given the numbers in the reverse order, she misapplied the rule.

It is also likely that students who rotely learn a rule will not use the relationship in reasoning about more complex algebraic expressions because they do not understand it. If children are given time to use more basic strategies and to think for themselves about the principles underlying these strategies and how those strategies can be made more efficient, then they will understand *why* $5 \div 8 = ⅝$. Students who understand why $5 \div 8 = ⅝$ have a relational understanding of fractions and division. (We define and provide further examples of Relational Thinking in Chapter 4.)

Less Common Strategies

Some children use strategies that make use of other mathematics concepts—such as ratios and common factors and multiples. These strategies can serve as springboards to investigate and reflect upon more sophisticated ideas.

Ratio Strategies. Equal Sharing problems can be solved by reducing the sharing situation to equivalent ratios involving smaller numbers of people sharing and things being shared. For example, Margie, a fifth grader, solved 8 children sharing 6 sticks of clay by halving the situation and then halving it again (Figure 1–15). She went from 8 sharing 6 to 4 sharing 3 to 2 sharing 1½. At that point, she figured how much each of the 2 sharers would get by splitting 1 stick of clay into 2 halves and the half stick into

Figure 1–15. *Margie's ratio strategy for 8 children sharing 6 sticks of clay*

2 fourths. Her final answer was ½ + ¼ = ¾. She reduced the situation from 6 sticks of clay for 8 children to 1½ sticks of clay for 2 people.

Margie essentially used a common factor, 2, to partition both quantities in the sharing situation into the same number of groups. Both the number of people sharing and the number of things she was sharing were divisible by 2. To help children generalize this strategy beyond repeated halving, teachers need to focus children's attention on the explicit goal of dividing both quantities into the same number of groups—whether it's 3, 4, 5, or more.

Kirk, a fourth grader, recognized the common factor 4 in 24 children sharing 8 pancakes equally. He wrote 4 × 6 = 24 and 4 × 2 = 8 and then drew 4 tables, putting 6 children and 2 pancakes at each table (Figure 1–16). Focusing on only one of the tables, he figured he would split each of the 2 pancakes into sixths, to give each child a share of ⅖. He knew that the shares at each of the other tables would be the same because the ratio of children to pancakes was the same. To help other students see the significance of what Kirk had done, his teacher pointed out how he used the common factor to split the sharing situation into 4 groups and then asked whether there was another way to split the pancakes and children into the same number of

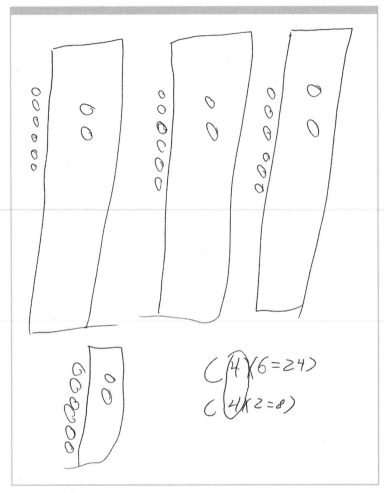

Figure 1–16.
Ratio strategy: simplifying 24 children sharing 8 pancakes to 4 tables each of 6 children sharing 2 pancakes

$(4 \times 6 = 24)$

$(4 \times 2 = 8)$

groups. If Kirk had chosen the greatest common factor, 8, his final share would have been in lowest terms (Empson 2001).

Even children who are able to recognize a common factor may find it hard to apply it in a ratio strategy. This is because children can have the tendency to interpret division in terms of a given sized chunk (how many groups of 4 in 24) rather than a given number of groups (how much in a group if 24 is split into 4 groups).

Summary of Strategy Development

The development of children's understanding of fractional quantities begins in the processes of creating fractional parts by drawing, cutting, folding, and splitting things and then reflecting on the results. By solving and discussing Equal Sharing problems, children come to understand that fractions are defined by a multiplicative relationship between two quantities. This relationship can be derived in several ways in an Equal Sharing situation. One way is by comparing the size of a fractional part to the whole unit. Another is by considering the ratio between the number of items shared and the number of people sharing. Yet another is by dividing the number of items to be shared by the number of people

The long-term goal for English language learners (ELL) is to meet the same math standards as monolingual students. ELL kids, like all kids, need word problems to learn math with understanding. When planning and writing problems for students, my colleagues and I consider what students can do rather than what they can't do. When possible, we assess what mathematics they understand when problems are posed in their first language. We also assess what English vocabulary and structures they understand. We then find or write problems at a level of linguistic and mathematical difficulty that works for our students. For example, although these problems address the same mathematical concept, the second is far more linguistically challenging than the first.

4 kids have 5 candy bars. How much can each kid have?

4 teenagers were going to the Monster Truck Show at the Coliseum. They bought 5 pounds of gumdrops from the concession stand. If they share the gumdrops equally, how many pounds of gumdrops would each teenager get?

We have lots of students who can solve the first problem and not the second one. The first problem is too simple for some ELL kids, but for kids who are just beginning to learn English, it's a great problem. As students learn more English, we gradually make the language of the problems more complex until they are able to solve problems like the second one. An additional benefit of problems with more basic language is that some monolingual students are able to solve these problems when they can't solve the problems that are linguistically more complex. Sometimes we provide two or three problems at different levels of linguistic complexity and allow each student to choose which problem would be best for them to solve.

Ellen Ranney

ELL teacher, John Muir School

Madison, WI

For more information on working with English learners in mathematics, see Maldonado et al. (2009) and Turner et al. (in press).

sharing (Figure 1–17). The strategies that children use to coordinate the quantities in Equal Sharing problems are based on their growing understanding of these multifaceted relationships. This understanding culminates in the knowledge that the division of a by b ($b \neq 0$) is the fraction $^a/_b$.

The goal is for children to understand fractions so that when they see a fraction written symbolically, a conceptual model is evoked and they do not rely on superficial features of the symbols to compute or reason.

Introducing Fraction Terms and Symbols

Naming Fractions

Fraction terminology is not part of children's intuitive knowledge of fractions. Children are familiar with halves and halving. However, many children overgeneralize this understanding and refer to any fractional part as "a half." For example, a third grader told her teacher that she "split the candy bar in threes and gave each person a half." She created three equally sized parts but called them each "a half" simply because they were pieces of a whole unit.

Children can solve Equal Sharing problems and represent their solutions without using fraction terms or symbols to describe the final share. For example, a child could represent the amount one person would get by shading in the amount of one share. This approach to designating the amount of a share is perfectly appropriate in young children's early learning about fractions.

Because terminology is not intuitive, you will need to introduce this language and the logic it follows. Questioning can help children make a connection between the size of a piece and its name. A traditional line of questioning starts with "How many pieces is the whole brownie cut into?" However, because it is the size of the part that determines the fraction's name rather than the number of parts into which the whole is partitioned, this line of questioning can lead to misconceptions.

If your questions focus on the size of the part relative to the whole, rather than the number of parts into which the whole is cut, children learn to look at the relationship between a part and the whole to name the part. Asking "How many of these parts fit into the whole brownie?" prompts children to focus on the relationship between the size of a fractional part and the whole to determine the value of the fraction. If you are consistent in asking this question, children learn that naming

Problem:	6 children are sharing 4 candy bars so that everyone gets the same amount. How much candy bar can each child have?
Strategy Name	**Strategy Description**
Non-Anticipatory Sharing	Child does not think in advance of both number of sharers and amount to be shared. For example, child splits each candy into halves because halves are easy to make. Gives each person ½. Child may or may not decide to split the last candy bar into sixths. *Each person gets ½ of a candy bar and a "little piece," if the last candy bar is split.*
Additive Coordination: –Sharing One Item at a time	Child represents each candy bar. Splits first candy bar into sixths because that is the number of sharers. Each person gets 1 sixth piece. Repeats process until all 4 candy bars are shared. *Each person gets ⁴⁄₆ of a candy bar altogether.*
Additive Coordination: –Sharing Groups of Items	Child represents each candy bar. Realizes that 6 pieces can be created by splitting 2 candy bars each into thirds. Each person gets ⅓. Child moves on to another group of items and continues similarly until all the candy bars are used up. *Each person gets ⅔ of a candy bar altogether.*
Ratio –Repeated Halving –Factors	Child may or may not represent all of the candy bars and people. Uses knowledge of repeated halving or multiplication factors to transform the problem into a simpler problem, 3 children sharing 2 candy bars. Solves the simpler problem. *Each child gets ⅔ of a candy bar.*
Multiplicative Coordination	Child does not need to represent each candy bar. Child understands that *a* things shared by *b* people is ᵃ⁄ᵇ, so 4 candy bars shared by 6 people means *each person gets ⁴⁄₆ of a candy bar.*

Figure 1-17. *Types of strategies children use to solve Equal Sharing problems*

a fractional quantity depends on the size of the part compared to the whole, rather than the actual number of parts into which the whole is cut.

Symbolizing Fractions

We recommend that you introduce fraction terms and symbols gradually, to ensure that children's use of mathematical terms and symbols keeps pace with their developing understanding of the meaning of fractions.

You can begin by presenting fraction terminology and encouraging children to use fraction terms—usually spelled out (halves, fourths, thirds, and so on)—in combination with counting numbers (1, 2, 3, …) to describe and quantify shares. When children understand fraction terms, distinguishing between the numerator (a counting number) and the denominator (a fraction term) in this way actually comes easily to them. For example, consider how the fraction symbol $\frac{2}{3}$ can refer to an amount of a candy bar. The numerator, 2, refers to the number of pieces in the share. The denominator, 3, refers to the size of the piece relative to the whole. To represent $\frac{2}{3}$, young children would write "2 thirds." When children begin to independently use correct fraction terminology to describe shares, you can introduce the standard fraction symbol ($\frac{a}{b}$). If you decide to represent fractional amounts on a number line, children will be best prepared to understand how a single point can represent an amount such as $\frac{2}{3}$ when they are able to relate fractional amounts to well known benchmark fractions, such as $\frac{1}{4}$ or $\frac{1}{2}$.

Figure 1–18 shows this progression in children's use of fraction terms and symbols in the context of Equal Sharing, from pictorial to symbolic.

A Note About Young Children's Drawn Partitions

Very young children may have some difficulty representing how they would split a cake or candy bar. Some of children's earliest partitions are literal in their representations of pieces. For example, a first grader used "sharks' teeth" to show how she would share a cake with four people (Figure 1–19a). Her drawing is inspired by what a cake might look like if the pieces were cut out one at a time—the way most cakes are served. She is thinking about cutting one piece at a time, disregarding the size of each piece and its relationship to the whole. Similarly, another first grader showed how he would share a piece of paper among 4 people by indicating each piece with a

Children's Representations for Fractions	Example: Representing ⅔ in solution to 3 children sharing 2 candy bars
Use diagrams and physical materials to represent amounts	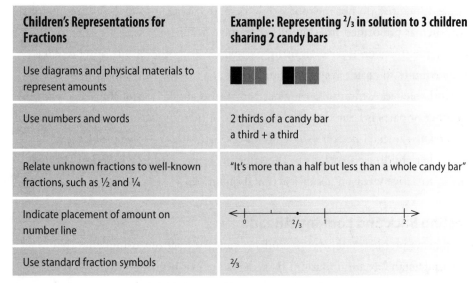
Use numbers and words	2 thirds of a candy bar a third + a third
Relate unknown fractions to well-known fractions, such as ½ and ¼	"It's more than a half but less than a whole candy bar"
Indicate placement of amount on number line	
Use standard fraction symbols	⅔

Figure 1-18. Progression of children's use of fractions words and symbols

separate shape (Figure 1–19b). He wanted to cut the paper into 4 parts, but did not think ahead about where each cut should be made to make the pieces equal.

Older children tend to be able to partition more accurately. But there are still many partitions such as into sevenths or tenths in which it is impossible to achieve more than roughly equal areas, even for adults.

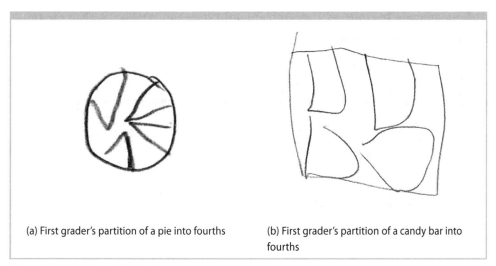

(a) First grader's partition of a pie into fourths

(b) First grader's partition of a candy bar into fourths

Figure 1-19. Young children's partitions

These difficulties do not mean it would be better for you to give children manipulatives such as preformed fraction pieces to solve problems. Learning how to create fractional quantities on their own using part-whole and other kinds of representations contributes to children's understanding of fractions in the long run, because to create workable representations, they need to reason about relationships, such as how the number of parts is related to the whole unit or how the ratio of sharers to shared items is related to each person's share. With opportunities to solve problems and observe other children's solutions to the same problems, children such as these two will learn to actively reason about fractional quantities.

Reflecting Back and Looking Ahead

Equal Sharing problems allow your students to learn fractions using what they already understand as a foundation. If students are just beginning to learn fractions, solving Equal Sharing problems makes it possible for them to draw on what they know about partitioning and sharing to create and reflect on fractional quantities. If students are further along in their understanding of fractions, solving and discussing Equal Sharing problems helps them use what they know about division and benchmark fractions to reason about increasingly sophisticated relationships between fractions and whole numbers. You can choose numbers for Equal Sharing problems that help students build on their current strategies, and students can deepen their understanding of fractions by connecting terminology and symbols to their solutions for Equal Sharing problems.

Equal Sharing problems are a productive way to begin fraction instruction with students in all of the elementary grades. In Chapter 2, we describe how teachers at two ends of this span of grades used Equal Sharing problems with their students.

Equal Sharing Problems

Here are some **Equal Sharing problems** that you may pose to your students. In general, the simpler problems are at the beginning of the list and the more challenging problems are at the end. Feel free to change the context or names in the problems so that your students will understand the problem situation. Also feel free to change the numbers in the problems to engage your students in the appropriate mathematics. For suggestions on numbers appropriate for your grade level, see pages 32–35.

The last problem is written with several number choices. Providing a variety of number choices is a common way to differentiate problems for students. The number choices here progress in difficulty from left to right. Teachers who give students problems in this format teach students to choose a pair of numbers and put the first number in the first blank and the second number in the second blank. When teachers use this format regularly, students learn to choose a set of numbers that is challenging but not overwhelming.

EQUAL SHARING PROBLEM	SHARING SITUATION
A. Kito and Frida have 13 cookies. If they share the cookies equally, how many cookies would each person get?	**2 share 13**
B. 4 children want to share 10 submarine sandwiches so that everyone gets the same amount. How much can each child have?	**4 share 10**

EQUAL SHARING PROBLEM	SHARING SITUATION
C. 4 children want to share 13 brownies so that each child gets the same amount. How much can each child get?	**4 share 13**
D. There are 11 yards of ribbon for 4 people to share. How many yards of ribbon can each person get if they share the ribbon equally?	**4 share 11**
E. 4 children want to share 3 oranges so that everyone gets the same amount. How much orange can each child have?	**4 share 3**
F. The teacher gave 4 sandwiches to 3 students to share. If the students shared the sandwiches equally, how many sandwiches would each student get?	**3 share 4**
G. 3 friends were at a Mexican restaurant. They were feeling hungry, so they ordered 8 burritos to eat. They want to share the burritos equally and eat them all. How much will each friend get to eat?	**3 share 8**
H. At the school carnival, Daniel won 6 chocolate cream pies. He plans to share them with his 7 friends. If all 8 people get the same amount of pie, how much pie can each person have?	**8 share 6**
I. Avery had 20 cupcakes at her birthday party for 6 children to share equally. How much cupcake can each child have?	**6 share 20**
J. Jayden has 18 sour cherry fruit strips. He and his 4 friends are going to share them all so that all 5 people get the same amount. How many fruit strips can each person have?	**5 share 18**
K. 12 children in art class have to share 8 packages of clay so that everyone gets the same amount. How much clay can each child have?	**12 share 8**
L. There are 3 liters of apple juice at a school party. 10 students want to drink all of the apple juice, and they all want to get exactly the same amount. How much apple juice can each student have?	**10 share 3**

EQUAL SHARING PROBLEM	SHARING SITUATION
M. 10 people want to share 84 pounds of candy so that each person gets the same amount. Exactly how many pounds of candy should each person get?	**10 share 84**
N. 20 children want to share 12 pounds of beads so that everyone gets the same amount. How much can each child have?	**20 share 12**
O. There were 36 campers at Camp Green Lake. They had 10 large cheese pizzas to share equally. How much pizza can each camper have?	**36 share 10**
P. 2 people want to share 1¾ submarine sandwiches so that each one gets the same amount. How much should each person get?	**2 share 1¾**
Q. 3 children want to equally share 6½ peanut butter sandwiches, with no leftovers. How much can each child have?	**3 share 6½**
R. Drake has _____ pounds of sunflower seeds. He and his friends are going to share them equally. There are _____ people altogether, including Drake. If everyone gets the same amount with nothing left over, what is the size of each person's share? (3, 6) (1½, 6) (3⁶⁄₇, 6) (3¾, 6)	**Various**

Instructional Guidelines for Equal Sharing Problems and Introducing Fractions

At several points in this book, we provide suggestions for problems and instructional goals at each grade level. In this section, we provide guidelines for posing and discussing Equal Sharing problems and introducing fraction terms and symbols. Grade levels are provided as a general guideline. Some children will be ready for problems at higher grades, and some children will need to work with problems designated for lower grades. If children have not had experience solving and discussing problems listed at earlier grades, start with them. You will most likely move through those problems fairly quickly. The important thing is that each child is engaged in solving and discussing problems at an appropriate level of challenge. We recommend that you read the suggestions for all of the grade levels rather than only for the grade level you teach. In many cases, we explain a concept only at one grade level.

KINDERGARTEN AND FIRST GRADE

✔ **Multiplication, Measurement Division, and Partitive Division with whole numbers to develop ideas of grouping and partitioning. For example:**

- *Juan has 5 baskets with 6 apples in each basket. How many apples does Juan have all together?*
- *4 children want to share 12 cans of play dough so that each child gets the same amount. How many cans of play dough should each child get?*
- *Steve has 12 dollars. A pack of trading cards costs 3 dollars. How many packs of cards can Steve buy?*

✔ Equal Sharing problems with remainders that can be shared. The number of sharers should be 2 and 4 for most children. Focus on problems with 1 or 2 remainders to be shared. For example:

- *2 children want to share 5 cupcakes so that each child gets the same amount. How many cupcakes should each child get?*
- *4 children want to share 10 cans of play dough so that each child gets the same amount. How much play dough should each child get?*

✔ Ask children about how they decide to split remainders.

✔ Introduce fraction names for shares (halves, fourths); $^a/_b$ notation is not necessary in these grades.

SECOND GRADE

✔ Multiplication, Measurement Division, and Partitive Division with whole numbers.

✔ Equal Sharing problems with remainders that can be shared. The number of sharers should be 2, 4, and 3 for most children. For example:

- *4 children want to share 22 cans of play dough so that each child gets the same amount. How many cans of play dough should each child get?*
- *3 children want to share 10 tamales so that each child gets the same amount. How many tamales should each child get?*

✔ Ask children about how they decide to share the leftovers.

✔ Introduce and reinforce fraction names for shares. For example:

- *"a half"*
- *"one-fourth"*
- *"three-fourths"*
- *"two-thirds"*

✔ Encourage children to represent shares (answer) with pictures, whole numbers, and fraction words (see Figure 1–18).

✔ Introduce the symbol for ½ once children learn to differentiate between halves, fourths, and thirds in words.

THIRD GRADE

✔ Equal Sharing problems with answers that are mixed numbers and fractions less than 1. The number of sharers should be 2, 4, 8, 3, 6, and 10 for most students. For example:

- *4 children are sharing 11 submarine sandwiches. If they want everyone to have the same amount, how much should each child have?*

- *There are 2 fruit strips for 3 children to share. If everyone gets the same amount, how much would each child get?*
- *6 children want to share 5 cupcakes equally. How many cupcakes would each child get?*
- *10 children want to share 1 cake. If everyone gets the same amount of cake, how much would each person get?*

✔ Introduce standard notation for unit fractions after ample work with pictures and fraction words.

- $\frac{1}{2}$
- $\frac{1}{4}$
- $\frac{1}{3}$

✔ Plan problems where students will get equivalent answers; discuss whether these answers represent the same amounts. For example:

- *If students solved a problem about 4 children sharing 2 cookies and some got $\frac{2}{4}$ and others got $\frac{1}{2}$, ask, "Is $\frac{2}{4}$ the same as $\frac{1}{2}$?")*
- *If students solved a problems about 8 children are sharing 6 cookies you might say "We have 3 different answers: $\frac{3}{4}$, $\frac{6}{8}$, and $\frac{1}{2}$ plus $\frac{1}{4}$. Are all of these the same amount?"*

✔ Introduce equations to represent students' answers. (See fifth and sixth grades for examples of other questions you may ask.)

- $\frac{1}{4} + \frac{1}{4} + \frac{1}{4} = \frac{3}{4}$ *("You found that each child would get $\frac{1}{4}$ of each of 3 cookies and that $\frac{1}{4}$ plus $\frac{1}{4}$ plus $\frac{1}{4}$ is the same as $\frac{3}{4}$. Does this number sentence show what you did?")*

FOURTH GRADE

✔ Equal Sharing problems with answers that are mixed numbers and fractions less than 1. Focus on 2, 4, 8, 3, 6, and 10 sharers, but include other numbers of sharers as well. Make sure students are working with nonunit fractions. For example:

- *3 children want to share 2 candy bars equally. How much candy bar should each child get?*
- *There are 4 burritos for 5 children to share. If they each want to have the same amount, how much burrito should each child get?*
- *8 children want to share 3 pies so they each have the same amount of pie. How much pie should each child get?*
- *We have 13 liters of juice for 10 children to share equally. How much juice should each child get?*

✔ If students have little to no prior experience solving Equal Sharing problems, you may need to spend a couple of weeks letting students represent shares with pictures, whole numbers, and fraction words before introducing and using standard fraction notation (see Figure 1–18).

✔ Plan problems where students will get equivalent answers; discuss whether these answers are the same (see third grade for examples of what questions you could ask to prompt discussion). Examples of appropriate problems include:

- *12 children are sharing 9 candy bars equally. How much candy bar would each child get?*
- *There are 6 candy bars for 8 children to share. If each child got the same amount, how much would each child get?*
- *20 children want to share 8 candy bars equally. How much should each child get?*

✔ Represent children's solutions with equations, with an emphasis on addition. (See third, fifth and sixth grades for examples of what questions you could ask.)

FIFTH AND SIXTH GRADES

✔ Equal Sharing problems with answers that are mixed numbers and fractions less than 1. Focus on problems with 4, 8, 3, 6, 10, and 12 sharers, but include other numbers of sharers as well, such as 15, 20, 100.

✔ Represent children's solutions with equations, with an emphasis on linking addition and multiplication and on equations that reflect a multiplicative understanding of fractions. For example, if students solved a problem about 8 children sharing 5 hamburgers you might write the following equations:

- $\frac{1}{8} + \frac{1}{8} + \frac{1}{8} + \frac{1}{8} + \frac{1}{8} = \frac{5}{8}$ (*"Kinga drew 5 hamburgers and gave each person an eighth of each hamwburger. She put the pieces together and said that $\frac{1}{8}$ plus $\frac{1}{8}$ plus $\frac{1}{8}$ plus $\frac{1}{8}$ plus $\frac{1}{8}$ is $\frac{5}{8}$. Does this equation show what Kinga did?"*)
- $5 \times \frac{1}{8} = \frac{5}{8}$ (*"Michaela drew 1 hamburger split it into 8 pieces. She said that each person would get $\frac{1}{8}$ of this hamburger. The other hamburgers would look just the same and she said that 5 groups of $\frac{1}{8}$ is the same as $\frac{5}{8}$."*)
- $5 \div 8 = \frac{5}{8}$ (*"Raymond said that he knows that when 5 things are shared by 8 people each person gets $\frac{5}{8}$."*)

✔ Represent the word problem situation using equations.

- *8 children are sharing 5 hamburgers equally. How much hamburger does one child get?*
  - $5 \div 8 = \square$
  - $8 \times \square = 5$

chapter 2

From the Classroom

Getting Started with Fractions

In Chapter 1, we introduced Equal Sharing problems and described the evolution of children's strategies. In this chapter, we show you how two teachers at opposite ends of the elementary years used Equal Sharing problems to teach fractions. Ms. Murphy teaches a multiage kindergarten and first-grade class at a school where about 70 percent of the children come from low-income families. Ms. Neha teaches seventh grade at a school in a prosperous part of town where none of the children come from low-income families. Even though these groups of students were quite different from each other, they both used a variety of strategies similar to the ones described in Chapter 1.

Equal Sharing in Kindergarten and First Grade

Most of Ms. Murphy's kindergarteners entered school with little knowledge of formal mathematics. Few of them could write the numbers one to ten and most could not count to twenty. Each year, Ms. Murphy begins mathematics instruction with simple word problems. In the first month of school, children solve problems like this:

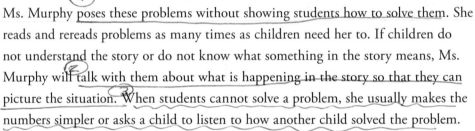

JASMINE HAD 2 BOOKS. She got 3 more books for her birthday. How many books did Jasmine have then?

JULIAN AND HIS SISTER have 6 cookies. How many cookies would Julian get if he and his sister shared the cookies equally?

Ms. Murphy poses these problems without showing students how to solve them. She reads and rereads problems as many times as children need her to. If children do not understand the story or do not know what something in the story means, Ms. Murphy will talk with them about what is happening in the story so that they can picture the situation. When students cannot solve a problem, she usually makes the numbers simpler or asks a child to listen to how another child solved the problem.

Ms. Murphy spends a lot of time listening to her students explain how they solved problems. Because these students are so young, watching what they do can be just as important as hearing what they say. After children have worked individually to solve a problem, Ms. Murphy chooses two or three children to explain or show their strategies to the rest of the class or small group. This way, while she listens she also supports her students to listen to each other.

When we talked with Ms. Murphy about introducing fractions to her kindergarten and first-grade students, she was interested but skeptical. The fourth- and fifth-grade teachers at her school struggled to teach fractions, and their students typically did not do well in fractions on standardized tests. She wondered if her students would be able to learn anything at all about fractions. Yet she was also optimistic because her children were able to solve division problems such as the one above about Julian and his sister sharing cookies. In general, she had learned that her students could solve word problems if they understood the story and were able to make sets to represent the quantities in the story.

Posing the First Fraction Problem

In January, Ms. Murphy posed the following problem to her students:

> SHERELLE AND TYRONE GOT 7 brownies at after-school club. Miss Carolyn told them that they could share the brownies as long as they each got the same amount. How many brownies would each person get?

She had printed the problem on a piece of paper for each child. Everyone had a pencil but no other materials. She read the problem several times for the children. None of her kindergarteners could read this problem and only three of her first graders could.

After about two minutes, Johnetta, one of the first graders, had something to say.

Johnetta: This is impossible! They are going to have to give the brownies back!

Ms. Murphy: Why do you think that?

Johnetta: Either Sherelle gets more or Tyrone gets more and Miss Carolyn said they had to be same!

Tommy: Miss Carolyn must have made a goof.

Ms. Murphy: [holds up 7 pieces of brown construction paper that she had hidden under her chair] Can we pretend that these are the 7 brownies? Sherelle and Tyrone, come on up here. You lucky kids are the ones who are getting the brownies, but you can only get them if you share them equally.

Tyrone, a kindergartener, took the 7 pieces of construction paper from Ms. Murphy and passed them out to Sherelle and himself, until they each had 3 pieces. He had 1 piece of paper left.

Tyrone: That one is left. If I take it, I have more, and if Sherelle takes it, she has more.

Ms. Murphy: I wonder if it is impossible. Miss Carolyn did say that they had to have the same. I wonder if there is anything we could do? [long pause in which none of the children offers a suggestion] In our family, sometimes we don't have enough for everyone to get a whole cookie. Like if we go to Subway and get cookies for dessert. I think those cookies are just too big and too expensive so I don't buy one for each person. Maybe if just Dan and I are going for cookies, I might just buy one cookie. Does that ever happen in your families? [The children said that it did.] What do your moms do when that happens?

Nadia: They break off little pieces for each person.

Ms. Murphy: Yes, anything else?

Simon: They give us each half.

Ms. Murphy: Half—what does that mean?

Simon: Half, like if you make 1 cookie and break it into 2.

Ms. Murphy: I wonder if that could help us with…

Ava: [interrupting] Oh, that's what Sherelle and Tyrone could do. Share the last one.

Ms. Murphy: Tell me more about that.

Ava: [in her excitement has walked to the front of the room] Is it OK if I ruin this paper?

Ms. Murphy: Sure.

Ava: [trying to carefully tear the paper into two equal pieces] I am trying to make it the same. They could do this, make 2 little brownies and each gets 1 little brownie.

Ms. Murphy: Wow, does that give you some ideas of what they could do?

Ava: Yes. They could each get 3 big brownies and a little brownie.

Simon: They each get 3 brownies and a half brownie.

Ms. Murphy: Ava, what do you think, do they each get 3 brownies and a half brownie?

Ava: Yes, that would work!

At this point, the conversation had lasted about fifteen minutes and several students were no longer paying attention. Ms. Murphy decided to stop there.

The next day, Ms. Murphy posed an Equal Sharing problem where 2 children were sharing 5 cookies. This time about 5 children immediately said that they could break the last cookie in half. By the end of the discussion, about half of the children had answers such as, "2 big cookies and 1 small cookie," "2 cookies and a piece" and a few children said, "2 cookies and a half." The rest of the children said that the extra cookie could be saved for later or given to the teacher.

Ms. Murphy continued to give Equal Sharing problems throughout the remainder of the school year. Some weeks, she would pose a couple of Equal Sharing problems. Sometimes weeks would go by without her posing any Equal Sharing problems. She only gave problems with either 2 or 4 people sharing.

Figure 2–1.
Adrianna's strategy for 2 people sharing 3 cookies

By the end of the year, all but two of her students were able to provide at least a pictorial answer such as the one shown in Figure 2–1 for situations where an odd number of items were shared by 2 people. In Figure 2–1, Adrianna shows how much each person would get if 2 people shared 3 cookies.

Some of the children provided both a picture and words to express their solutions to these problems. Figure 2–2 shows how Ava solved the problem about 2 people sharing 3 cookies.

Many of the children were able to solve Equal Sharing problems with 4 sharers. Figure 2–3 shows how Adrianna solved a problem where 4 children were sharing 3 cakes.

Ava solved this same problem by dividing the first two cakes in half and the last cake in fourths. She concluded that each person would get "a half and a little half."

Ms. Murphy's students were able to solve simple Equal Sharing problems with

Figure 2–2.
Ava's strategy for 2 people sharing 3 cookies

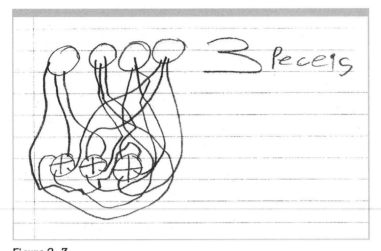

Figure 2–3.
Adrianna's strategy for 4 people sharing 3 cakes

2 or 4 sharers, involving situations with which the children were familiar. They usually did not provide answers that included fractional terms, but they were able to show how much each sharer would get. Solving and discussing these problems helped the children begin to understand how parts were related to wholes, whether it was a brownie, a cookie, or something else.

Equal Sharing in Seventh Grade

Ms. Neha teaches seventh grade at a school in a prosperous neighborhood of a midsized city. Like Ms. Murphy, Ms. Neha's class is focused on students' ideas. She uses a mathematics curriculum that is problem based and encourages students to use a variety of strategies. Students spend a lot of time talking about their mathematical ideas with each other.

Even though her students typically do well on standardized mathematics tests, Ms. Neha felt that they had gaps in their understanding of fractions. We talked with her about problems to use to develop students' understanding of fractions and she decided to start with Equal Sharing. She began by giving this problem and, like Ms. Murphy, offered no instruction on the specific strategies for students to use:

8 PEOPLE WANT TO SHARE 5 pizzas so that each person gets the same amount. How much pizza would each person get?

Her students used almost all of the strategies described in Chapter 1. Sarah and Ethan used Nonanticipatory strategies. Sarah at first tried splitting each pizza in half, found that she had a leftover, then tried fourths, and again found that she had a leftover, and then finally tried eighths and found that she was able to give out all of the parts so that each person got $\frac{5}{8}$ of a pizza. Ethan began by splitting all 5 of the pizzas in half. He gave each student a half and had 1 pizza left. He split that pizza in eighths and said that each person would get a half and an eighth. (See Figure 2–4.)

Most students used an Additive Coordination strategy in which they shared each item. They drew all 5 pizzas, split them into eighths, and found that each person would get $\frac{5}{8}$ of a pizza. Figure 2–5 shows what Josh did.

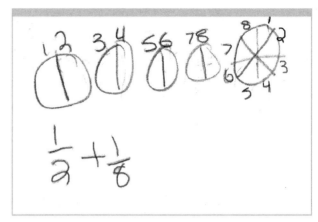

Figure 2–4.
Ethan's Nonanticipatory strategy in which he started by partitioning all of the pizzas in halves

Mindy used a transitional strategy. (See Figure 2–6.) She split the first pizza into eighths and then said that each person would get $\frac{1}{8}$ of that pizza and then $\frac{1}{8}$ of each remaining pizza for a total of $\frac{5}{8}$ of a pizza.

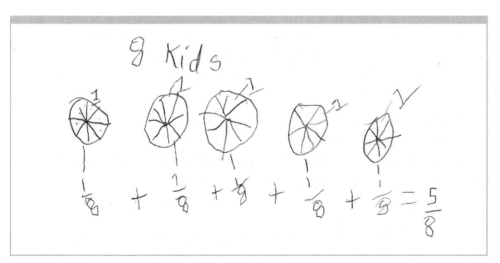

Figure 2–5. *Josh's Additive Coordination strategy in which he represented sharing each pizza with all of the people*

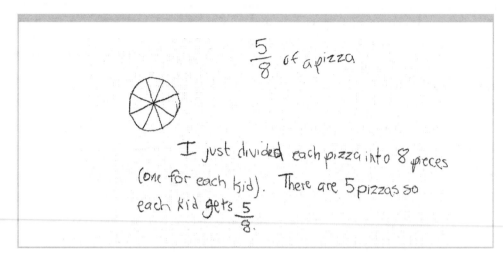

$\frac{5}{8}$ of a pizza

I just divided each pizza into 8 pieces (one for each kid). There are 5 pizzas so each kid gets $\frac{5}{8}$.

Figure 2–6. *Mindy's strategy showing her thinking making a transition from Additive to Multiplicative Coordination*

Only two students, Andy and Kara, immediately figured that each person would get ⅝, without drawing any of the pizzas. They were the only students who used Multiplicative Coordination and understood a fraction as a quotient.

Ms. Neha's students were accustomed to discussing their ideas and were able to describe their strategies and compare their solutions. They realized that Ethan's answer of ½ and ⅛ was the same as ⅝ by reasoning that ½ is the same as ⁴⁄₈ so ½ and ⅛ would be the same as ⁴⁄₈ and ⅛, which is ⅝. Several students who used strategies like Sarah's or Ethan's liked Mindy's idea about splitting 1 pizza into eighths and then deducing that the remaining pizza would each yield ⅛ for each person. In general, the students were perplexed when Kara and Andy shared that they just knew each person would get ⅝ pizza. Andy said, "It's 5 pizzas divided by 8 people, so it's ⅝." Other students listened and asked questions but did not seem convinced.

Solving this problem and discussing some possible solutions took about 25 minutes. Ms. Neha had time for one more problem. She posed this one:

16 KIDS NEED TO SHARE 12 pounds of clay. If they share the clay equally, how much clay would each kid get?

This problem is harder than the first problem. As before, only Kara and Andy used a Multiplicative Coordination strategy and immediately said $^{12}/_{16}$. Some of the students who used less efficient strategies on the first problem adopted Mindy's strategy for this problem. A few children used a Ratio strategy and reasoned that 16 sharing 12 was the same as 8 sharing 6, which was the same as 4 sharing 3, and then drew 3 items and found that each person would get $^3/_4$.

Making Sure Students Are Prepared for High School Algebra

When Ms. Neha saw that so few used Multiplicative Coordination to arrive at an immediate answer, she realized that although her students knew a lot about fractions, they did not understand the multiplicative relationship between the numerator and the denominator. These children would be studying algebra next year, and Ms. Neha

knew that understanding concepts such as slope or algebraic expressions such as $\dfrac{3x^2}{6x}$

would be challenging without a firm understanding of the multiplicative relationship between numerator and denominator. She supplemented the fraction units in her

Figure 2–7. *Listening to a classmate share her strategy*

curriculum with Equal Sharing problems and the other types of problems discussed later in this book. In some cases, she substituted these problems for the fraction activities in her textbook because she found that the problems prompted richer discussion and allowed for a greater variety of solution strategies than the fraction activities did. By the end of the year, most of her students were able to use Multiplicative Coordination to solve Equal Sharing problems. She felt her students were much better prepared for algebra than they would have been if they had not solved and discussed these problems.

Reflecting Back and Looking Ahead

Equal Sharing problems can be used by teachers in any grade to assess students' understanding of fractions and to build students' understanding of fractional quantities. Younger students can solve Equal Sharing problems by drawing on their intuitive understanding. You can use Equal Sharing problems with older students to refine and deepen their understanding of fractions.

Once students have a basic understanding of fractions, you can move on to more challenging problems. In Chapter 3, we introduce Multiple Groups problems. These types of problems help students refine their understanding of fractional quantities and to begin to conceptualize multiple groupings of fractions.

Student Commentary

Last year I had a teacher who was telling me what to do. He told me all these different things to do with fractions. It took me a long, long time to learn his ways. This year my teacher allows me to try to do everything myself. She helps me, but she doesn't show me exactly what to do. I am working hard this year figuring out how to solve problems, but I kinda like it.

Selma, seventh grader

chapter 3

Multiple Groups Problems and Children's Strategies for Solving Them

a typical curriculum sequence follows the introduction of
fractions with the topics of equivalent fractions and then addition
and subtraction of fractions. We recommend a departure from this sequence
and propose that once students can create and name fractional quantities in
their solutions to Equal Sharing problems, they work on *Multiple Groups* word
problems involving a whole number of equal groups of fractional amounts.
These problems are special cases of multiplication and division of fractions.
Multiple Groups problems help children reinforce and extend their understanding of fractions in terms of mathemat-
ical relationships, which is foundational to
understanding equivalence and to operating
on fractions—adding, subtracting, multiplying, and dividing them.

In this chapter, we introduce Multiple
Groups problems and then examine the
types of strategies that children use to
solve these problems.

Types of Multiple Groups Problems

In Chapter 1, we introduced a framework for classifying multiplication and division story problems based on whether the unknown was the number of groups, the amount in each group, or the total amount. In this chapter, we expand that framework to encompass what we call Multiple Groups problems. Multiple Groups problems are multiplication and division word problems that involve a whole number of groups, with a fractional amount in each group. You can use these problems to strengthen children's understanding of fractions and provide an introduction to computation with fractions.

Here are two examples of Multiple Groups problems:

EACH SMALL CAKE TAKES ¾ of a cup of frosting. If Bety wants to make 24 small cakes, how much frosting will she need?

EACH SMALL CAKE TAKES ⅔ of a cup of frosting. If Bety made 8 cups of frosting, how many small cakes can she frost?

Before you read on, we invite you to take a minute to identify the known and unknown quantities in each problem and write an equation that could represent each situation, using the numbers in the problem.

In the first problem, the given information includes the amount in each group (¾ of a cup) and the number of groups (24). This problem asks us to figure out how much 24 groups of ¾ are. The *total amount* of frosting is unknown, so the problem is Multiple Groups Multiplication. In the second problem, the given information includes the amount in each group (⅔ of a cup) and the total amount of frosting (8 cups). The problem asks us to find how many groups of ⅔ are in 8. The *number of groups* (small cakes) that can be frosted is unknown, and so the problem is Multiple Groups Measurement Division (Figure 3–1).

These problems are similar to whole-number multiplication and division problems involving equal groups in that they can be solved by repeated addition or

Problem Type	Number of Groups (Whole Number)	Amount per Group (Fraction)	Total	Possible Equation*
Equal Sharing (Multiple Groups, Partitive Division) 12 children are sharing 9 peanut butter and jelly sandwiches. How much sandwich would each child get?	12	Unknown	9	$12 \times a = 9$
Multiple Groups: Multiplication I need to make peanut butter and jelly sandwiches for 12 children. I want to make $\frac{3}{4}$ of a sandwich for each child. How many sandwiches do I need to make?	12	$\frac{3}{4}$	Unknown	$12 \times \frac{3}{4} = b$
Multiple Groups: Measurement Division I have 9 peanut butter and jelly sandwiches. How many children could I feed with these sandwiches if I give $\frac{3}{4}$ of a sandwich to each child?	Unknown	$\frac{3}{4}$	9	$c \times \frac{3}{4} = 9$

*When we write $n \times m$ for a Multiple Groups problem, we let n stand for the number of groups and m stand for the amount per group.

Figure 3–1. *Multiple Groups problem types*

subtraction. But instead of groups that contain a collection of objects that can be counted, children deal with groups that contain a fractional amount. These problems are solvable by children well before the point in the mathematics curriculum when multiplication and division of fractions are typically introduced.[1]

In contrast to Equal Sharing, these problems incorporate fractions in the problem statement. To make sense of these problems, then, children need to have some basic

---

[1] In Chapter 8, we discuss multiplication and division of fractions in which the solution is not modeled through repeated addition or subtraction of groups and students need to deal with fractions of fractions—for example, $\frac{1}{3} \div \frac{2}{3} = \frac{1}{2}$ or $\frac{3}{4} \times \frac{8}{9} = \frac{6}{9}$. These problems are more difficult to solve.

understanding of fractions in place. This understanding does not need to be fully developed. Simpler versions of these problems involving unit fractions such as $\frac{1}{3}$ and $\frac{1}{4}$ can be used to help children learn to reason explicitly about the relationship between a unit fraction and its whole. The frog food problem in the next section is an example of such a problem.

Using Multiple Groups Problems to Reinforce Basic Fraction Relationships

To illustrate the use of Multiple Groups problems to develop children's understanding of basic fraction relationships, we present a vignette from a third-grade classroom where the children solved a Measurement Division problem. The teacher, Ms. Thomas, decided to have the class solve a problem involving a unit-fraction quantity to encourage children to work on developing their understanding of the relationship $n \times \frac{1}{n} = 1$—in this problem, the specific relationship was 3 groups of $\frac{1}{3}$ is equal to 1. The class was beginning their third week of studying fractions. They had solved and discussed Equal Sharing problems, and Ms. Thomas knew that several of her students were still building their understanding of basic fractions relationships. She gave them this problem:

THE ZOOKEEPER HAS 4 CUPS of frog food. His frogs eat $\frac{1}{3}$ cup of food each day. How long can he feed the frogs before the food runs out?

This problem is a Measurement Division problem, because the total amount of food—4 cups—is known and the goal is to find how many measures of $\frac{1}{3}$ cup the total contains. Ms. Thomas had posed many whole-number Measurement Division problems to her students before this lesson. The children did not think of this problem explicitly as division; instead, they drew upon their understanding of fraction relationships to solve it. As a matter of routine, Ms. Thomas expected and encouraged her students to rely upon their own reasoning to solve problems such as this one.

Jack drew 4 rectangles to represent the 4 cups of food, and then split each rectangle into thirds (Figure 3–2). He said that $\frac{1}{3}$ of a cup could feed the frogs for 1

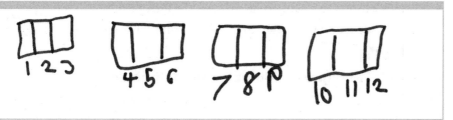

Figure 3-2. *Jack's strategy for the frog problem*

day, and then numbered all of the thirds to count the total number of days that the frogs could be fed. His answer was 12. Jack's strategy is a Direct Modeling strategy because he represents the situation and every quantity in the problem.[2]

Kay started with the relationship $\frac{1}{3} + \frac{1}{3} + \frac{1}{3} = 1$. She continued to add $\frac{1}{3}$ cups of food until she had created a total of 4 cups (Figure 3–3). She then went back and counted the number of thirds she had added and got a total of 12.

Solving this problem helped Jack and Kay consolidate their

$$\frac{1}{3} + \frac{1}{3} + \frac{1}{3} = 1 \qquad 3 \text{ days}$$

$$1 + \frac{1}{3} = 1\frac{1}{3}$$

$$1\frac{1}{3} + \frac{1}{3} = 1\frac{2}{3}$$

$$1\frac{2}{3} + \frac{1}{3} = 2$$

$$2 + \frac{1}{3} + \frac{1}{3} + \frac{1}{3} = 3$$

$$3 + \frac{1}{3} + \frac{1}{3} + \frac{1}{3} = 4$$

Figure 3-3.
Kay's strategy for the frog problem

understanding of $\frac{1}{3}$ as relational, because they repeatedly constructed 3 groups of $\frac{1}{3}$ to make 1 in their solutions. Jack constructed this relationship with a drawing; Kay constructed this relationship symbolically with an equation, $\frac{1}{3} + \frac{1}{3} + \frac{1}{3} = 1$. Ms. Thomas' goal was to reinforce for children the relationship that 3 groups of $\frac{1}{3}$ is 1. Recall Holly's attempt to solve a similar problem, described in Chapter 1 (p. 5). Lack of a grasp of the basic relationship $\frac{1}{2} + \frac{1}{2} = 1$ prevented Holly from combining

---

[2] For more on Direct Modeling see Chapter 1, *Children's Mathematics: Cognitively Guided Instruction* (Carpenter et al. 1999).

halves into wholes. This vignette shows how the use of Multiple Groups problems can help children develop a relational understanding that n groups of $\frac{1}{n}$ is 1.

Children's Strategies for Multiple Groups Problems

Multiple Groups problems can also be used to develop more sophisticated understandings of fraction relationships and operations. Students are capable of generating their own strategies for Multiple Groups problems fairly early in the course of instruction in fractions. These strategies reflect and reinforce their growing understanding of fraction relationships. Younger children, such as second or third graders, tend to use more basic strategies, such as Direct Modeling and Repeated Addition. Older children may use these more basic strategies if they have not been exposed to Multiple Groups problems. But when instruction supports them to reflect on the mathematical relationships they use in their strategies, they are able to more quickly develop sophisticated ways of thinking about these types of problems. In the sections that follow, we describe the strategies that students use to solve Multiple Groups problems and how these strategies reflect an increasingly sophisticated understanding of fraction relationships.

Representing Each Fractional Quantity Individually: Direct Modeling and Repeated Addition

Direct Modeling and Repeated Addition are the most basic strategies for Multiple Groups problems. When children use these strategies, they represent all of the quantities in the problem and count or add (or occasionally for Measurement Division problems, subtract) to figure a final answer. To produce even the most elementary strategies, students need to be able to represent and reason about fraction relationships, such as $\frac{1}{4} + \frac{1}{4} + \frac{1}{4} + \frac{1}{4} = 1$ and $3 \times \frac{1}{3} = 1$. Children's understanding of these relationships is often implicit and not directly represented in their solution.

For example, two fourth graders were given the following Measurement Division problem:

NINA HAS 10½ YARDS of fabric to make pillows. If each pillow takes ⅜ of a yard of material, how many pillows can Nina make before she runs out of fabric?

Grace used a Direct Modeling strategy. She began by drawing 10½ yards of material represented as rectangles. She partitioned each yard into eighths, and then marked off sections of ⅜ each to show each pillow that could be made (Figure 3–4). The final half-yard was partitioned into 4 equal segments, because Grace knew that ½ = 4⁄8. Counting each section that she had made by grouping eighths, she got a final answer of 28 pillows.

Grace's strategy implicitly used two basic relationships. She understood that $1 = \frac{1}{8} + \frac{1}{8} + \frac{1}{8} + \frac{1}{8} + \frac{1}{8} + \frac{1}{8} + \frac{1}{8} + \frac{1}{8}$ and that $\frac{1}{8} + \frac{1}{8} + \frac{1}{8} = \frac{3}{8}$, as indicated by how she partitioned each yard and grouped sets of 3 eighths pieces together to make each pillow (see Figure 3–4).

Children's Repeated Addition strategies are similar to Direct Modeling strategies with the exception that they represent the relationships with fraction symbols rather than pictures. Grace's classmate Luke also represented each pillow individually but as single addends rather than as groupings of eighths. He repeatedly added ⅜ until he reached 10½ (Figure 3–5). In

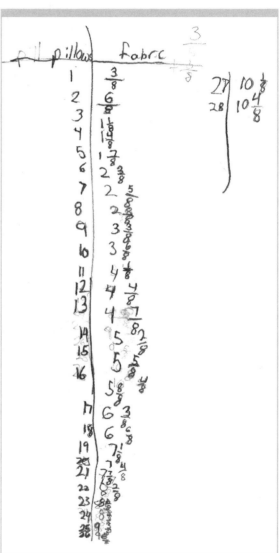

Figure 3–4.
Grace's strategy for 10½ ÷ ⅜

Figure 3–5.
Luke's strategy

the left column, he kept track of each pillow as it was incorporated into the running total to the right. As he created his running total, he used $\frac{8}{8}$ = 1 to regroup. For example, when he added $\frac{3}{8}$ to $\frac{6}{8}$ early in his strategy (line 4), he said that he knew that $\frac{6}{8} + \frac{2}{8}$ was $\frac{8}{8}$ or 1 and that $\frac{1}{8}$ more made $1\frac{1}{8}$.

Even though these two strategies are fairly basic compared to the strategies that follow, they make use of critical fraction relationships. Grace and Luke were reinforcing their understanding of these relationships. Furthermore, this type of strategy requires considerable problem-solving skill to monitor and keep track of all the groups that are created and counted. It's easy to lose track of a count or running sum when the representation of the strategy has so many parts.

Fifth-grader Shawn used a transitional strategy to solve this multiplication problem:

EACH LITTLE CAKE TAKES $\frac{3}{4}$ of a cup of frosting. If Bety wants to make 20 little cakes for a party, how much frosting will she need?

She began the way Luke did, by adding each fraction individually. But when she got to $3\frac{3}{4} + \frac{3}{4}$, she crossed off what she had written and in its place, she wrote "$\frac{3}{4}$" 20 times, in a 4-by-5 array (Figure 3–6). She added the first row of 4 groups of $\frac{3}{4}$ cup of frosting to get 3 cups and then realized that each row after that would also add to a subtotal of 3 cups. Finally, she skip-counted by threes to get a total of 15 cups of frosting that Bety needed for her 20 little cakes.

Like the more basic strategies described above, Shawn's strategy incorporates an understanding of fractions in terms of relationships: $\frac{3}{4} = 3 \times \frac{1}{4}$ and $4 \times \frac{1}{4} = 1$. Shawn also showed an emerging understanding that when we multiply fractions, we can simplify the process by forming groupings of fractions—in this case, $4 \times \frac{3}{4} = 3$—and then combining the groupings. This strategy is transitional because she represented every fraction individually, but then combined the fractions in each row to equal to 3. Finally, Shawn knew that the problem could be represented by multiplication (note the line "$\frac{3}{4} \times 20$" on her page) but reported that she could not think of any other way to approach this calculation other than what she had done.

Grouping and Combining Strategies

As children strive to use strategies that are more efficient than Direct Modeling and adding fractions individually, they become more strategic in the use of mathematical relationships like the one that Shawn used. They realize that they do not need to represent all of the quantities in a problem and begin to develop ways to group and count sets of fractions that involve "friendlier" amounts. These friendlier amounts, or groupings, are usually whole numbers. For example, a set of 4 groups of ¾ can be thought of as 3 instead of ¾ + ¾ + ¾ + ¾. Finding these groupings and which ones work well at first may be a matter of chance—as for Shawn. As children solve and discuss Multiple Groups problems, they begin to look for more efficient groupings to use in their solutions.

$$\frac{3}{4} \times 20$$

$$\begin{array}{ccccc} & 1\frac{1}{2} & 2\frac{1}{4} & 3 & \\ \frac{3}{4} & \frac{3}{4} & \frac{3}{4} & \frac{3}{4} & 3 \text{ cups} \\ \frac{3}{4} & \frac{3}{4} & \frac{3}{4} & \frac{3}{4} & 3 \text{ cups } 6 \\ \frac{3}{4} & \frac{3}{4} & \frac{3}{4} & \frac{3}{4} & 3 \text{ cups } 9 \\ \frac{3}{4} & \frac{3}{4} & \frac{3}{4} & \frac{3}{4} & 3 \text{ cups } 12 \\ \frac{3}{4} & \frac{3}{4} & \frac{3}{4} & \frac{3}{4} & 3 \text{ cups } 15 \text{ cups} \end{array}$$

Bety would need 15 cups.

Figure 3–6.
Shawn's strategy

For example, fifth-grader Cam was given this multiplication problem:

IT TAKES ⅔ OF A YARD of material to make a pillow. How many yards of material would it take to make 15 pillows?

The first thing she did was double the amount of fabric required for 1 pillow to find that 1⅓ yards of material could be used to make 2 pillows. She added another ⅔ of a yard to make 3 pillows (Figure 3–7), and then saw a grouping—3 pillows uses 2 yards of material—that she could use to count the pillows more efficiently. Each time she added 2 more yards of material, she could make 3 more pillows. She continued to build the total number of pillows up to 15 using this relationship until she concluded that she needed 10 yards of material to make all of the pillows.

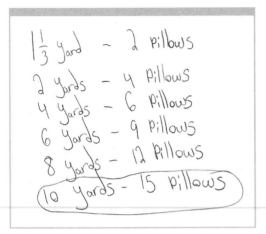

Figure 3–7.
Cam's grouping and combining strategy

Cam's grouping can be represented by this relationship:

$$3 \times \tfrac{2}{3} = 2$$

Although she did not use this equation explicitly in her solution, her strategy was based on the fact that 3 groups of ⅔ is equal to 2. Her use of this relationship is notable because it helped her count fractions without representing each fraction individually. As students begin to use more complex relationships such as this one in their solutions, you can help them learn to recognize, verbalize, and symbolize these relationships.

Because her grouping resulted in a whole number (2), it was easier to work with and made the strategy less prone to calculation or counting errors. To use this strategy effectively, Cam had to understand that the grouping incorporated 3 pillows. The two-column table helped her keep track of this relationship.

Children do not necessarily work with whole-number groupings or groupings that are all the same size in these intermediate strategies. For example, seventh-grader Nishi was given a Measurement Division problem similar to the one above that involved figuring how many pillows could be made with 10½ yards of material if each pillow required exactly ⅜ of a yard. After thinking, she decided, "I'll just add ⅜ until it equals 10½." She began skip-counting by ⅜, writing:

$$\tfrac{3}{8}, \quad \tfrac{6}{8}, \quad 1\tfrac{1}{8}, \quad 1\tfrac{4}{8}$$

Then she recognized that 1⅘ = 1½ and realized she could use this grouping to more efficiently build up to 10½. "This means 1½ yards equals 4 pillows. So 3 yards would be 8 pillows, and 6 yards would be 16 pillows." Then rather than doubling again, she combined the grouping 3 yards for 8 pillows with what she already had to get 9 yards for 24 pillows. Finally, she saw that she only needed 1½ more yards to go from

9 yards to 10½ yards and so she split the grouping 3 yards for 8 pillows in half to get 1½ yards for 4 pillows. Combining this with her running total, she concluded she could make 28 pillows with 10½ yards of fabric (Figure 3–8).

Similarly to Cam, Nishi's first goal for solving this problem was to individually add the amount of fabric for each pillow. But when she reached a number that was easy to combine, she realized that groupings could be used to combine the amount of fabric for more than 1 pillow at a time.

Multiplicative Strategies

Children's most sophisticated strategies for Multiple Groups problems are marked by the formation of groupings that are multiplicatively related to each other and that go beyond doubling and halving. Children shift from thinking additively about combining and counting groupings to thinking multiplicatively.

$$10\tfrac{1}{2} \div \tfrac{3}{8}$$

$$\tfrac{3}{8} \cdot X = ?$$

$$\tfrac{3}{8} \quad \tfrac{6}{8} \quad \tfrac{9}{8} = 1\tfrac{1}{8} \quad 1\tfrac{4}{8} = 1\tfrac{1}{2}$$

$$1\tfrac{1}{2} \ne 4 \text{ pillows}$$

$$3 \ne 8 \text{ P}$$

$$6/16 \text{ P}$$

$$9/24 \text{ P}$$

$$\boxed{1\tfrac{1}{2} + 9 = 10\tfrac{1}{2}/28 \text{ pillow}}$$

Figure 3–8. *Nishi's strategy*

For example, Julie, a fifth grader, solved the multiplication problem about pillows using multiplicative relationships:

IT TAKES ⅔ OF A YARD of material to make a pillow. How many yards of material would it take to make 15 pillows?

She said, "This is 15 groups of ⅔. So that's the same as 30 groups of ⅓. And then if I divide by 3, because there are 3 thirds in a yard, I get 10 yards." She wrote:

$$15 \times \tfrac{2}{3} = 15 \times 2 \div 3 = 10$$

Fifth-grader Trenton was given this Measurement Division problem:

MR. T HAS 12 CUPS of frog food. His frogs eat 1½ cups of food each day. How long can he feed the frogs before the food runs out?

He began by writing "12" and "1½" and then said, "2 times 1½ is 3, because 2 × 1 is 2, and 2 × ½ is 1, and then 2 + 1 is 3. So the frogs eat 3 cups of food in 2 days. A lot of people know that 12 divided by 3 is 4. … If each 3 cups of food would last 2 days, then 4 times as much food would last 8 days" (Figure 3–9).

Trenton saw right away that 3 was related to the amount of food the frogs could eat in a day *and* it was also related to the total amount of food that Mr. T had. He used this insight to go from a known relationship (1½ cups of food for 1 day) to an unknown relationship (12 cups of food for how many days). First he doubled 1½ cups to get 3 cups for 2 days. Then he related this grouping to the total amount of food by multiplying both the amount of food and number of days by 4. His reasoning essentially followed the structure in Figure 3–10, although he did not represent it in this way. Trenton implicitly drew upon the associative property of multiplication to relate what he knew to what he did not know.

Some children represent their thinking with equations as they work. Sixth-grader Kylie was given the pillow problem to solve, in which Nina had 10½ yards of material, and each pillow took ⅜ yard. She started with the following grouping, explaining that she knew that 8 pillows would take 3 yards of material:

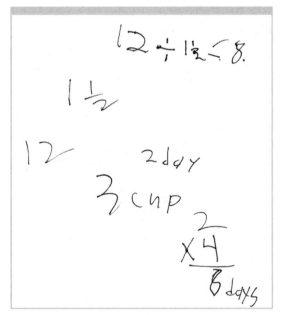

Figure 3-9. *Written parts of Trenton's strategy*

$$\frac{3}{8} \times 8 = 3$$

Trenton's Thinking	Possible Equation to Represent Trenton's Thinking
If we double 1½ it's 3.	$2 \times 1\frac{1}{2} = 3$
Since 4 times 3 equals 12, we can times 2 by 4 and we can make that into what it will end up to be … 8 days.	$4 \times (2 \times 1\frac{1}{2}) = 4 \times 3$ $(4 \times 2) \times 1\frac{1}{2} = 4 \times 3$ $8 \times 1\frac{1}{2} = 12$

Figure 3-10. Trenton's thinking and the relationships that guided his thinking

Kylie's goal was to figure out how many pillows 10½ yards of fabric could make. She saw that she could get close to 10½ yards by tripling 3 yards. She knew that this also meant that the number of pillows that 3 yards would make also had to be tripled. She wrote:

$$\tfrac{3}{8} \times 24 = 9$$

Finally, similarly to Nishi, she reasoned that to go from 9 yards to 10½ yards, she needed 1½ more yards of material, which would make half as many pillows as 3 yards would make:

$$\tfrac{3}{8} \times 28 = 10\tfrac{1}{2}$$

Trenton verbalized the relationships he was using but did not write them out fully. In contrast, at each step, Kylie kept track of the number of pillows she could make by writing an equation to show how many yards of material the pillows would require. Similarly to Trenton, Kylie drew on the associative property of multiplication to transform one equation into another. These properties were implicit to her reasoning.

We also note that Kylie began her strategy with a relationship—$8 \times \tfrac{3}{8} = 3$—that was familiar to her. It is an example of a type of efficient grouping that children learn to generalize as they solve Multiple Groups problems. In Chapter 4, we discuss the evolution of relationships such as this one and children's use of fundamental properties of operations and equality in their reasoning. With the teacher's support—addressed in Chapter 5—children learn to represent the grouping relationships they

Multiple Groups Problem	I have 12 peanut butter and jelly sandwiches. How many children could I feed with these sandwiches if I give ¾ sandwich to each child? (Measurement Division)
Represents Each Group —*Direct Modeling* —*Repeated Addition*	Child represents each fractional group, either by drawing or by a fraction. For example, draws 12 sandwiches. Partitions each into fourths. Groups 3 fourths portions together and counts as 1 child. Continues this process until all 12 sandwiches are used up. Can feed 16 children.
Grouping and Combining Strategies	Child does not represent each fractional group. Creates a more efficient grouping by combining fractional groups. Uses these groupings to count number of groups. For example:

¾ + ¾ = 1½	2 kids
1½ + 1½ = 3	4 kids
3 + 3 = 6	8 kids
6 + 3 = 9	12 kids
9 + 3 = 12	16 kids

| **Multiplicative Strategies** | Child does not represent each fractional group. Relates fractional group or a grouping to total, using multiplication. For example, "4 groups of ¾ is 3. There are 4 threes in 12 so there are 4 times 4 or 16 groups of ¾ in 12 so you could feed 16 children." |

Figure 3–11. *Children's strategies for Multiple Groups problems*

> ## Teacher Commentary
>
> *Teaching fractions by starting with Equal Sharing problems and moving to other story problems with fractions is the only approach I see as working for special education students. There was a time when I taught fraction procedures to my special education kids. We would start with coloring in pictures to show fractions and then move to procedures*

for adding fractions. It never worked. I could teach them the procedure 100 times and it wouldn't work. Kids with learning disabilities or other special education issues often have memory issues. My students would remember the procedure for three days in a row and then on the fourth day, they wouldn't have it. When I had students for two years in a row, we always had to start all over again with fractions in the second year. There was no retention because they didn't understand it.

Students with learning disabilities or other issues need to see things in context in order to understand them. Story problems are one of the best ways to give these kids the context. A lot of kids with learning disabilities have language issues, which can cause some challenges when working with story problems. When my kids are working with story problems, I work with them to help them understand the context. I ask them to draw out what they know about the story. Yesterday I had a boy working on a problem where 4 kids were sharing 3 cakes. He was stuck so I read the problem to him and asked him to draw what the problem was about. He drew the kids and the cakes and then said, "Oh, I can do this," and he went on to solve the problem.

Now that I teach fractions through Equal Sharing and other story problems, my kids are doing really well. They solve these problems without my telling them what to do. When I have kids two years in a row, they always remember some things from the year before. It helps that teachers at our school start fraction work with Equal Sharing problems in kindergarten. Special education kids especially need to start fraction work early. It is too much for them to learn what a fraction is and learn how to add and subtract fractions all in one year.

Tammy Hughes
Special Education Teacher
John Muir School
Madison, WI

(For more information on CGI and Special Education students, see Behrend (2003) and Moscardini (2009).)

work with by writing equations. These equations, in turn, become objects for them to reason about and transform in their solutions, as illustrated in Kylie's solution.

Reflecting Back and Looking Ahead

In this chapter, we focused on two types of word problems involving multiple equal groups—Multiplication and Measurement Division—that teachers could use to consolidate students' understanding of fractional quantities as relational and to elicit children's use of strategic relationships. Reasoning about situations that involve decomposing units, such as whole cups, into fractional units and then recombining these fractional units provides children a chance to develop their understanding of these relationships. Because these problems involve equal groups, children need to combine fractional units in their solutions. Striving for efficiency in their solutions leads children to begin to apply strategies that involve multiplicative relationships and fundamental properties of operations and equality. We call such strategies *Relational Thinking strategies* and discuss them in depth in the following chapter.

Multiple Groups Problems

Here are some Multiple Groups problems to pose to your students. The problems are generally arranged from easiest to most difficult. You can change the numbers in these problems to meet the needs of your students. Refer to the instructional guidelines on pages 69–71 for suggestions of possible number substitutions for different grade levels.

PROBLEM	POSSIBLE EQUATION
A. Ms. Jones wants to feed each of the children she babysits a half sandwich for lunch. If she babysits 8 children, how many sandwiches should she make?	$8 \times \frac{1}{2} = \square$
B. Nick made 6 small cakes for his birthday party. He thinks each person at the party will eat half of a cake. How many people can be at the party, if everyone eats this much?	$\square \times \frac{1}{2} = 6$
C. Carla has 9 cans of paint. It takes $\frac{1}{2}$ can of paint to paint a chair. How many chairs can she paint with her 9 cans of paint?	$\square \times \frac{1}{2} = 9$
D. It takes $\frac{1}{4}$ yard of fabric to make a pillow. How many pillows could I make with 3 yards of fabric?	$\square \times \frac{1}{4} = 3$
E. Each student needs $\frac{3}{4}$ stick of clay to do an art project. If 14 students wanted to do this art project, how many sticks of clay would they need?	$14 \times \frac{3}{4} = \square$

	PROBLEM	POSSIBLE EQUATION
F.	Bernice uses ⅔ yard of ribbon for each bow she makes. How much ribbon would she use if she made 7 bows?	$7 \times ⅔ = \square$
G.	Tyrone eats ⅜ pound of cheese each day. How many days will it take him to eat 3 pounds of cheese?	$\square \times ⅜ = 3$
H.	A kitten eats ³⁄₁₀ cup of kitten food. How much kitten food would you need if you wanted to feed 15 kittens?	$15 \times ³⁄₁₀ = \square$
I.	Eric has 6 bags with ⅚ pound of candy in each bag. How many pounds of candy does he have altogether?	$6 \times ⅚ = \square$
J.	Emma drinks ⅔ cup of water for every mile she hikes. Her water bottle holds 4 cups of water. How many miles can she hike before her water runs out?	$\square \times ⅔ = 4$
K.	Elena has 12 pounds of clay. It takes ¾ pound of clay to make a bowl. How many bowls can she make with the clay that she has?	$\square \times ¾ = 12$
L.	It takes ⅜ cup of sugar to make a loaf of bread. How much sugar would you need to make 16 loaves of bread?	$16 \times ⅜ = \square$
M.	Megan has 16 half dollars. How many whole dollars does she have?	$16 \times ½ = \square \times 1$
N.	It takes ⅗ yard of ribbon to make a bow. How many bows could you make with 7½ yards of ribbon?	$\square \times ⅗ = 7½$
O.	Eve's gecko eats ²⁄₇ jar of baby food a day. She has 10 jars of baby food. How many days can she feed her gecko with this food?	$\square \times ²⁄₇ = 10$
P.	Kennedy has _____ pounds of M&Ms to make party favors. It takes _____ pound of M&Ms to fill 1 bag. How many bags of M&Ms can Kennedy fill with her M&Ms? (4, ⅓) (8, ⅔) (20, ⅝) (44, ⅜)	$\square \times ⅓ = 4$

PROBLEM	POSSIBLE EQUATION

Q. A dressmaker has ___ yard of lace. It takes ___ yard of lace to decorate a pocket. How many pockets can she decorate with the piece of lace that she has?

$\square \times \frac{1}{4} = \frac{3}{4}$

$(\frac{3}{4}, \frac{1}{4})$ $(\frac{8}{10}, \frac{1}{5})$ $(\frac{3}{4}, \frac{3}{16})$ $(\frac{8}{10}, \frac{4}{15})$

Open Number Sentences

In Chapter 5, we describe how Ms. Perez introduces and uses equations to represent students' strategies. In Chapters 6 and 7, we describe how a teacher can pose equations as problems for students to solve. However, as soon as students are able to readily solve Multiple Groups problems as discussed in Chapters 3 and 4, teachers can introduce simple equations for them to solve, such as the following. These equations are similar in structure to Multiple Groups problems. If students have difficulty solving them, it may mean they need more experience solving word problems, such as the ones listed above.

A. $\frac{1}{2} + \frac{1}{2} + \frac{1}{2} + \frac{1}{2} + \frac{1}{2} = \square$

B. $\square = \frac{1}{3} + \frac{1}{3} + \frac{1}{3} + \frac{1}{3} + \frac{1}{3} + \frac{1}{3}$

C. $4 \times \frac{1}{4} + 3 \times \frac{1}{4} = \square$

D. $8 \times \frac{1}{2} = \square$

E. $\square \times \frac{1}{2} = 10\frac{1}{2}$

F. $\square \times \frac{1}{4} = 1\frac{1}{4}$

G. $\frac{1}{3} + \frac{1}{3} + \frac{1}{3} + \frac{1}{3} = \square \times \frac{1}{3}$

H. $8 \times \frac{1}{5} = \square + \frac{3}{5}$

I. $\frac{3}{4} + \frac{3}{4} = \square + \frac{1}{2}$

J. $4 \times \frac{3}{4} = \square$

K. $5 = \square \times \frac{5}{8}$

L. $7 \times \frac{7}{8} = \square - \frac{7}{8}$

M. $\square = 16 \times \frac{3}{4}$

N. $\square \times \frac{7}{8} = 14$

O. $\square = 10 \times \frac{2}{3}$

P. $\square \times \frac{3}{8} = 9 \frac{3}{8}$

Given an Equation, Write a Story Problem

Pose an equation to students and ask them to write a story problem for it.

A. $6 \times \frac{1}{2} = \square$

B. $10 \div \frac{1}{2} = \square$

C. $3 \div \frac{1}{4} = \square$

D. $8 \div \frac{2}{3} = \square$

E. $4 \times \frac{3}{4} = \square$

Instructional Guidelines for Multiple Groups Problems

In this section, we provide guidelines for posing, discussing, and extending Multiple Groups problems. We presented these problems in Chapter 3 and continue to discuss them in Chapters 4 and 5. You may find that your understanding of these problem types and how to use them in the classroom will be enhanced after you read Chapters 4 and 5.

At all grade levels, children should work with Equal Sharing problems before working with Multiple Groups problems. Grade levels are provided as general guidelines. Consider the Equal Sharing problems your students are able to solve when choosing which Multiple Groups problems to give them. Make sure the fraction in the problem statement is a quantity that your students understand. We recommend that you read the suggestions for all of the grade levels rather than only for the grade level you teach.

FIRST GRADE

✔ Multiple Groups problems with ½ in each group—for example:

- Multiplication: *There are 6 children and I want to give them each a half of a banana. How many bananas do I need?*
- Measurement Division: *I have 2 slices of cheese. It takes half of a slice of cheese to make a snack. How many snacks can I make?*

✔ Multiple Groups problems with ½ or ¼ in each group—for example:

- Multiplication: *There are 6 children and I want to give them each one-fourth of a banana. How many bananas do I need?*
- Measurement Division: *I have 2 slices of cheese. It takes one-fourth of a slice of cheese to make a snack. How many snacks can I make?*

✔ Multiple Groups problems with ½, ¼, ¾, ⅓, and ¹⁄₁₀ in each group, and mixed numbers including these fractions in each group—for example:

- Multiplication: *There are 6 children and I want to give them each ¾ of a sandwich. How many sandwiches do I need?*
- Measurement Division: *I have 7 cans of paint. It takes 2¼ cans of paint to paint a fence. How many fences can I paint?*

✔ Multiple Groups problems: focus on problems with ½, ¼, ¾, ⅓, ⅔, and ¹⁄₁₀ in each group, and mixed numbers including these fractions, but include other amounts in a group as well—for example:

- Multiplication: *There are 6 teenagers and I want to give them each 1⅔ sub sandwiches. How many sub sandwiches do I need?*
- Measurement Division: *I have 3½ cans of paint. It takes ⅔ can of paint to paint a chair. How many chairs can I paint?*

✔ Open Number Sentences[3]: focus on relationships between unit fractions and 1: focus on equations with groups of ½, ¼, and ⅓—for example:

- $\frac{1}{2} + \frac{1}{2} + \frac{1}{2} + \frac{1}{2} + \frac{1}{2} + \frac{1}{2} = \square$
- $\square \times \frac{1}{4} = 2$
- $3 \times \frac{1}{3} + 2 \times \frac{1}{3} = \square$

---

[3] We address equations such as these in several different places later in this book. See Chapter 7 for information on introducing Open Number Sentences to your students.

✔ Open Number Sentences that focus on relationships between fractions less than 1 and whole numbers—for example:

- $4 \times \frac{3}{4} = \square$
- $\square \times \frac{5}{8} = 8$
- $\square \times \frac{2}{3} = 3$
- $3 \times \frac{1}{3} + 2 \times \frac{1}{3} = \square$

✔ Look for students who use relationships to solve these word problems and equations. (For example, if the problem is about 16 groups of ¾, most fourth graders will repeatedly add three-fourths—notice when a student does something more efficient, such as adding 4 three-fourths to get 3 and then using that information to solve the problem. Highlight the use of relationships as Ms. Perez does in Chapter 5.)

FIFTH AND SIXTH GRADES

✔ Multiple Groups Problems: focus on problems where the amount in each group is expressed with halves, fourths, thirds, tenths, eighths, or sixths; include amounts in each group that are less than 1 as mixed numbers—for example:

- Multiplication: *There are 16 teenagers and I want to give them each ⅝ of a large sub sandwich. How many sub sandwiches do I need?*
- Measurement Division: *I have 6¾ cans of paint. It takes 1⅜ cans of paint to paint a door. How many doors can I paint?*

✔ Open Number Sentences that focus on the relationships between fractions and whole numbers, for example:

- $8 \times \frac{3}{8} = \square$
- $\square \times \frac{3}{4} = 15$
- $\square \times 1\frac{2}{3} = 25$

✔ Highlight students' strategies that use multiplicative relationships to solve these problems (For example, listen for students who say things like, "I know that 8 groups of ⅛ is 1 so 8 groups of ⅜ is 3," or, "I know that 4 groups of ¾ is 3 so 20 groups of ¾ would 5 times 3 or 15." Highlight the use of these relationships as Ms. Perez does in Chapter 5.)

chapter 4

Relational Thinking

Connecting Fractions and Algebra

in this chapter, we step back to examine the deeper structures of children's mathematical thinking. A small set of mathematical relationships governs how numbers, operations, and equations work in arithmetic as well as in algebra. We call these relationships the *fundamental properties of operations and equality*. When children are encouraged to use their own strategies to solve problems involving fractions, they intuitively draw on these fundamental properties. When teachers encourage such strategies and create opportunities for students to reflect on the mathematics relationships that they used, learning fractions serves as a foundation for learning algebra with understanding. We call the strategies in which children draw upon these fundamental properties, whether implicitly or explicitly, *Relational Thinking* strategies

To begin to use Relational Thinking strategies, children need to understand fractional quantities as relational. We begin the chapter by describing what this understanding is and how Equal Sharing and Multiple Groups problems support its development. We then introduce Relational Thinking and revisit children's strategies for Multiple Groups problems to highlight when and how they involve Relational Thinking. We conclude by discussing how Relational Thinking enables students to understand the connections between learning arithmetic and algebra.

Relational Understanding of Fractions

Students who can express a number in terms of other numbers and operations on those numbers hold a *relational understanding of the number.* Understanding numbers relationally helps students use mathematical relationships to solve problems. For example, a child who understands that 5 can be decomposed into 2 and 3 can use that understanding to solve 8 + 5 = *n* by first adding 8 + 2 to get 10 and then adding 3 more to get *n* = 13. Similarly, a child who understands that 45 can be thought of as 4 tens and 5 ones, and 36 as 3 tens and 6 ones, can use this understanding to add 45 and 36 by combining tens, combining ones, and then combining the results: 40 + 30 = 70; 5 + 6 = 11; so 45 + 36 = 70 + 11 = 81. In both of these examples, students used an understanding of how one amount could be expressed in terms of other amounts to simplify the problem and facilitate a solution.

As children solve Equal Sharing problems, they deal with two distinct types of relationships that are essential to a *relational understanding of fractions.* First, children learn to relate the process of partitioning a whole unit into *n* equal parts with the size of a part, $\frac{1}{n}$, that results. We call this understanding a *relational understanding of unit fractions.* Second, children learn that they can combine unit fractions to make *fractions that are multiples of unit fractions,* such as $\frac{3}{4}$ and $\frac{5}{4}$, as well as mixed numbers, such as $1\frac{7}{8}$. We refer to this understanding as a *relational understanding of fractions as composite.*

Relational Understanding of Unit Fractions

A unit fraction is any fraction that has the form $\frac{1}{n}$ (where *n* is any positive whole number not equal to 0). A unit fraction is defined by its relationship to the whole and the two interconnected ideas that 1 unit can be divided into any number of equal parts *and* those parts can be recombined to make 1 again. For example, if *n* people are sharing 1 thing equally and completely, each person gets a share that is exactly $\frac{1}{n}$ of that thing:

$$1 \div n = \frac{1}{n}$$

If all of the shares are recombined, the whole thing is reconstituted:

$$n \times \frac{1}{n} = 1$$

The multiplicative relationship between a part and its whole is reversible in the sense that the whole can be broken apart into unit fractions and the unit fractions can be put back together to make the whole. This essential understanding becomes abbreviated for children as:

$$\frac{n}{n} = 1$$

We described in Chapter 1 how young children tend to separate the process of creating equal shares ($1 \div n$) from the resulting fractional share ($\frac{1}{n}$). They may say, as one child did, "I split the candy bar in threes [i.e., into 3 equal parts] and gave each person a half." As children learn to coordinate the process of partitioning with the result of the partitioning—"I split this candy bar into 3 equal parts and gave each person a third of it"—they begin to think flexibly of unit fractions in terms of a reversible relationship with the whole unit. They think of the whole as a unit that can be partitioned. You can help children express that relationship as "1 split into 3 equal groups is $\frac{1}{3}$" and "3 groups of $\frac{1}{3}$ is 1." As children reflect on these relationships when they use them in their solutions to Multiple Groups problems, these different ways of thinking about thirds become consolidated in the relationship "$\frac{3}{3}$ is the same as 1." You can assist this development by listening closely as children explain their reasoning and by providing mathematical phrasing or number sentences to represent these emergent relationships.

Relational Understanding of Fractions as Composite

Equal Sharing problems provide a natural context for children to combine unit-fraction quantities. They learn in the context of solving problems and representing their solutions that any fractional share $^m/_n$ can be expressed in terms of unit-fraction amounts. These unit-fraction amounts do not need to come from the same whole—only from a set of wholes that are equal in size. For example, $^3/_8$ of 1 candy bar is the same as $^1/_8$ of each of 3 candy bars (Figure 4–1).

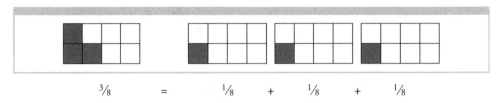

$$\frac{3}{8} \quad = \quad \frac{1}{8} \quad + \quad \frac{1}{8} \quad + \quad \frac{1}{8}$$

Figure 4–1. $^3/_8$ of 1 is the same as $^1/_8$ of 1 three times.

In other words, Equal Sharing helps children begin to understand the fraction $^m/_n$ in terms of the relationships between a whole unit, that unit segmented into equal parts, and some combination of those parts from different units of the same size. Children first think of this composite relationship as additive and later as multiplicative:

$$\underbrace{\frac{1}{n} + \frac{1}{n} + \frac{1}{n} + \ldots + \frac{1}{n}}_{m \text{ times}} = \frac{m}{n}$$

$$m \times \frac{1}{n} \qquad = \frac{m}{n}$$

Students might state this idea as, "m groups of one-nth is the same as m $n$ths." There is no limit to the value of m in $^m/_n$. The relationship holds equally well for $^4/_{17}$ and $^{17}/_4$. Solving problems that involve two or more wholes, as recommended in Chapter 1, helps children generalize this relationship.

As children's understanding of these fraction relationships grows, they begin to use their understanding in combination with the fundamental properties of operations and equality to think relationally about adding, subtracting, multiplying, and dividing fractions.

Introduction to Relational Thinking

Characterizing Relational Thinking

When children use *Relational Thinking* to solve problems, they are drawing upon a small set of fundamental properties that govern how operations and equations work

(Carpenter et al. 2003; Empson et al. in press). Children's strategies often reflect an intuitive understanding of these properties as they use them to enact solutions and to structure their thinking.

Adults, like children, often use Relational Thinking intuitively. We invite you to stop for a moment to think about how you would figure the total amount of money spent on 5 stuffed bears each costing $14 without writing anything down.

A third grader reasoned that 5 groups of $10 would be $50, and then 5 groups of $4 would be $20, for a total of $50 + $20 = $70 for the bears. If you reasoned similarly, then you used Relational Thinking. One way to represent the logic underlying this thinking is:

$$5 \times 14 = (5 \times 10) + (5 \times 4)$$

That is, 5 groups of 14 can be transformed into 5 groups of 10 plus 5 groups of 4. The fundamental property represented by this equation is the *distributive property of multiplication over addition* (often simply called "the distributive property"). The third grader had never heard of this property, nor had he been explicitly taught to use this property to multiply. Instead, his understanding of base-ten numbers and how multiplication worked guided his thinking about this calculation.

Other students may use different types of Relational Thinking to solve the same problem. For example, a sixth grader solved the problem and explained, "When I have to multiply a number by 5, I just multiply half of the number by 10, so 5 times 14 is 70." A way to represent his thinking is:

$$5 \times 14 = 5 \times (2 \times 7) = (5 \times 2) \times 7 = 10 \times 7 = 70$$

The fundamental property represented by this equation is the *associative property of multiplication*. Like the third grader, the sixth grader had not been explicitly taught to use this property to multiply. His understanding about how multiplication works guided his thinking about this calculation.[1]

---

[1] For more examples of how children's strategies for multiplication and division of whole numbers are based on these properties, see Baek, 2008.

Children use Relational Thinking in their solutions to whole-number and fraction problems before they learn to write equations to represent the relationships or use conventional terms to describe their thinking. Equations such as $5 \times 14 = (5 \times 10) + (5 \times 4)$ help us identify and represent the logic behind a child's thinking. Conventional terms such as *the distributive property* help us describe and classify this logic. In this chapter, we use equations and conventional terms to represent the deep structure of children's thinking and the kinds of explicit understanding students can attain. The way we use equations and terms in this chapter differs in some ways from how we use equations and conventional terms with children. In Chapter 5, we discuss how and when you can introduce equations to children and use them in instruction.

Because children's understanding of these fundamental properties of operations and equality is contained in how they *relate* one numerical expression—such as 5×14—with another—such as $(5 \times 10) + (5 \times 4)$—we call it *Relational Thinking*. To see the possibility of this relationship in 5×14 requires both a generalized understanding of how multiplication and addition are related and the use of this understanding to guide the solution for this specific computation. When children solve problems involving fractions, they draw upon the same fundamental properties combined with their understanding of specific fraction relationships.

Relational Thinking and Fractions

Consider what a group of first graders was able to do without having been taught a procedure for adding fractions with unlike denominators (Empson 1999)—a topic that appears much later in the elementary curriculum. At the conclusion of five weeks of instruction that focused on solving and discussing Equal Sharing problems, they were given this story problem, a type of problem they had never solved before:

 TINA AND TONY PAINTED PICTURES this afternoon. Tina used half a jar of blue paint for her picture. Tony used three-fourths of the same size jar of blue paint for his picture. How much blue paint did Tina and Tony use altogether for their paintings?

To combine ½ and ¾, 8 out of the 17 first graders thought of ¾ as equal to ½ + ¼ and reasoned that ½ plus another ½ was equal to 1, and then plus another ¼ was 1¼. These children could not have used this strategy if they had not been able to think of ¾ as an amount that was equal to ½ + ¼. The logic of the children's thinking can be represented by the equations in Figure 4–2.

The first graders worked from what they understood to solve a new type of problem. They did not need to be shown a procedure to combine these two fractions because they understood how to decompose ¾ and figured out how to use this decomposition to help them add ½ + ¾. This strategy involved the implicit use of the associative property of addition, which states that if three numbers are to be added, either the first and second numbers or the second and third numbers can be

We provide tables such as Figure 4–2 to highlight the deep structure of children's thinking and the kinds of explicit understanding of mathematics that students can attain. Although we encourage you to spend some time connecting children's strategies with equations and properties, we want you to know that you do not need to make these connections right now to continue reading this book or experimenting with the ideas in it. Some readers may wish to attend only to descriptions of children's strategies at this point and some may wish to concentrate on the fundamental properties in children's reasoning. Either way is fine. The important thing is to try some problems with your students and study their strategies. With experience, you will find it easier to make connections between children's strategies, equations, and the fundamental properties of operations and equality.

Children's Thinking	Possible Equation to Represent Children's Thinking	Fundamental Property That Is Basis of Children's Thinking
"¾ has ½ and ¼ in it."	$\frac{3}{4} = \frac{1}{2} + \frac{1}{4}$ $\frac{1}{2} + \frac{3}{4} = \frac{1}{2} + (\frac{1}{2} + \frac{1}{4})$	Relational understanding ¾ as equal to ½ + ¼
"½ and ½ make a whole."	$\frac{1}{2} + (\frac{1}{2} + \frac{1}{4}) = (\frac{1}{2} + \frac{1}{2}) + \frac{1}{4}$	Associative property of addition
"A whole plus 1 extra fourth is 1 and 1 fourth."	$(\frac{1}{2} + \frac{1}{2}) + \frac{1}{4} = 1 + \frac{1}{4} = 1\frac{1}{4}$	Relational understanding of 1 as equal to ½ + ½

Figure 4–2. *Using Relational Thinking to add fractions*

added first. It is an example of how fraction instruction can help students develop their understanding of mathematical relationships and how a focus on mathematical relationships can help students learn fractions with understanding.

Younger children's emergent use of Relational Thinking is remarkable in light of the fact that older students often have difficulty learning to explicitly recognize and apply the very same fundamental properties in their solutions to algebraic equations. For example, when we taught high school algebra, many of our students struggled to apply the distributive property to multiply 4 by the sum of x and y in the expression $4(x + y)$. They would incorrectly conclude that $4(x + y) = 4x + y$ rather than $4(x + y) = 4x + 4y$. Similarly, students would inappropriately apply the associative and commutative properties to subtraction and conclude that $8x - (8 - 4x)$ was equal to $4x - 8$ rather than $12x - 8$. Cultivating children's use of Relational Thinking prepares them to understand algebraic concepts and manipulations such as these.

Relational Thinking emerges early in children's thinking about whole numbers and fractions. Most children use some form of Relational Thinking to solve addition and subtraction problems by the end of second grade, even in classrooms where the teacher does not focus on it. But without teacher guidance, children do not continue to develop their capacity to think relationally. In many cases, it atrophies, as it seemed to have done for our high school students, and students abandon making sense of mathematics.

In the following section, we revisit children's solution strategies for Multiple Groups problems to draw your attention to the emergence and use of Relational Thinking.

Thinking Relationally About Multiple Groups Problems

As children come to understand fractions as relational, they begin to use fundamental properties of operations and equality to reason about operations and computations involving fractions. In Chapters 1 and 3, we introduced the types of strategies children use to solve Multiple Groups problems. In this section, we focus on the deep structure of these strategies by examining how children's strategies depend upon the use of Relational Thinking. We distinguish between the type of strategy that a child uses and how that strategy draws on Relational Thinking. For example, a child may use a grouping strategy to solve a problem, but the way the child forms groupings and combines them can reflect the use of different fundamental properties of operations and equality—that is, different forms of Relational Thinking. Children's use of Relational Thinking emerges as they begin to use grouping strategies to simplify their calculations and continues to develop as their strategies become more sophisticated.

Relational Thinking in Children's Grouping and Combining Strategies

Cam solved a Multiple Groups multiplication problem involving 15 groups of $\frac{2}{3}$ of a yard of fabric by combining groupings that related 3 pillows and 2 yards (see Figure 3–7). Her work is represented in the first two columns of the table in Figure 4–3. Each line of Cam's table represents a relationship between the number of pillows, the amount of fabric needed for 1 pillow, and the total amount of fabric used for the number of pillows. We show these relationships in the third column using equations. Cam did not write equations, but she understood that she was working with the relationship between groupings of pillows and the total amount of fabric needed for the

Cam's Work		Equation
Yards	Pillows	
$\frac{2}{3}$	1	$1 \times \frac{2}{3} = \frac{2}{3}$
$1\frac{1}{3}$	2	$2 \times \frac{2}{3} = 1\frac{1}{3}$
2	3	$3 \times \frac{2}{3} = 2$
4	6	$6 \times \frac{2}{3} = 4$
6	9	$9 \times \frac{2}{3} = 6$
8	12	$12 \times \frac{2}{3} = 8$
10	15	$15 \times \frac{2}{3} = 10$

Figure 4–3. *Equations to represent the relationships between amount of fabric and number of pillows in Cam's table*

grouping. (Before looking at the entire table you might cover the rightmost column and try to write an equation that represents the relationship between the number of pillows and amount of fabric used.)

The way Cam used her table to solve the problem shows an *implicit* understanding of the distributive property. For example, she combined 4 yards for 6 pillows with 2 yards for 3 pillows to get 6 yards for 9 pillows. Each of those groupings involves a multiple of ⅔—the amount of fabric for a single pillow—and so combining groupings involves combining multiples of ⅔. 6 groups of ⅔ combined with 3 more groups of ⅔ is the same as 9 groups of ⅔ (Figure 4–4). Because 6 groups of ⅔ is equal to 4 and 3 groups of ⅔ is equal to 2, 9 groups of ⅔ is equal to 4 + 2 or 6:

$$9 \times \tfrac{2}{3} = 6$$

Cam applied this property repeatedly throughout her strategy whenever she combined another 3 groups of 2.

Cam knew that she did not need to represent each fractional amount individually. She created more efficient groupings of fractional amounts and then combined the groupings on the basis of fundamental properties of operations and equality.

Cam's Thinking	Possible Equation to Represent Cam's Thinking	Fundamental Property That Is Basis of Cam's Thinking
"If 6 pillows can be made with 4 yards, and 3 pillows can be made with 2 yards, then 9 pillows can be made with 6 yards."	$(6 \times \tfrac{2}{3}) + (3 \times \tfrac{2}{3}) = (6 + 3) \times \tfrac{2}{3}$ $= 9 \times \tfrac{2}{3}$	*Distributive property*

Figure 4–4. *Using Relational Thinking to solve a Measurement Division problem*

Relational Thinking in Multiplicative Strategies

Trenton solved a Measurement Division problem that involved finding how many groups of 1½ cups were in 12 cups of frog food (Figure 4–5). His goal was to count the number of one and one-halves in 12.

He began building up from $1\frac{1}{2}$ by doubling $1\frac{1}{2}$ using the distributive property. He said that 2 groups of $1\frac{1}{2}$ could be figured by multiplying 2×1 and then $2 \times \frac{1}{2}$ and adding them together.

Next he drew upon the associative property to relate that grouping, 2 groups of $1\frac{1}{2}$ cups is 3 cups, to the total amount of frog food, 12 cups, in the following way. He doubled $1\frac{1}{2}$ to make 3 cups, and then multiplied that by 4 to make 12 cups. To keep track of the number of one and one-halves he had used to build up to 12, he had to keep track of the relationship between $1\frac{1}{2}$ cups and 12 cups as he related 3 cups for 2 days to 12 cups for 8 days. Because multiplication is associative, he was able to regroup 4 groups of $2 \times 1\frac{1}{2}$ into 4×2 groups of $1\frac{1}{2}$. Figure 4–5 shows each step of Trenton's strategy, equations that could be used to represent his thinking, and the fundamental properties that Trenton drew upon.

Kylie used a basic fraction relationship in her solution that many children come to use in multiplying and dividing fractions (see pp. 60–61 in Chapter 3). She wanted to figure how many groups of $\frac{3}{8}$ were in $10\frac{1}{2}$. She began with the knowledge that 8 groups of $\frac{3}{8}$ is 3:

$$8 \times \frac{3}{8} = 3$$

Trenton's Thinking	Possible Equation to Represent Trenton's Thinking	Fundamental Property That Is Basis of Trenton's Thinking
"2 days uses 3 cups of food."	$2 \times 1\frac{1}{2} = (2 \times 1) + (2 \times \frac{1}{2})$ $= 2 + 1$ $= 3$	Distributive property Fractions as multiples of units fractions
"8 days uses 12 cups of food, because if I multiply 2 days by 4 to get 8 days I need to multiply 3 cups by 4 to get 12 cups."	$4 \times (2 \times 1\frac{1}{2}) = 4 \times 3$ $(4 \times 2) \times 1\frac{1}{2} = 4 \times 3$	Associative property
	$8 \times 1\frac{1}{2} = 12$	Multiplication

Figure 4–5. *Relational Thinking in Trenton's strategy*

Figure 4–6. *Thinking relationally*

When we asked her how she knew that 8 groups of ⅜ was 8, she said, "I just know that if I multiply a fraction by the denominator it equals the number in the numerator. One way to show that this works is to think 8 groups of ⅛ is 1, so 8 groups of ⅜ will be 3." The relationship $b \times \frac{a}{b} = a$ is true for all fractions, $\frac{a}{b}$, as long as $b \neq 0$. Many students justify it on the basis of the commutative and associative properties of multiplication as Kylie did. Figure 4–7 represents this reasoning with equations and the fundamental properties that justify the relationships from one equation to the next. We invite you to identify how the rest of Kylie's strategy embodied Relational Thinking.

Julie's strategy for figuring 15 groups of ⅔ yard of fabric each (p. 59) drew on the associative property of multiplication. She said that 15 groups of ⅔ was the same as 30 groups of ⅓, which was equal to 10 yards. Her thinking is represented in Figure 4–8.

Some of the most sophisticated Relational Thinking strategies for Multiple Groups problems involve reasoning about equations. For example, a sixth grader was given this problem:

EACH LITTLE CAKE TAKES ¾ of a cup of frosting. If Bety wants to make 20 little cakes for a party, how much frosting will she need?

He immediately recognized the situation as multiplication and wrote:

$$20 \times \frac{3}{4} = p$$

He said, "I can halve the number of groups and double the size of each group," and wrote:

$$20 \times \frac{3}{4} = 10 \times 1\frac{1}{2}$$

Possible Equation	Fundamental Property That Is Basis of Children's Thinking
$8 \times \frac{3}{8} = 8 \times (3 \times \frac{1}{8})$	Relational understanding of $\frac{3}{8}$ as multiple of unit fraction $\frac{1}{8}$
$= 8 \times (\frac{1}{8} \times 3)$	Commutative property of multiplication
$= (8 \times \frac{1}{8}) \times 3$	Associative property of multiplication
$= 1 \times 3$	Relational understanding of $\frac{1}{8}$ and 1
$= 3$	Identity property of multiplication

Figure 4–7. *Justification of a generalizable fraction relationship*

He then said, "I can do that again and then it would be easy to multiply." He continued writing:

$$20 \times \frac{3}{4} = 10 \times 1\frac{1}{2} = 5 \times 3 = 15$$

Like the strategies above, this one embodied the use of fundamental properties of operations and equality. For example, the first transformation from 20 groups of $\frac{3}{4}$ to 10 groups of $1\frac{1}{2}$ can be justified by the associative property of multiplication. 20 is decomposed into two factors (first line) and then one of the factors is grouped with $\frac{3}{4}$ (second line):

$$20 \times \frac{3}{4} = (10 \times 2) \times \frac{3}{4}$$
$$= 10 \times (2 \times \frac{3}{4})$$
$$= 10 \times 1\frac{1}{2}$$

Possible Equation	Fundamental Property That Is Basis of Children's Thinking
$15 \times \frac{2}{3} = 15 \times (2 \times \frac{1}{3})$	Fraction as a multiple of unit fraction
$= (15 \times 2) \times \frac{1}{3}$	Associative property of multiplication
$= 30 \times \frac{1}{3} = 30 \div 3$	Inverse relationship between multiplication and division

Figure 4–8. *Julie's Relational Thinking strategy*

The strategies presented in this chapter tend to involve the use of fairly efficient relationships. But when children first start using Relational Thinking to solve a particular type of problem, they do not always choose very efficient relationships. Lynne, a fifth grader, used the strategy in Figure 4–9 to solve a problem that asked her to compute $26 \times \frac{3}{8}$. She started with the goal of figuring out how much 10 groups of $\frac{3}{8}$ would be. When we asked her why she chose 10, she said, "When I multiply I like to find out how many 10 groups there are. Then to find out how many 20 groups would be really easy." Ten is often a good number to start with when multiplying a whole number by a whole number, but for this problem, ten was not a very efficient number of groups to start with.

The associative property can also be used to justify transforming 10 groups of $1\frac{1}{2}$ to 5 groups of 3. This strategy is similar to the one described at the beginning of this chapter to solve 5 groups of 12 by using $5 \times 12 = 10 \times 6$.

Children use the fundamental properties of operations and equality naturally in their strategies for problem solving. The use of these properties increases children's understanding of fraction computation at the same time that it increases their understanding of mathematical relationships such as the associative and distributive properties.

As students grow in their use of Relational Thinking, they learn to analyze a problem to determine which relationships would be most efficient in solving that particular problem. Students first need experience deciding for themselves what relationships to use, even if their choices are inefficient, before they can be expected to analyze problems to determine which relationships are best suited to a particular problem. Students refine their anticipatory thinking skills by using relationships to solve problems and hearing how other students used relationships to solve problems.

Relational Thinking Throughout the Mathematics Curriculum

Recognizing and cultivating students' use of Relational Thinking is key to helping them build a deep understanding of fractions and operations on fractions. Profound understanding of arithmetic is marked by the ability to use Relational Thinking to make sense of numbers, operations, and equations. Developing students' Relational Thinking as they are learning fractions integrates their knowledge of whole-number arithmetic with fraction arithmetic, and it lays a critical foundation for future algebra learning.

To appreciate the significance of Relational Thinking across the mathematics curriculum, consider how children might simplify the following expressions and what they have in common (Empson et al. in press):

70 + 40

$^7/_5 + {^4/_5}$

Children who understand place value will see the first expression in terms of combining groups of tens. They would see 70 as 7 groups of 10 and 40 as 4 groups of 10 and figure that together they made 11 groups of 10, or 110. We can represent the "groups of" notion using multiplication:

$$70 + 40 = (7 \times 10) + (4 \times 10)$$
$$= (7 + 4) \times 10 = 110$$

Children who understand fractions will see the second expression similarly. That is, $^7/_5$ can be thought of as 7 groups of $^1/_5$ and $^4/_5$ as 4 groups of $^1/_5$. Altogether, there are 11 groups of $^1/_5$ or $^{11}/_5$:

$$^7/_5 + {^4/_5} = (7 \times {^1/_5}) + (4 \times {^1/_5}) =$$
$$(7 + 4) \times {^1/_5} = {^{11}/_5}$$

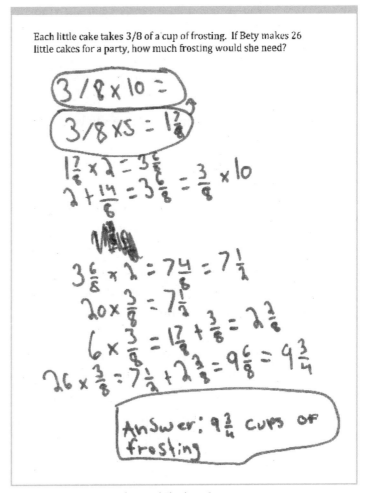

Each little cake takes 3/8 of a cup of frosting. If Bety makes 26 little cakes for a party, how much frosting would she need?

Figure 4–9. *Lynne's Relational Thinking Strategy*

Each computation is based on the same fundamental property of operations and equality—the distributive property of multiplication over addition. When children work from a well-connected understanding of number and operations, their thinking is based on properties such as this one.

Further, children's understanding of these mathematical properties is the basis for algebra. Consider the justification for simplifying this algebraic expression:

7a + 4a

Why does it simplify to 11*a* and not 11*aa* or 11(*a* + *a*)? Like the two computations above, it involves the implicit use of the distributive property:

$$7a + 4a = (7 \times a) + (4 \times a) = (7 + 4)a = 11a$$

7*a* denotes 7 times *a*, which can be thought of as 7 groups of size *a*; similarly, 4*a* can be thought of as 4 groups of size *a*. Combined, this makes 11 groups of size *a*, or 11*a*. If children learn the addition of whole numbers, fractions, and decimals as a series of rules without also understanding the underlying algebraic basis of the operation—as they so often do—then they will not be prepared to understand algebra and why 7*a* + 4*a* = 11*a* rather than 11*aa* or 11(*a* + *a*). However, if they learn these operations in the context of developing Relational Thinking strategies, they are much more likely to understand the connections between arithmetic and algebra and be able to reason on the basis of mathematical relationships, without a rigid dependence on a fixed set of rules.

The Fundamental Properties of Operations and Equality

Students who use Relational Thinking are using a relatively small set of fundamental properties of operations and equality and related principles to establish connections between quantities, operations on quantities, and equalities between quantities in word problems as well as equations. We have discussed examples of children's use of several of these properties. In Figure 4–10 we provide a list of these properties, which hold for all numbers, including positive and negative whole numbers and fractions, as well as variables representing arbitrary rational numbers. In upcoming chapters, we discuss more instances of children's spontaneous use of these properties in the context of solving problems and performing computations. Children's strategies often make use of more properties than we explicitly identify. You may enjoy the challenge of identifying how children use fundamental properties to guide their thinking beyond the ones that we highlight for a given strategy.

Children's understanding of fractions as relational can be seen as special cases of these properties. For example, understanding that $1 \div n = \frac{1}{n}$ and $n \times \frac{1}{n} = 1$ is a special case of understanding multiplication and division as inverse operations.

We have found in our district that fractions are often the barrier to understanding algebra. High school teachers don't have time to develop the concepts of fractions. If kids don't learn fractions and really understand them in elementary and middle school, there is little chance to learn fractions in high school. Students often get to algebra and only think of fractions as a picture. They don't see fractions as numbers, and they don't have multiple ways of thinking about fractions. This causes all kinds of difficulties. When you get to solving equations like

$$\frac{x + 2}{2} = 7$$

and you don't understand that fractions are related to division, all you can do is memorize that when you see an equation like this, you multiply each side of the equation by the quantity on the bottom. At some point, memorizing falls apart. Students get to problems that don't match the memorized formulas that they have in their heads, and then they can't solve the problems. Teaching fractions so that students develop Relational Thinking opens the door to higher-level mathematics. Memorizing how to compute does not provide students with the basis for understanding number and operations needed for advanced mathematics. Students who understand fractions are able to make connections, and if they don't remember the rules, they can reason things out and figure out problems. If they get to a problem they haven't seen before, they can often figure out a way to solve it. We are really missing the boat by giving children pictures to color and thinking we are teaching fractions.

Chris Nugent

PK-8 Mathematics Coordinator

Dubuque, Iowa

At some point, students need to also learn that addition and multiplication are associative, but division and subtraction are not:

$$24 \div (12 \div 4) \neq (24 \div 12) \div 4$$
$$(92 - 57) - 7 \neq 92 - (57 - 7)$$

And addition and multiplication are commutative, but subtraction and division are not:

$$3 - \tfrac{1}{2} \neq \tfrac{1}{2} - 3$$
$$3 \div 2 \neq 2 \div 3$$

Reflecting Back and Looking Ahead

In this chapter, we introduced Relational Thinking and discussed its role in developing students' understanding of fractions. We described how solving and discussing Multiple Groups problems can reinforce concepts of fractions as relational and introduce operations involving fractions. Children develop Relational Thinking strategies as they strive for efficiency in their solutions. When students use Relational Thinking to solve fraction computation problems, they increase their understanding of fraction computation at the same time that they increase their understanding of the fundamental properties of operations and equality. Teaching with a focus on mathematical relationships transforms instruction in fractions into a critical site for the development of algebraic thinking.

Teachers play a necessary role in making the Relational Thinking in children's strategies explicit by writing equations to represent children's thinking and then questioning students about connections between these equations and their thinking. As children develop the ability to use equations to represent their strategies, they gradually learn to reason about equations as objects with mathematical properties— as they need to do when they solve algebraic equations. In Chapter 5, we discuss the teacher's role in eliciting children's Relational Thinking and helping it become an object of reflection. At first, you may simply want to note for yourself how children's strategies make use of Relational Thinking. However, for students to realize the full potential of Relational Thinking, you will need to help them learn to recognize and represent these relationships and use them explicitly in their reasoning.

Properties of Addition		Examples
Identity	$a + 0 = a$	$\frac{3}{8} + 0 = \frac{3}{8}$
Inverse	For every real number a there is a real number $-a$ such that $a + (-a) = 0$	$\frac{1}{3} + (-\frac{1}{3}) = 0$
Commutative	$a + b = b + a$	$\frac{1}{6} + \frac{1}{2} = \frac{1}{2} + \frac{1}{6}$
Associative	$a + (b + c) = (a + b) = c$	$\frac{4}{5} + (\frac{1}{5} + \frac{1}{2}) = (\frac{4}{5} + \frac{1}{5}) + \frac{1}{2}$

Properties of Multiplication		Examples
Identity	$a \times 1 = a$	$\frac{4}{3} \times 1 = \frac{4}{3}$
Inverse	For every real number a, $a \neq 0$, there is a real number $\frac{1}{a}$ such that $a \times \frac{1}{a} = 1$	$8 \times \frac{1}{8} = 1$
Commutative	$a \times b = b \times a$	$9 \times \frac{2}{3} = \frac{2}{3} \times 9$
Associative	$a \times (b \times c) = (a \times b) \times c$	$(5 \times 4) \times \frac{3}{4} = 5 \times (4 \times \frac{3}{4})$

Distributive Property of Multiplication over Addition		Example
	$a \times (b + c) = (a \times b) + (a \times c)$	$6 \times 2\frac{1}{3} = 6 \times (2 + \frac{1}{3}) = (6 \times 2) + 6 \times \frac{1}{3}$

Other Properties of Operations		Examples
Addition and Subtraction are Inverse Operations	If $a + b = c$, then $c - b = a$	$\frac{3}{4} + \frac{1}{4} = 1$, so $1 - \frac{1}{4} = \frac{3}{4}$
Multiplication and Division are Inverse Operations	If $a \times b = c$, then $c \div b = a$	$8 \times \frac{3}{4} = 6$, so $6 \div \frac{3}{4} = 8$

Properties of Equality		Examples
Addition Property of Equality*	If $a = c$, then $a + b = c + b$	$\frac{1}{3} = \frac{1}{6} + \frac{1}{6}$, so $\frac{1}{3} + \frac{1}{6} = (\frac{1}{6} + \frac{1}{6}) + \frac{1}{6}$
Multiplication Property of Quality*	If $a = c$, then $a \times b = c \times b$	$3 \times \frac{2}{3} = 2$, so $5 \times (3 \times \frac{2}{3}) = 5 \times 2$

*We do not include a subtraction property of equality or a division property of equality, even though they are true properties, because subtraction can be expressed in terms of addition and division in terms of multiplication.

Figure 4–10. *Fundamental properties of operations and equality*

chapter 5

From the Classroom

Making Relational Thinking Explicit

In Chapters 1, 3, and 4, we described children's thinking about fractions and the types of problems that teachers can use to build understanding of fractions. We focused on problems and strategies that lead to the development of Relational Thinking, because thinking relationally is fundamental to understanding fractions.

Although some students use Relational Thinking whether or not the teacher encourages them to, most students need teacher support to use Relational Thinking flexibly and consistently. Virtually all students are capable of using Relational Thinking with support. In this chapter, we shift our attention to the teaching practices that support children to use Relational Thinking and make it explicit. We focus in particular on teachers' use of equations to represent the relationships that children use in their strategies. We illustrate these practices by describing a lesson in Ms. Perez's fifth-grade class and her decision making as she teaches.

A New Role for Many Teachers

When teachers encourage students to use their own strategies to solve problems, they are often astonished to realize that new mathematical ideas emerge with regularity in students' thinking. These ideas often involve Relational Thinking. Realizing that children are capable of creating new ideas can lead teachers to rethink their role from the one who demonstrates Relational Thinking to the one who sets the stage for students to use and develop their own forms of Relational Thinking. This new role involves:

1) Carefully planning the problems you pose to students, focusing in particular on the kinds of strategies that students could use in combination with the mathematics that could be addressed,

2) Facilitating communication among students so that students can express their ideas and reflect on each other's strategies,

3) Assessing students' thinking on an informal and ongoing basis and using information about your students' thinking to guide your choice of problems and how you help students' express their ideas.

Although all three of these aspects of the teacher's role are illustrated in this chapter, we especially focus on how teachers can help students express their mathematical ideas and reflect on each other's strategies. Equations are an especially powerful tool for communicating and reflecting on mathematical ideas during discussions of students' strategies because they can be used to represent the problem situation, strategies to solve the problem, and the fundamental relationships on which students' strategies are based.

Supporting the Development of Relational Thinking

We illustrate the teacher's role in the development of students' Relational Thinking with a snapshot of Ms. Perez's teaching, narrated from her point of view. It is an example of how one teacher enacted the ideas in this book. Our aim is to help you reflect on your own teaching practices, rather than prescribe specific teaching practices. Different teachers will have different ways of using information about children's thinking based on their teaching preferences and the needs of their students.

For the second year in a row, Ms. Perez is teaching fractions based upon the framework for problem types and solution strategies provided in this book. She started this unit on fractions by having her students explore Equal Sharing and Multiple Groups problems. On this day, she teaches a lesson in which she plans to highlight and allow students to reflect as a class upon the Relational Thinking in a couple of students' strategies. She provides some background and then explains her thinking as she was planning and teaching this lesson.

Ms. Perez's Fifth-Grade Lesson

My fifth-grade class has been studying fractions for about six lessons. Although the students had a unit on fractions last year, in many ways this was the first time they have really been pushed to think about the deep ideas of fractions. At the beginning of the unit, a lot of my students didn't think about fractions as numbers and most of them didn't connect fractions with what they knew about division of whole numbers.

Getting Started

I started fraction instruction by having students solve Equal Sharing problems. Because we had already established a routine for solving and discussing problems and my students were used to tackling problems on their own, I didn't show them what to do. I just used a context they were familiar with and told them that I wanted them to solve the problem in any way that made sense to them. I try to make time each day to let students share their strategies so they can learn from each other. All of my students were able to solve these problems, although some of them struggled at first with the conventional names for the resulting share. After working with Equal Sharing problems, all of my students were able to correctly name fractional amounts for mixed numbers and for fractions less than one, and they understood that fractions were numbers.

I then moved on to Multiple Groups problems. I started with multiplication problems with a unit-fraction amount in each group. For example, we solved the problem:

I AM MAKING SUB SANDWICHES for some friends. There will be 13 of us eating sub sandwiches. I want to serve each person ¼ of a sub sandwich. How many sub sandwiches do I need to make all together?

Many of my students used Relational Thinking strategies to solve this problem. For example, they would say "4 one-fourths are a whole, so 8 one-fourths would be 2 sandwiches, and 12 one-fourths would be 3 sandwiches, and then you only need another one-fourth of a sub. You would need 3¼ sandwiches to feed your friends." After working with several Multiple Groups problems—both Multiplication and Measurement Division—where students were combining unit fractions, we moved on to this multiplication problem with groups of nonunit fractions:

MR. DAVIS IS PLANNING an art project for his class. Each student will need ¾ of a package of clay to do this project. If Mr. Davis has 12 students in his class, how many packages of clay would he need?

My first goal in giving this problem was for each and every student to solve the problem using a strategy that made sense to him or her. My second goal was to find some students who used Relational Thinking strategies and have them share those strategies with the class. I knew a lot of students would either draw out every ¾ package of clay or repeatedly add three-fourths. Although these are valid strategies for solving this problem, I was hoping to find some students who used Relational Thinking. For example, maybe they would see that 2 groups of ¾ was 1½ and then combine groups of 1½ rather than groups of ¾. I was also hoping that someone might even recognize that 4 groups of ¾ was 3 and then be able to quickly combine groups of 3 while still keeping track that 3 packages of clay would represent what 4 students would get. When the students who used Relational Thinking shared their strategies with the class, I planned to introduce equations to help other students understand the Relational Thinking.

I started the lesson by reading the problem to the class and giving each student a sheet of paper with the problem written on it. I walked around the room as the students were solving the problem and mostly just watched what they were doing. If students were frustrated or stuck, I asked if they needed help. Sometimes they said no and I just moved on. If they said yes, I asked them to tell me the story in their own words. If they couldn't retell the story, we worked on understanding what was happening in the problem. I have some struggling readers and English language learners who often need some support to understand what is happening in the problem. I started by checking in with these students to see if they understood the story. I asked them to show me how much 1 person would get. Some students drew ¾ of a package of clay and others just wrote ¾. I then said, "Can you show me what would 2 people get?" I didn't need any other probes today to help students get started. For my students who really had to work to show me what 2 people would get, I asked them to solve the problem for 6 students rather than 12. For students who solved the problem quickly, I asked them to figure out how much clay would be needed for 21 students rather than 12.

Checking in on Students' Strategies

Once everyone was started working, I began to look for evidence of Relational Thinking. I noticed that Sonya and Lamar used Relational Thinking.

Figure 5–1 shows Sonya's paper. When I asked Sonya to explain to me what she had done, she said, "¾ plus ¾ is what 2 kids would get. I knew that was 1½. It is really easy to add 1½ and 1½. That is how much 4 kids would get and it is 3 packages. (She pointed to the numbers in the second row as she said this.) Then another 1½ packages would be 2 more kids, so 6 kids, and that is 4½ packages. I just kept adding 1½ packages, which is always for 2 more kids, and kept figuring out how much clay that would be. I stopped when I had 12 kids." Her way of writing her strategy was confusing, but her strategy made sense and used Relational Thinking.

Lamar's paper is shown in Figure 5–2. When I asked him to explain his strategy, he said, "¾ plus ¾ is 1½, so 1½ packages is 2 people, double that, 3 packages is 4 people, double that, 6 packages is 8 people, but if I double again, I get too many people. I need clay for 4 more people, so 3 more packages. 6 plus 3

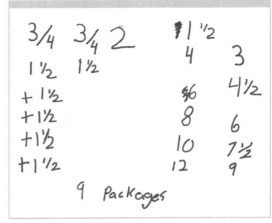

Figure 5–1. *Sonya's strategy for 12 groups of ¾*

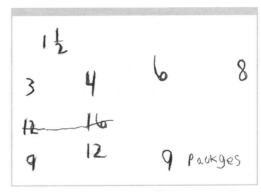

Figure 5–2. *Lamar's strategy for 12 groups of ¾*

is 9, so 9 packages." Lamar used a more efficient Relational Thinking strategy than Sonya. Again, his way of writing his strategy was pretty confusing, but his strategy made sense.

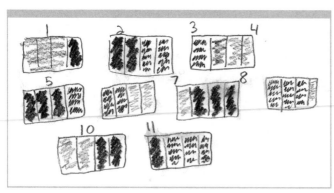

Figure 5–3. *Alex's strategy for 12 groups of ¾*

Sharing Strategies: Helping Students Make Connections

After the students had been working on solving this problem for about twenty minutes, I got their attention and told them that we were going to listen to how each other solved the problem. Alex solved the problem by drawing out groups of ¾ and I had him share first (Figure 5–3 shows what Alex drew on the board). I wanted to start with a basic strategy like his because all students would be able to understand it, and I wanted a strategy pictured so that we could refer back to it when the Relational Thinking strategies were shared.

Alex said, "I wasn't sure how many packages we would need so I just started drawing packages and cutting them into fourths. I got kinda tired of drawing packages. I went back and colored in what one kid would get—see here is what one kid would get—then here is what another kid would get, then here is what another kid would get. And then I thought, I need to remember how many kids are getting clay. That is when I put the numbers on the top. When I got to 12, I knew I could stop. All I had to do was count the packages. I got 9."

At this point, I was thinking about the students like Lucas who had struggled with the problem and I wanted to make sure they understood Alex's solution. Lucas had drawn out separate groups of ¾ and gotten an answer of ³⁶⁄₄. I had Lucas go up to Alex's drawing and show me the clay that Alex gave the first person, and then the clay Alex gave the second person. Since Alex used color, Lucas was easily able to do this. I asked Lucas, "When Alex gave clay to 2 people, how many packages did he use?" At first Lucas answered six-fourths. Through conversation and input from other students, Lucas was able to see that this could also be one and two-fourths or 1½ packages.

After discussing Alex's strategy, we moved on to Sonya. I wanted Sonya to share her strategy before Lamar because I thought it would be easier to understand than Lamar's. Since the way that Sonya wrote her strategy was pretty confusing, my plan was to introduce equations to help others understand her strategy. These equations would also help us focus on the relationships that Sonya used.

Ms. Perez: Sonya is going to share next. Sonya, I'm not going to have you show us what you wrote on your paper. I want you to tell us how you solved the problem. I am going to be the recorder, and I am going to write what you did using equations. Everyone is going to have to listen and watch really carefully because I want to make sure that what I write matches how Sonya solved the problem. OK, Sonya, what did you do first?

Sonya: First I knew that ¾ and ¾ is 1½. That is how much 2 kids would get.

Ms. Perez: She said ¾ *and* ¾. Does anyone have an idea how we could write that in an equation? Peter?

Peter: She added them, ¾ plus ¾ is 1½.

Ms. Perez: OK, does this equation [writing on the board] show what Sonya did?

$$ ¾ + ¾ = 1½ $$

Students: Yes.

Sonya: But that was 2 kids, you need to write *2* or you might forget.

Ms. Perez: Good point, should we write *2 kids* next to this?

$$ ¾ + ¾ = 1½ \qquad 2 \ kids $$

Sonya: Yes, you can't forget that that is how much for 2 kids.

Ms. Perez: OK, so we have 2 kids would use 1½ packages of clay. Claire, can you go up to Alex's picture and show me where he shows that 2 kids would get 1½ packages of clay? [Claire goes up the board and uses her finger to circle the first package and a half of Alex's picture.] Claire, what number does Alex have up there by that part of his strategy?

Claire: *2, for 2 kids.*

Ms. Perez: OK, Sonya, what did you do next?

Sonya: 1½ and 1½ is really easy for me to add. It is 3. So I got 3 packages, but I had to remember that 3 packages is for 4 kids.

Ms. Perez: OK, let's see if this equation represents what you just told me:

$$1\tfrac{1}{2} + 1\tfrac{1}{2} = 3$$

Sonya: But you need the *4*, you can't forget the 4 kids.

Ms. Perez: OK, let me write that.

$$1\tfrac{1}{2} + 1\tfrac{1}{2} = 3 \qquad 4 \text{ kids}$$

Ms. Perez: Is that what you have done so far?

Sonya: Yes.

Ms. Perez: Alex, did you also find that 4 kids would use 3 packages?

Alex: Yes, I did [walks to the board]. Here is where I wrote the 4 kids and look, they get 3 packages of clay [with his finger, circles the first 3 packages of clay and the numeral *4* above it].

It is really important to have kids like Alex make connections between the more basic strategy and the Relational Thinking strategy. I need to ask questions to students to help them think about the strategies that other students are sharing. Even though my questions help students listen and pay attention, the more important purpose behind them is to help students draw connections between the strategies. This helps students to see the relationships and maybe even to use the relationships in their next strategy.

Next I wanted to focus on how Sonya moved from 2 kids using 1½ packages of clay right to 4 kids using 3 packages of clay without needing to figure out how much clay 3 kids would need. Many students didn't understand what she did. I asked questions of students such as Terry and Peter, because I thought they were close to understanding, and with a little additional support, could understand the strategy.

Ms. Perez: Sonya went right from 2 kids to 4 kids. She never figured out how much clay for 3 kids. With Alex's strategy, I saw how much 3 kids would get but I don't see it here with Sonya's strategy. Terry, can you tell me what you think she did?

Terry: I am confused. No one gets 1½ packages, they each get ¾.

Sonya: No, but 2 kids get 1½ packages so 4 kids get 3 packages. It is easier to add 1½ than to add ¾.

Terry: I still don't get it. I got 4 kids get 3 packages too, but I added ¾ 4 times.

Tyrone: I think I get it. It's like you double both: if 2 kids get 1½ packages, the 4 kids get double what 2 kids get, they get 3 packages.

Terry: [long pause] Oh, you double both, kids and packages. Oh, that is a good idea!

Ms. Perez: Sonya, what did you do next?

Sonya: I didn't add another ¾, I added another 1½, 4 plus 1½ is 5½, that is 6 kids.

Ms. Perez: Terry, what do you think about this? She didn't add another ¾.

Terry: No, she adds what 2 more kids would get, that is a good idea!

Ms. Perez: Peter, what do you think is the difference between what Terry did and what Sonya did?

Peter: I did it like Terry, but I think I get what Sonya did. It is easier to add one and one-halves than three-quarters, so she added what 2 kids would get each time.

I was pretty sure that Alex, Terry, and Peter now had an intuitive grasp of Sonya's strategy. The conversation probably helped other students to gain some understanding too. Now I focused on the equations that could represent Sonya's strategy.

Ms. Perez: Sonya, do you think you could write the next step with an equation? [Sonya writes at board:]

$$4 + 1\tfrac{1}{2} = 5\tfrac{1}{2} \quad 6 \text{ kids}$$

Terry: She did it again, she added what 2 kids would get.

Lamar: I thought she would double the whole thing. That's what I did.

Ms. Perez: Lamar, we will look at yours soon, but let's finish Sonya's here.

We continued with Sonya's strategy until we had the following written on the board:

$$\tfrac{3}{4} + \tfrac{3}{4} = 1\tfrac{1}{2} \qquad 2 \text{ kids}$$
$$1\tfrac{1}{2} + 1\tfrac{1}{2} = 3 \qquad 4 \text{ kids}$$
$$3 + 1\tfrac{1}{2} = 4\tfrac{1}{2} \qquad 6 \text{ kids}$$
$$4\tfrac{1}{2} + 1\tfrac{1}{2} = 6 \qquad 8 \text{ kids}$$
$$6 + 1\tfrac{1}{2} = 7\tfrac{1}{2} \qquad 10 \text{ kids}$$
$$7\tfrac{1}{2} + 1\tfrac{1}{2} = 9 \qquad 12 \text{ kids}$$

If Sonya had shared without my writing anything down, only a few students would have been able to understand her strategy. Not only did these equations help other students understand her strategy, they also helped us focus on the mathematical relationships she used. Students need to learn how to write equations to show their ideas. My goal is for students to connect equations to strategies and problem situations and to eventually be able to use equations to communicate mathematical ideas.

My work introducing equations to represent solution strategies reminds me of my literacy instruction when I taught first grade. My first graders had all these ideas and my role was to introduce conventions that would help them communicate their ideas. For example, I taught them about spacing between words, capital letters, periods to mark off sentences, some standard spellings, and so on. It is much the same when I introduce equations to these older students. They have these great ways of solving problems, and my job is to introduce conventions so that they can represent and communicate these ideas.

Next I asked Lamar to share his strategy. I chose not to have him share what he wrote because I wanted to continue to introduce equations to represent solution strategies, and I knew that equations would focus on relationships in a way that Lamar's notation did not. I started by having Lamar explain how he solved the problem. He is a student who needs to get his whole idea out there, so I didn't interrupt him with notation right away.

Ms. Perez: Lamar, could you share how you solved this problem?
Lamar: I did ¾ plus ¾ is 1½. 1½ packages would be what 2 people would get. If I double it, I have 3 packages and 4 people. If I double it again, I have 6 packages

is 8 people. I tried to double the whole thing and I got 16 people and 12 packages, but that is too many people. With 6 people and 8, I need clay for 4 more people, so 3 more packages. 6 plus 3 is 9, so 9 packages for 12 people.

Ms. Perez: OK, can someone tell me what Lamar did?

Terry: It was too fast!

Ms. Perez: Yes, it was fast. Sometimes it is hard to communicate our ideas only with talking. Today, Alex used a picture to help us understand how he solved the problem, and when Sonya shared, we wrote equations to help us understand how she solved the problem. We are going to try to write equations to help us understand Lamar's strategy. Lamar, why don't you start again? This time I am going to try to write some equations to show what you did. Everyone needs to listen and watch really closely because I want to make sure that what I write matches how Lamar solved the problem. OK, Lamar, why don't you tell us the first part about what you did?

Lamar: First, I found that 2 kids would need 1½ packages, ¾ plus ¾ is 1½.

Ms. Perez: OK, does this equation show what you did at first?

$$\tfrac{3}{4} + \tfrac{3}{4} = 1\tfrac{1}{2}$$

Lamar: Yes.

Ms. Perez: How about the rest of you, does this show what Lamar just said?

Sonya: What about the 2? He said there were *2* packages and you don't have that.

Ms. Perez: Good point, I think we had this same problem when we started with yours. How can we write an equation where we show that Lamar had 2 groups of ¾?

Claire: You could write *2 kids* like we did with Sonya.

Ms. Perez: Yes, I could do that. I am going to challenge you here though. Is there a way that I could write an equation with a *2* in it that shows what he did?

Since Sonya's strategy was about adding what 2 students would get each time, I didn't feel compelled to get the students to write a multiplication equation for her strategy. Lamar did a lot of doubling and the best way to show doubling is with multiplication equations. I was hoping that we would be able to write a multiplication equation, so I didn't accept the suggestion that we write *2 people* off to the side like I did with Sonya.

Peter: It isn't ¾ plus 2. That isn't right.

Lamar: No, I didn't add 2, I did 2 kids.

Ms. Perez: And how much did each kid get?

Lamar: ¾ package.

Ms. Perez: So you have 2 kids and each gets ¾. Can anyone think of an equation that would go with 2 kids, each getting ¾? [Long pause in which no one volunteers.] What if instead of ¾ of a package each kid got 5 packages, can you think of how we could use an equation to show that 2 kids each get 5 packages?

Tyrone: We talked about this before, it could be 5 plus 5, but it could also be 2 times 5—2 groups of 5.

Ms. Perez: [writes *2 × 5* on the board] Tyrone says that this shows 2 groups of 5. Now with the problem that you all just solved, did we have 5 packages for each student?

Chorus: NO!

Claire: We had ¾ for each kid.

Ms. Perez: How could we write 2 groups of ¾? Remember, this one shows 2 groups of 5.

Tyrone: How about 2 times ¾?

Ms. Perez: [writes *2 × ¾*] How does that look for a start? What does this mean? Lamar, what does this mean?

Lamar: 2 groups of ¾. That is what I did, 2 groups of ¾ is 1½.

Ms. Perez: So is this a way of writing Lamar's first step?

$$2 \times \text{¾} = 1\text{½}$$

We discussed for quite some time why this equation fit with what Lamar did. I knew this equation would challenge a lot of my students since many of them entered fifth grade writing addition equations for simple multiplication story problems. For example, if the problem was something like, "I have 5 buckets with 43 marbles in each bucket, how many marbles do I have?" they would write:

$$43 + 43 + 43 + 43 + 43 = n$$

as the equation that goes with this problem. Of course this equation isn't wrong, but I wanted them to know that

$$5 \times 43 = n$$

also represents with this problem. If they have a problem like 87 buckets with 43 marbles in each bucket, the only practical equation they can write to go with this problem is a multiplication equation. Almost all of my students can now write multiplication and division equations to represent story problems with whole numbers, but writing multiplication and division equations to represent situations that involve fractions is a new challenge for them.

The Discussion Continues

Ms. Perez: OK, Lamar, let's get back to your strategy. You started with 2 groups of ¾ is 1½. Then what did you do?

Lamar: Then I just doubled it. If 2 kids is 1½ packages, then 4 kids would be 3 packages. I wrote *3* and *4* on my paper.

Ms. Perez: So, I am wondering if there is an equation we could write that would show this idea, that 4 kids would get 3 packages of clay.

Lamar: It is just like the one you wrote, but this time you have 4 groups of ¾ is the same as 3.

Ms. Perez: Do you want to come up and write it?

Lamar: Sure.

Ms. Perez: Write it here, right under where we wrote the other equation.

Lamar: OK.

$$2 \times \tfrac{3}{4} = 1\tfrac{1}{2}$$
$$4 \times \tfrac{3}{4} = 3$$

Ms. Perez: OK, can someone read what Lamar just wrote and tell me what it means?

Terry: 4 groups of ¾ is 3. He said he doubled both, the kids and the clay.

Ms. Perez: Does that work?

Terry: Yeah, if 2 kids have 1½, 4 kids will have 3. You double both.

Ms. Perez: Tyrone, what do you think?

Tyrone: I think it's right—4 groups of ¾ is 3. Double the kids and double the packages.

Ms. Perez: OK, then what did you do next?

Lamar: Hmm. I don't remember what I already told you and what I didn't tell you yet.

Ms. Perez: Sometimes it is hard to remember just one part of how you solved the problem. See if you can use the equations that we are writing to help you remember where you are.

Lamar: Oh, yeah, I doubled it one time, then I doubled it again, if 4 kids would need 3 packages, then 8 kids would need 6 packages.

I was happy that Lamar could look at the equations we had written and figure out what he had already explained to us. I hope eventually students will see that equations not only help us communicate with others but also can help us solve problems. Many students already use equations to solve problems with whole numbers. My goal is for them to be able to transfer this to their work with fractions.

Ms. Perez: OK, how about someone else, can someone else tell me what the equation for this part would be? Alex, do you have an idea?

Alex: It has to have an 8 and a 6.

Ms. Perez: Yes, it does. Do you remember what Lamar said about the 8 and the 6?

Alex: 8 kids would need 6 packages?

Ms. Perez: Yes, and how much does each kid get?

Alex: ¾ of a package.

Ms. Perez: OK, so 8 kids each get ¾ of a package and that is 6 packages. Is this right?

Alex: Yes.

Ms. Perez: And how could we write that in an equation?

Alex: I am not sure.

Jessie: I have an idea. [Comes to the board and writes.]

$8 \times \frac{3}{4} = 6$

Ms. Perez: Why do you think that would work, Jessie?

Jessie: Because 8 groups of $\frac{3}{4}$ is 6. That is what Lamar said.

Ms. Perez: OK, what do you think, Alex?

Alex: That is probably right.

Ms. Perez: OK, Lamar, what did you do next?

Lamar: [long pause, looking at the equations on the board] OK, I see where I am. I doubled it again. If 8 kids get 6 packages, then 16 kids get 12 packages, but that is too many kids so I crossed it off.

Ms. Perez: OK, Does this show what you did?

$16 \times \frac{3}{4} = 12$

Lamar: Yes, but that was too many kids, so I went back to 8 kids and 6 packages. I only need 4 more kids to get 12 kids and I already know that 4 kids need 3 packages, so I just kind of added them together and got 12 kids would need 9 packages.

Ms. Perez: You just said a lot. Let's break that down a little. Look at this equation [pointing], $16 \times \frac{3}{4} = 12$. Why did Lamar say that he couldn't use this?

Peter: That is for 16 kids. It's too many kids.

Ms. Perez: OK, so what did he do?

Peter: He said he went back to 8 kids need 6 packages.

Ms. Perez: [points to $8 \times \frac{3}{4} = 6$] OK, so he went back to there.

Peter: Yeah and he added 4 more kids. Oh, he has that up there! 4 times $\frac{3}{4}$ is 3.

Lamar: It is kinda like I added two equations together.

Ms. Perez: Let's look at that:

$4 \times \frac{3}{4} = 3$

$8 \times \frac{3}{4} = 6$

You added those together?

Lamar: Yeah, kinda, the way I think about it is, I had 4 groups of $\frac{3}{4}$ and then 8 groups of $\frac{3}{4}$, and that is like 12 groups of $\frac{3}{4}$ altogether.

Ms. Perez: Now that is interesting. What do the rest of you think? Would 4 groups of ¾ plus 8 groups of ¾ be the same as 12 groups of ¾?

Peter: It would have to be!

Terry: I need to hear it again.

Ms. Perez: Would 4 groups of ¾ plus 8 groups of ¾ be the same as 12 groups of ¾?

Terry: Yes, it would, it is like what 4 kids get plus what 8 kids get would be the same as what 12 kids get!

Ms. Perez: I am going to write this idea in an equation to see if that helps more people think about it.

$$4 \times \tfrac{3}{4} + 8 \times \tfrac{3}{4} = 12 \times \tfrac{3}{4}$$

Ms. Perez: I know this is a long equation here but let's look at it together. 4 groups of ¾ plus 8 groups of ¾ is the same as 12 groups of ¾. Is that true?

Lamar: Yes, and that is what I did.

Sonya: Oh, I get it now! He did 4 people's clay and 8 people's clay is 12 people's clay. That's right.

Ms. Perez: So, Lamar, does this show what you did?

Lamar: No, I need to show the answer, I need to show the 9 packages.

Ms. Perez: Oh, of course you do. I got so excited about this equation that I forgot about that! How could you show it?

Lamar: Could I just write = 9 at the end? Can you have two equal signs?

Ms. Perez: Actually you can, why don't you do that?

$$4 \times \tfrac{3}{4} + 8 \times \tfrac{3}{4} = 12 \times \tfrac{3}{4} = 9$$

Figure 5–4 shows what our board looked like.

I was really excited that Lamar said something about adding equations together. Although that isn't one of our standards at fifth grade, I know that in high school algebra, students will eventually need to understand how they can add equations together. I was also excited that the equation we wrote showed the distributive property with a fraction amount in each group.

That was a really complex equation and several students were able to talk about it. It was my sense at this point that about a third of the class understood this equation. When we work with complex ideas like this, I don't expect everyone to understand them the first time. And you never really know what small seeds are planted for some students who appear not to understand at all. We will return to this idea often, and I expect everyone to grow in their understanding of these equations.

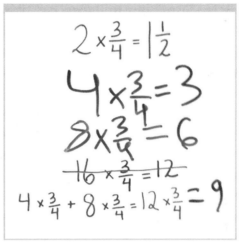

Figure 5–4. *The board after Ms. Perez and Lamar finished writing equations to represent his strategy*

Figure 5–5. *Students discuss their strategies*

Using Equations to Represent Word Problems, Strategies, and Relationships

Equations can be used to represent various aspects of students' thinking about word problems and their solutions.

Equations to Represent Word Problems and Children's Strategies

The easiest types of equation for children to write are those that represent the *strategy* they have used to solve a word problem, even if the strategy does not involve number sentences. It is harder for children to write an equation to represent a *word problem*, because it involves viewing the situation in its entirety and relating the given quantities and the unknown quantity without solving the problem (Carey 1991).

For example, consider this problem:

JAY IS MAKING FLOWER POTS. It takes ¾ of a package of clay to make 1 flower pot. How many flower pots can Jay make with 4½ packages of clay?

The most likely equations we would use to represent the relationship between the total amount of packages of clay (4½), the amount of a package of clay it takes to make a flowerpot (¾), and the number of flower pots (y) are:

$$4\frac{1}{2} \div \frac{3}{4} = y \text{ and } y \times \frac{3}{4} = 4\frac{1}{2}$$

However, fourth-grader Mei Lein solved the problem by reasoning "¾ plus ¾ is 1½, that's 2 pots; plus another ¾ is 2¼, that's 3 pots; plus another ¾ is 3 that's 4 pots, plus ¾ is 3¾, that's 5 pots, plus ¾ is 4½ and that's 6 pots." The equation that she wrote to show how she solved the problem was,

$$\frac{3}{4} + \frac{3}{4} + \frac{3}{4} + \frac{3}{4} + \frac{3}{4} + \frac{3}{4} = 4\frac{1}{2}$$

Students eventually need to be able to write equations that represent how a problem was solved *and* equations that represent the situation in a problem. With many opportunities to solve problems and write equations to represent their solutions, children learn to read a word problem and to write an equation to represent the problem before they have solved it. This capacity develops for addition and subtraction word problems before multiplication and division word problems and for word problems involving whole numbers before word problems involving fractions. In the middle grades, students can learn to write equations to represent problems and then use the equations as tools to help them solve the problem. In algebra, many problems cannot realistically be solved without first writing an equation to represent the problem.

Equations That Highlight Mathematical Relationships

After Lamar shared his strategy for solving the packages of clay problem, the teacher wrote this equation:

$$4 \times \tfrac{3}{4} + 8 \times \tfrac{3}{4} = 12 \times \tfrac{3}{4}$$

This equation highlights the distributive property, one of the fundamental properties that Lamar used to solve this problem. You can use equations like this one to highlight the mathematical relationships that students use to reason about a problem. This equation is powerful both for what it contains and what it does not contain. Unlike informal notation, which can contain extraneous information, this equation contains exactly what is essential to understanding how the distributive property was used to solve this problem. Equations that highlight mathematical relationships do not necessarily describe how the problem was solved but rather highlight the relationships that were used in solving the problem.

Using Equations to Communicate and Reflect on Thinking

Equations are usually a better tool for recording solution strategies than the informal notation that children generate on their own. Equations can help students communicate their thinking to teachers as well other students. Once students develop skill in using equations to represent their thinking, equations can serve as powerful tools for reflection. Students can refer back to equations to catch errors. If students lose track of where they are when solving a problem, equations enable them to pick up where they left off and complete the problem. Sometimes students refer back to equations they used to record how they solved a problem to help them generate a strategy for a similar problem.

Some Relational Thinking strategies are not well suited to being represented with equations. For example, Katrin solved $12\frac{1}{2} - 3\frac{3}{4}$ as follows: "$12\frac{1}{2}$ minus 3 is $9\frac{1}{2}$ then minus as $\frac{1}{2}$ is 9 then 9 minus $\frac{1}{4}$ is $8\frac{3}{4}$." Although the following equations could be used to represent Katrin's strategy,

$$12\frac{1}{2} - 3 = 9\frac{1}{2}$$
$$9\frac{1}{2} - \frac{1}{2} = 9$$
$$9 - \frac{1}{4} = 8\frac{3}{4}$$

the notation below with arrows better reflects the fact that Katrin kept a running difference as she worked.

$$12\frac{1}{2} - 3 \rightarrow 9\frac{1}{2} - \frac{1}{2} \rightarrow 9 - \frac{1}{4} \rightarrow 8\frac{3}{4}$$

It is important to use a symbol other than an equal sign to separate the expressions in the notation above because $12\frac{1}{2} - 3$ does not equal $9\frac{1}{2} - \frac{1}{2}$ and so on. The arrow is not a universally recognized mathematical symbol as the equal sign is, but it is a useful symbol for recording the process of children's thinking. For more information about developing students' understanding of the equal sign see Chapter 2 of *Thinking Mathematically*, Carpenter, et al (2003).

Some teachers ask students to communicate their mathematical thinking in words. For example, some teachers would want Sonya to write a description (see Figure 5–6) to show how she solved the problem.

Although there are problems that require students to explain their thinking in words, this problem is not one of them. Equations are more useful than words for communicating Relational Thinking strategies because they highlight the critical mathematics used in these strategies and help students focus on what is essential in understanding these strategies.

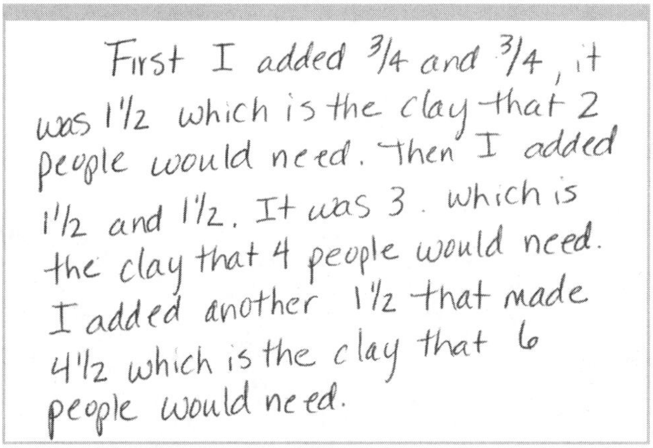

Reflecting Back and Looking Ahead

When teachers learn about children's intuitive strategies for solving problems, many decide to decrease or eliminate the time they

First I added 3/4 and 3/4, it was 1½ which is the clay that 2 people would need. Then I added 1½ and 1½. It was 3. which is the clay that 4 people would need. I added another 1½ that made 4½ which is the clay that 6 people would need.

Figure 5–6. *A written description of Sonya's strategy obscures the mathematical relationships she used*

spend demonstrating and explaining computation and problem-solving procedures to students. Some teachers then wonder what their role in the classroom could be if it is not focused on demonstrating and explaining strategies to students and monitoring students' progress in using these strategies. In this chapter, we examined the active role that teachers can take to foster Relational Thinking strategies among their students. This new role centers on helping students communicate strategies to other students, directing questions to specific students to help them draw connections between these strategies and more basic strategies, introducing equations to represent students' strategies, and highlighting the fundamental properties of operations and equality that underpin these strategies.

In upcoming chapters, we illustrate how you can use these same practices as you teach fraction equivalence and order (Chapter 6) and operations involving fractions and decimals (Chapters 7 and 8) as well as what it means to understand these topics.

chapter 6

Understanding Fraction Equivalence and Order

in this chapter, we describe how children can use their understanding of relationships between fractions to build their understanding of fraction equivalence and order. The teacher plays an active role in helping students extend their understanding. This role includes asking probing questions, introducing equations, and choosing number combinations for problems with specific purposes in mind.

We begin the chapter with a discussion of how some of the usual approaches to teaching equivalent fractions can be problematic. We then show how students' first opportunities to reason about equivalent fractions can emerge in discussions of Equal Sharing problems and how this reasoning is fundamentally relational in nature. Equations can be a tool to help make these relationships explicit for students. We then discuss how word problems and equations can be used to further develop and refine children's understanding, Next we discuss how children's growing understanding of equivalence can be linked to formal mathematical representations and definitions. We conclude by describing the variety of informal strategies that students use to compare fractions.

Some Issues with Common Approaches to Teaching Equivalence

Fraction Manipulatives

The use of fraction manipulatives to teach equivalence and order is popular. However, students can use manipulatives such as fraction bars or divided circles to solve fraction problems without understanding the mathematical basis for the relationship. For example, a fourth grader used fraction bars to figure out that $\frac{3}{4}$ was bigger than $\frac{2}{3}$ saying, "I know the red ones are fourths and I know the orange ones are thirds, so I got 3 red and 2 orange and see—the 3 red put together are bigger than 2 orange" (Figure 6–1). Her explanation makes no reference to mathematical relationships between thirds and fourths or between the fractions and whole units. If the goal is for children to understand fractions, manipulatives such as these are not necessarily helpful, because children can use them to solve problems without reasoning about critical relationships. Rather than supporting children to think, these types of manipulatives can eliminate the need for children to think mathematically.

A striking example of this kind of unhelpful use of fraction manipulatives was described by Laura Brinker Kent writing about how fifth graders used fraction strips to add fractions with unlike denominators (Brinker 1997). To figure $\frac{2}{5} + \frac{2}{8}$, Jay first laid out the eighths fraction strip, then the fifths strip next to it, lined up at the $\frac{2}{5}$ mark (Figure 6–2). He saw that the two fractions together made what looked to him like $\frac{5}{8}$. Although $\frac{5}{8}$ is an estimate of the actual sum, Jay did not distinguish between an approximate sum and an exact sum. He was not aware that his answer was not correct, because he thought he was using the fraction strips correctly. Several students in this fifth-grade class used the tool the way Jay did, leading Kent to conclude that the use of fraction strips interfered with students' ability to rely on fraction relationships in their reasoning.

Children need only a few simple tools to solve problems involving fractions. These tools include paper and pencil for drawing or notating, cutout pieces of paper for folding or cutting, colored pencils or markers for allocating shares, and linking cubes for representing discrete quantities such as the people or candy bars in a problem. These tools allow students to work with fractional quantities in a manner that reflects and reinforces their understanding of fraction relationships.

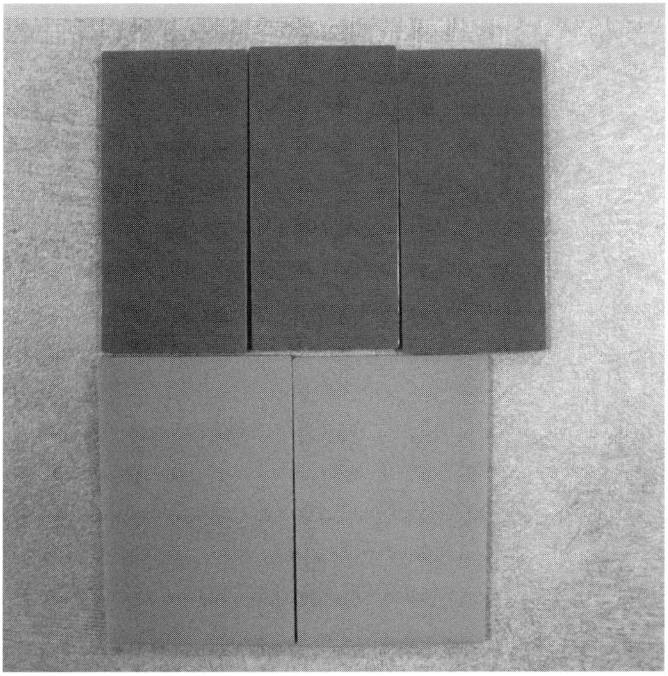

Figure 6–1. *Using fraction bars to show $\frac{3}{4} > \frac{2}{3}$ does not require reasoning about mathematical relationships*

If students use these relatively unstructured tools to solve problems and represent fractional quantities, they will be free to attend to the mathematical features of fractions. Children's use of these simple tools can also provide the teacher with a window into how children are thinking about fractions that is absent when they use more structured materials that have some of the critical problem-solving decisions—such as how to create thirds—designed into them. Recall what we learned about the limitations of Ernesto's understanding of $\frac{1}{4}$ at the beginning of Chapter 1 when we saw how he created a representation for $\frac{1}{4}$. If he had been using fraction manipulatives, we may not have learned that he had a limited understanding of $\frac{1}{4}$.

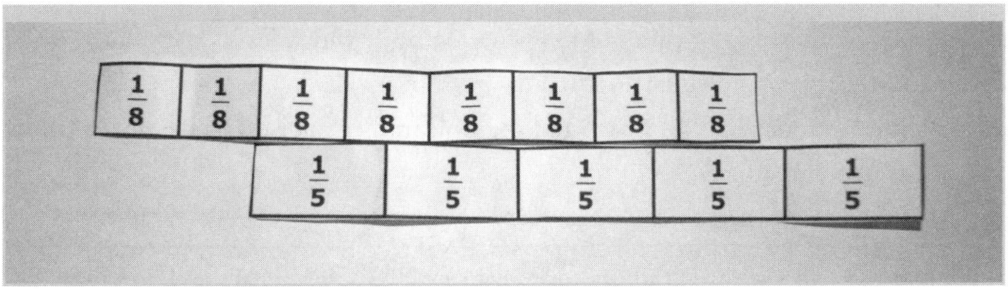

Figure 6–2. *Using fraction strips to figure, mistakenly, that $\frac{2}{5} + \frac{2}{8}$ is $\frac{5}{8}$*

Symbolic Manipulations

In many curriculum programs, instruction on fractions transitions quickly from the use of manipulatives to the use of abstract symbolic procedures. A fourth grader whose teacher used such a program brought home a worksheet that involved reducing fractions to lowest terms. At the top of the page was an example:

$$\frac{6}{8} = \frac{6 \div 2}{8 \div 2} = \frac{3}{4}$$

He knew that equivalence had to do with covering the same amount of area and knew how to divide whole numbers. But he did not understand why dividing the numerator and denominator by same number led to an equivalent fraction. And when it came to figuring out how to reduce $\frac{6}{15}$ on his own, he could not do it. With tears welling up in his eyes, he asked his mom how he was supposed to know what number to divide by.

Although the steps of this procedure may be easy to teach, its mathematical justification is sophisticated. Consider this informal justification:

$$\frac{a}{b} = \frac{a}{b} \div 1$$

$$\frac{n}{n} = 1, n \neq 0$$

$$\frac{a}{b} = \frac{a}{b} \div \frac{n}{n} = \frac{(a \div n)}{(b \div n)}$$

The procedure is usually introduced to students before multiplying and dividing a fraction by a fraction have been introduced, reinforcing the mistaken notion that a fraction is two separate numbers rather than a single number with a single value. Students tend to think of division by $\frac{3}{3}$, for example, as two separate whole-number divisions by 3. They do not think of it as division by 1, which leaves the value of the fraction unchanged. And when children do learn to divide any two fractions, they learn a different procedure, to invert and multiply, rather than to divide numerators and divide denominators.[1]

---

[1] Both procedures are correct. Dividing across is not taught because it usually leads to a more complicated fraction (i.e., a fraction with a fraction in the numerator or denominator).

What can you do instead? In the next section, we show how you can support the development of a relational understanding of equivalence and avoid the difficulties in understanding to which overly structured manipulatives and poorly understood procedures can lead.

Using Equal Sharing Problems to Introduce Equivalent Fractions

First Encounters with Equivalence: Comparing Solutions

It was the eighth day of instruction on fractions in Ms. Keller's first-grade classroom.[2] The children had solved and discussed a variety of Equal Sharing problems over the previous seven days. On this day, Ms. Keller posed a single problem to the children:

> SIX CHILDREN HAVE ORDERED blueberry pancakes at a restaurant. The waiter brings 8 pancakes to their table. If the children share the pancakes evenly, how much can each child have?

Most students were easily able to figure out that each child would get 1 pancake and then the 6 children would share the remaining 2. Many students partitioned the last 2 pancakes into either thirds or sixths. Ernie showed the group how he split the last 2 pancakes into thirds, so that each child got 1 pancake and ⅓ of a pancake altogether (Figure 6–3a). Carmen explained that she had cut

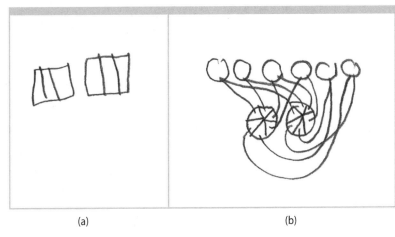

Figure 6–3. *(a) Ernie shows how he would partition 2 pancakes in thirds (he said that he made squares because they were easier to draw than circles); (b) Carmen's strategy for sharing 2 pancakes among 6 children*

---

[2] This vignette was reported in full in Empson (1999).

each of the last 2 pancakes into sixths, so that each child got 1 pancake and ⅔ of a pancake altogether.

Because the children had found two different ways to share the 2 pancakes, Ms. Keller asked the class whether the amounts were the same. Marie responded, "I knew it would be a sixth, because there's 6 people, and if you wanted to divide them evenly, you could do it in sixths … but I would rather do the thirds." Ms. Keller pressed Marie for a reason:

Ms. Keller: OK, you did it by sixths, but you'd rather do it by thirds? Why would you rather do thirds and not sixths?

Marie: Because thirds gets bigger pieces.

Ms. Keller: Is that right? What do you think, Carmen?

Carmen: Well, if there was, if you each get 2 of these (sixths) and you put them together, it would be a half.

Ms. Keller: Can you show me what you mean?

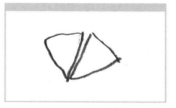

Figure 6–4. *Carmen shows why she thinks that ⅖ would be sort of like ½*

Carmen drew Figure 6–4, adding, "It would be sort of like a half."

Ms. Keller then went to get two large, circular cutouts (about fifteen inches in diameter). She sat down on the rug, with the children gathered around her, and began to cut the first circle into thirds. Her plan was to cut out one circle into thirds and the other into sixths and then compare ⅓ and ⅖. As the interaction unfolded, however, the children articulated a far more powerful form of reasoning about equivalence than physically comparing the size of thirds and sixths. As you read the following, we invite you to identify what Ms. Keller says and does to encourage the children to think of fraction relationships.

Ms. K: This is my big pancake. I went to this restaurant, look at the biggest pancakes you've ever seen. OK, watch this. This one is going to be a little difficult. I'm going to do it like Sally [a student who drew a circle and split it into thirds] did, try to anyway [cutting circle into thirds]. And in your case, everyone got what, Sally?

Sally: A third.

Ms. K: But when Carmen split her pancakes [starts to cut the second circle] …

Sally: [interrupting] All you have to do is cut those [thirds] in half.

Ms. K: Well, wait a second.

Sally: So you can make those [thirds] first and then cut each one in half, and it'll make 6.

Ms. K: What?! Wait a minute. Let me try this. [To group] Did you hear what she just said? Let me see, I'm trying this [cutting thirds by laying cutout on top of already cut pieces and looking through the paper at them].

Tim: Now just cut those in half.

Sally: OK, now take those 3 and cut each one of those in half, and you'll have sixths.

Ms. K: You will?

Sally: Yeah.

Ms. K: [to others] You agree?

Others: [loud] Yeah!

Ernie: Yeah, 'cause [counting on thirds], 2, 4, 6.

Ms. K: Really? OK, but Carmen, how many sixths do they get?

Carmen: 2.

Jennifer: That makes 1 of these [a third].

Ms. K: They each get a third.

Sally: It's still the same amount.

Ms. K: But Marie said she'd rather be in this group [thirds], because this [a third] is bigger.

Marie: Yes, they're bigger pieces.

Kaitlin and others: No.

Jennifer: You still get the same amount.

Ms. K: Wait, Jennifer, why do you think that?

Jennifer: If you get 2 of these [sixths], it'll be, if you cut 1 of these [thirds] in half, it'll be one—same thing.

Ms. K: But Marie didn't say that, did you, Marie? [Marie shakes her head.] See, Marie doesn't agree. Marie still thinks that this is bigger, right, Marie?

Marie: Yep.

Kaitlin: Nope, I disagree with Marie.

Ms. K: Why?

Kaitlin: Because if you cut that [third] in half, it'll just equal 2 of these [sixths].

Ms. K: You mean ⅓ equals ²⁄₆?

Students: Yeah.

Ms. K: I don't know, Marie, do you think that's right? They say that a person in this group gets 2 of these [sixths], 'cause they get 1 from this one, and 1 from this one, but in the other group, they only get 1 [third]. I don't know. Which one would you rather have, Marie?

Marie: [pointing to 2 sixths pieces] It's still the same amount.

Ms. K: So you're telling me ⅓ is the same as 2 of these sixths?

Marie: Yeah.

In this episode, a teacher who was skilled at listening responsively to her students heard their emergent ideas about how the two fraction amounts were related and helped them articulate these ideas. It began when Ms. Keller asked Ernie and Carmen to put the two different fractional solutions to an Equal Sharing problem on the board and then asked the class whether the fractional amounts (²⁄₆ and ⅓) were equal or not. Marie focused only on the size of a single piece and claimed that a third was bigger than a sixth. Carmen realized that one of the shares consisted of 2 pieces and speculated that if the 2 sixths pieces were put together, it would make half of a pancake. To investigate these claims with the class, Ms. Keller began to cut two paper pancakes. However, as she was in the process of cutting, the children saw how thirds were related to sixths and they told Ms. Keller that rather than starting with the whole circle to cut sixths, she could take each third of a circle and cut it in half. Ms. Keller then asked more questions to get more children involved and to help them articulate this relationship.

The line of thinking that if you cut a third of a pancake in half it will make 2 sixths of a pancake is a far more powerful justification for equivalence than the demonstration that 2 sixths fits perfectly when it is laid on top of 1 third. It is based on mathematical relationships rather than a relationship between physical materials. Although she did not choose to do so today, Ms. Keller could have written an equation to summarize this relationship and asked, "So you're telling me that 1 third is the same as 2 of these sixths?"

$$\tfrac{1}{3} = \tfrac{1}{6} + \tfrac{1}{6}$$

Ms. Keller's questioning helped her students express and reflect on their thinking. In particular, she continually pressed the students for reasons, even when the reasons might have been obvious to her. Asking students to share reasons along with their answers helped them verbalize what they understood and provided opportunities for other students to hear it and reflect on it.

Using Equations to Compare Solutions

Teachers working with older students can use equations to represent students' claims about relationships between different fractional answers for Equal Sharing problems. Mr. Li, a fifth-grade teacher, gave this problem to his class:

 A TEACHER BROUGHT 6 little pineapple cakes for his students to share. If there are 9 students, and they all want the same amount, how much cake can each student have?

The class solved the problem using a variety of strategies to arrive at three different fractional answers: $\tfrac{6}{9}$, $\tfrac{2}{3}$, and $\tfrac{1}{2} + \tfrac{1}{6}$. Most students found only one of these answers. Mr. Li had Randy and Silvia share their solutions so that the class could compare the resulting amounts:

Randy: I drew 6 circles for the cakes then I saw that I could just take 3 of them and cut them into thirds to make 9 pieces. And I did it again. So each person gets $\tfrac{2}{3}$ of a cake.

Silvia: I just knew to cut each cake into ninths so each person got $\tfrac{1}{9}$ from every cake. That's $\tfrac{6}{9}$ for everyone.

After each student's explanation, Mr. Li wrote an equation to represent the final share. For Randy's solution, he wrote:

$$\tfrac{1}{3} + \tfrac{1}{3} = \tfrac{2}{3}$$

For Silvia's solution, he wrote:

$$\tfrac{6}{9} = \tfrac{1}{9} + \tfrac{1}{9} + \tfrac{1}{9} + \tfrac{1}{9} + \tfrac{1}{9} + \tfrac{1}{9}$$

He then recapped their solutions: "Randy worked with 3 cakes at a time. He found that each student could get $\tfrac{1}{3}$ of a cake from the first 3 cakes and another $\tfrac{1}{3}$ of a cake from the second 3 cakes. Silvia worked with all 6 cakes and cut them into ninths. She found that everyone could get $\tfrac{1}{9}$ of each cake, which made $\tfrac{6}{9}$ of a cake." And then he posed a new question: "Do you think that Randy and Silvia came up with the same amount of cake for each person? Do you think that $\tfrac{2}{3}$ and $\tfrac{6}{9}$ represent the same amounts of cake? To help you think about it, let's look at an equation." He wrote:

$$\tfrac{1}{3} + \tfrac{1}{3} = \tfrac{1}{9} + \tfrac{1}{9} + \tfrac{1}{9} + \tfrac{1}{9} + \tfrac{1}{9} + \tfrac{1}{9}$$

"$\tfrac{1}{3}$ plus $\tfrac{1}{3}$ is what Randy said each person would get. All those one-ninths added together is what Silvia said 1 person would get. Do you think this equation is true?"

A student said, "It's true, because $\tfrac{1}{3}$ is equal to $\tfrac{1}{9} + \tfrac{1}{9} + \tfrac{1}{9}$." Mr. Li grouped the ninths in the equation using parentheses:

$$\tfrac{1}{3} + \tfrac{1}{3} = \left(\tfrac{1}{9} + \tfrac{1}{9} + \tfrac{1}{9}\right) + \left(\tfrac{1}{9} + \tfrac{1}{9} + \tfrac{1}{9}\right)$$

and asked the class, "How do you know $\tfrac{1}{3}$ is equal to $\tfrac{1}{9} + \tfrac{1}{9} + \tfrac{1}{9}$?" Silvia volunteered that when she was solving the problem, she made ninths, and to make ninths, she first split a cake into thirds, then each third into three parts. Mr. Li asked her to illustrate her thinking at the board. As she drew (Figure 6–5), she reiterated, "I think $\tfrac{1}{3}$ is equal to $\tfrac{1}{9} + \tfrac{1}{9} + \tfrac{1}{9}$ because if you split one of these thirds into 3 pieces, you get ninths, because that's 9 pieces altogether, 3 in each piece."

Mr. Li reiterated her explanation, "So, Silvia says that $\frac{1}{3}$ equals 3 groups of $\frac{1}{9}$," and wrote to the side:

$$\frac{1}{3} = 3 \times \frac{1}{9}$$

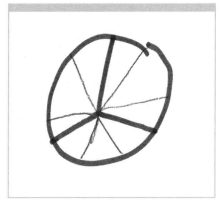

Figure 6-5. *Silvia splits each third into three equal parts to create ninths*

Tabriz then said, "So I think the equation with adding all those amounts is true, because if 1 third equals 3 ninths, then 2 thirds is equal to 6 ninths, and then that's what you have, 2 one-thirds on one side and 6 one-ninths on the other." Other students agreed. Alana chimed in. "Yeah, it's like if you just take each of those thirds and split it into 3, you're making ninths."

Mr. Li wrote *true* beside the first equation and then asked, "Is there a way you could write an equation that uses multiplication rather than addition to show that Silvia's and Randy's answers represent the same amount? Remember you told me that you thought that this equation was true." He pointed to:

$$\frac{1}{3} + \frac{1}{3} = \left(\frac{1}{9} + \frac{1}{9} + \frac{1}{9}\right) + \left(\frac{1}{9} + \frac{1}{9} + \frac{1}{9}\right) \qquad TRUE$$

Omar volunteered, "Well, you have 2 one-thirds, that's like 2 times $\frac{1}{3}$, and 6 one-ninths, that is 6 times $\frac{1}{9}$, so I think it could be—could I come to the board and write it?" He wrote:

$$2 \times \frac{1}{3} = 6 \times \frac{1}{9}$$

Mr. Li said, "Let's look at this. Omar says that 2 groups of $\frac{1}{3}$ is the same as 6 groups of $\frac{1}{9}$. Is this a true equation? What do you think, Alana?" Alana said, "Of course it is true, it is just the same as the other equation, but you don't write out all of the groups; you just use multiplication." The class agreed. Omar added, "I could have written this a different way—it's the same as $\frac{2}{3}$ equals $\frac{6}{9}$."

"OK," Mr. Li agreed. "So another way to write this relationship is …"

$$\frac{2}{3} = \frac{6}{9}$$

Mr. Li's approach to introducing equivalent fractions was to elicit students' thinking about mathematical relationships that they knew to be true. He began by having students present two different solutions to the same Equal Sharing problem and then asked the class whether they represented the same amount. He used equations to represent the relationships. Students used Relational Thinking to reason about how a more basic equation, $\frac{1}{3} = 3 \times \frac{1}{9}$, was related to the equation that they were examining.

By asking students to reason about the relationships represented in fraction equations, Mr. Li was encouraging them to build a rich, relational understanding of equivalent fractions. This approach contrasts with the approaches described at the beginning of the chapter, where children use manipulatives to cover equal areas or practice the procedure of dividing the numerator and denominator by the same number.

Ms. Keller and Mr. Li both played critical roles in making students' ideas about equivalence relationships explicit. Ms. Keller worked actively to move the discussion along by questioning students and eliciting their reasoning. Mr. Li used equations to represent students' claims about how fractions are related and asked the students to evaluate their truth.

Number Choices for Equal Sharing That Lead to Equivalent Solutions

Ms. Keller and Mr. Li were able to lead discussions about equivalent fractions because their students got different but equivalent solutions to an Equal Sharing problem. They thought carefully about what numbers to put into the problem. They wanted a number combination that would be likely to produce two or more fractional answers so that they could introduce concepts of equivalence by asking students to compare the different amounts.

Take a look at the following problem and the two different number choices. Which do you think is more likely to lead to several equivalent fractions as answers?

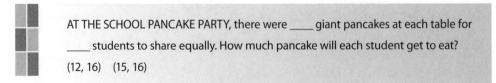

AT THE SCHOOL PANCAKE PARTY, there were _____ giant pancakes at each table for _____ students to share equally. How much pancake will each student get to eat?

(12, 16)   (15, 16)

The first number combination leads to a greater variety of equivalent fractions than the second, because $^{12}\!/_{16}$ has more equivalent fractions than $^{15}\!/_{16}$ where the terms are less than or equal to the *quantities in the problem*. Common answers for 16 students sharing 12 include $^{12}\!/_{16}$, $^{6}\!/_{8}$, $^{3}\!/_{4}$, and $^{1}\!/_{2} + ^{1}\!/_{4}$. Common answers for 16 students sharing 15 include $^{15}\!/_{16}$ and $^{1}\!/_{2} + ^{7}\!/_{16}$. Even though children could cut the pancakes into thirty-seconds, for example, they hardly ever do.

Figure 6–6 lists some Equal Sharing problems with some different number combinations and the common answers that students produce, to give you an idea of the equivalent fractions that the class could discuss after sharing their solutions. Number combinations for the first problem have only one common factor (besides 1, which is considered a "trivial" factor); when children solve these problems, they usually arrive at one of two fractional answers. The number combinations for the second problem have two or more common factors; when children solve these problems, they usually arrive at one of three or more fractional answers.

Problem	Numbers	Common Answers
At a restaurant, the waiter brings ___ submarine sandwiches for ___ children to share so that everyone gets the same amount. How much can each child have?	(2, 8)	$^{2}\!/_{8}$, $^{1}\!/_{4}$
	(6, 8)	$^{6}\!/_{8}$, $^{3}\!/_{4}$
	(6, 9)	$^{6}\!/_{9}$, $^{2}\!/_{3}$
	(5, 15)	$^{5}\!/_{15}$, $^{1}\!/_{3}$
Eric has ___ pounds of jellybeans to share equally with his friends. If there are ___ people altogether, how much can each person have?	(12, 18)	$^{12}\!/_{18}$, $^{6}\!/_{9}$, $^{4}\!/_{6}$, $^{2}\!/_{3}$
	(15, 45)	$^{15}\!/_{45}$, $^{5}\!/_{15}$, $^{3}\!/_{9}$, $^{1}\!/_{3}$
	(60, 100)	$^{60}\!/_{100}$, $^{30}\!/_{50}$, $^{15}\!/_{25}$, $^{12}\!/_{20}$, $^{6}\!/_{10}$, $^{3}\!/_{5}$

Figure 6–6. *Equal Sharing problems that lead to comparisons of equivalent fractions*

We did not include compound fractions such as ½ + ¼ among the possible solutions even though students will generate them as answers. Incorporating this type of expression in discussions of equivalence can focus students' attention on fractions equivalent to ½.

More Problem Types for Exploring Equivalence

As students begin to reason explicitly about equivalent fractional amounts, you can use other types of problems to help them develop and refine this reasoning. These problem types include word problems and Open Number Sentences.

Equivalencing and Comparison Word Problems

Proportional word problems in which there are two sharing situations to complete or compare can draw students' attention to relationships between two fractions or ratios. In the following Equivalencing problem, for example, children need to complete the sharing situation for the second group so that the people at both tables get equivalent shares:

 AT A CLASS PARTY, the teacher gave a table of 5 students 2 large brownies to share equally. How many large brownies does she need for the remaining 15 students, if she wants to be sure that everyone gets exactly the same amount?

Some children will solve a problem like this by figuring how much brownie each child gets at the first table and then using that amount to build up the set of brownies that 15 children need to get. For example, each of the 5 children at the first table gets ⅖ of a brownie; so the number of brownies needed at the second table can be determined by calculating 15 groups of ⅖. The notion of equivalence is "same amount for each person." A more sophisticated strategy for solving this problem involves reasoning about the relationships between the 2 tables of children. Since 15 is 3 times bigger than 5, the 15 children need 3 times as many brownies as the 5 children, which is 6 brownies altogether. The notion of equivalence here is "same multiplicative relationship between the number of people as between the number of brownies at the two tables."

Comparison problems also involve two situations but instead of a finding a missing value, students need to compare two ratios:

 WHO GETS MORE CHOCOLATE: a child at a table where 3 children are sharing 2 small chocolate bars or a child at a table where 6 children are sharing 4 small chocolate bars?

Children can solve these problems by figuring out how much a person in each situation would get and then comparing them or by reasoning about relationships. For example, a fourth grader reasoned about relationships to solve this problem: "If you have twice as many children and twice as many chocolate bars, the kids get the same amount at both tables."

Changing the quantities in the problem can change the difficulty of the problem. In the following problem, children essentially need to compare two unequal fractions with unlike denominators. It is much more difficult than the previous one.

 WHO GETS MORE CHOCOLATE: a child at the red table where 3 children are equally sharing 2 small chocolate bars or a child at the blue table where 4 children are equally sharing 3 small chocolate bars?

Students can still reason about relationships to solve problems like this. For example, a fifth grader said:

At the red table, everyone could get half a candy bar and there would be a half more for the 3 kids to share. At the blue table, everyone could get half a candy bar and then there is a whole candy bar for 4 kids to share. If 4 kids share a whole candy bar, they each get ¼. With the 3 kids sharing half a candy bar, there isn't enough for everyone to get ¼. So the kids at the blue table get more than the kids at the red table.

Other students might draw on more sophisticated relationships to solve this problem. For example, a sixth grader said, "At the red table, each person gets ⅔, and at the blue table, everyone gets ¾. ¾ is more than ⅔ because ¾ is only ¼ less than a whole but ⅔ is ⅓ less than a whole."

Equivalencing and Comparison problems can be set in more abstract contexts, such as price or rate, and play an important role in the development of proportional reasoning. We mention them only briefly here but encourage you to try them in your own classroom to investigate the possibilities.[3]

Open Number Sentences

In Chapter 5, we described how equations could be used as tools to communicate students' Relational Thinking strategies and to highlight the mathematical relationships underlying those strategies. Ms. Perez in Chapter 5 and Mr. Li in this chapter used equations in these ways.

Equations with unknown values can also be posed as *problems* to develop students' ability to think relationally about equivalence. We call equations with unknown values *Open Number Sentences*. The unknown can be represented with a letter or a box. Here are two examples:

$$\tfrac{1}{3} = 2 \times a$$
$$j \times \tfrac{1}{12} = \tfrac{3}{4}$$

Students can solve these types of problems without using standard algebraic procedures. They use Relational Thinking and draw on what they know about fraction relationships. Eve, a fourth grader, was asked to find the value for j that made the second equation true. She said, "How many groups of $\tfrac{1}{12}$ is the same as $\tfrac{3}{4}$? I know that 3 groups of $\tfrac{1}{12}$ is the same as $\tfrac{1}{4}$. So 9 groups of $\tfrac{1}{12}$ would be the same as 3 groups of $\tfrac{1}{4}$. So j is 9."

---

[3] Further information about missing-value equivalence problems and other kinds of proportional problems can be found in Kaput and West (1994) and Lamon (1993, 1999).

Sixth-grader Kareem solved the first problem as follows: "$\frac{1}{3}$ is the same as 2 groups of what? $\frac{1}{6}$ is half as big as $\frac{1}{3}$, so 2 groups of $\frac{1}{6}$ would be $\frac{1}{3}$. So a has to be $\frac{1}{6}$."

Each student's solution was based on their understanding of the relationship between two different unit fractions and how multiples of those unit fractions could be combined to produce equal amounts ($\frac{1}{4} = 3 \times \frac{1}{12}$ for Eve, $\frac{1}{3} = 2 \times \frac{1}{6}$ for Kareem). This type of reasoning is at the heart of a relational understanding of equivalence.

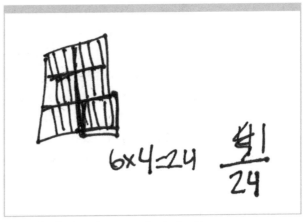

Figure 6–7. *Jenny's strategy for* $4 \times k = \frac{1}{6}$

Students can solve Open Number Sentences using more concrete strategies. For example, to solve $4 \times k = \frac{1}{6}$, fifth-grader Jenny drew a rectangle partitioned into sixths. Then she subdivided each of the sixths into 4 equal parts and wrote $6 \times 4 = 24$ to designate the total number of parts in the rectangle (Figure 6–7). She used this fact to reason that $\frac{1}{6} \div 4 = \frac{1}{24}$ and, because she knew that division and multiplication were inverse operations, that $4 \times \frac{1}{24} = \frac{1}{6}$, which meant k was equal to $\frac{1}{24}$. You do not need to wait until all of your students can use Relational Thinking before posing these problems to your class.

Before focusing on Open Number Sentences, students need experience solving Equal Sharing and Multiple Groups problems and using number sentences to represent their solutions. These experiences help them establish an understanding of fractions as relational and to connect formal mathematical notation with their intuitive thinking. Both are necessary to solve Open Number Sentences. (See how one teacher introduced Open Number Sentences to her class in Chapter 7, p. 162).

Open Number Sentences that include expanded representations of fractions help children develop their understanding of equivalence. These expanded representations help children distinguish between the size of a fractional part and the number of fractional parts. Representing $\frac{4}{7}$, for example, as $\frac{1}{7} + \frac{1}{7} + \frac{1}{7} + \frac{1}{7}$ or as $4 \times \frac{1}{7}$ helps children see the different roles that 4 and 7 play in this fraction.

There are many possible variations on Open Number Sentences that support students' emerging understanding of fraction equivalence and basic operations. Figure 6–8 includes examples of Open Number Sentences written loosely from simplest to more complex to indicate some of this variety. We include only one of many possible Relational Thinking strategies for each problem.

Using Variables in Open Number Sentences

We prefer to represent the unknown in Open Number Sentences with variables, such as a, rather than a box and have found that even first and second graders are able to

Open Number Sentence	Sample Relational Thinking Strategy
Number sentences where one unit fraction is twice the size of the other	
$\frac{1}{3} = n \times \frac{1}{6}$	"n is 2 because $\frac{1}{6}$ plus $\frac{1}{6}$ is $\frac{1}{3}$."
$\frac{2}{5} = h \times \frac{1}{10}$	"h is 4 because $\frac{1}{10}$ plus $\frac{1}{10}$ is $\frac{1}{5}$."
$\frac{2}{3} = \frac{4}{y}$	"y is 6 because $\frac{1}{6}$ plus $\frac{1}{6}$ is $\frac{1}{3}$."
Number sentences where one unit fraction is a multiple of the other	
$\frac{3}{8} + m = \frac{1}{2}$	"m is $\frac{1}{8}$ because $\frac{4}{8} = \frac{1}{2}$."
$\frac{2}{j} = \frac{6}{15}$	"j is 5 because $\frac{1}{5}$ is 3 times as big as $\frac{1}{15}$ and 6 is 3 times as big as 2."
Number sentences where unit fractions are not multiples of each other	
$\frac{1}{3} + t = \frac{1}{2}$	"t is $\frac{1}{6}$; $\frac{1}{3}$ is $\frac{2}{6}$ and $\frac{1}{2}$ is $\frac{3}{6}$."
$\frac{7}{10} = \frac{f}{15}$	"f is $10\frac{1}{2}$; $\frac{1}{10}$ is $1\frac{1}{2}$ times as big as $\frac{1}{15}$ so f is $1\frac{1}{2}$ times 7."

Figure 6–8. *Open Number Sentences that progress in difficulty and sample Relational Thinking strategies*

read and use this type of notation. By convention in algebra, multiplication between a number and a variable is represented without a multiplication sign: $3a$. We use the multiplication sign because it makes the operation clearer for children: $3 \times a$. As students become experienced using this kind of representation, middle-grades teachers may decide to omit the multiplication symbol.

Figure 6–9. *Students volunteer to share strategies*

We revisit Open Number Sentences in Chapter 7 to see how they can be used to support children's reasoning about decimals and again in Chapter 8 to see how they can be used to develop children's thinking about operations.

The Mathematics of Equivalence: What Stays the Same

Lola was asked to find different ways of writing ⅓. She wrote the list in Figure 6–10. When asked how she came up with it she said, "I thought of ⅓ of a cake. Then I thought, I could split the third in half and would get sixths and then I would have 2 of them. If I split each sixth in half, I could make twelfths and I would get 4 of them. You can just keep going on like this forever."

$$\frac{1}{3} = \frac{2}{6} = \frac{4}{12} = \frac{8}{24} = \frac{16}{48}$$

Figure 6–10. *Lola's list of equivalent fractions*

$$\frac{1}{3} = \frac{2}{6} = \frac{3}{9} = \frac{4}{12} = \frac{5}{15} = \frac{100}{300}$$

Figure 6–11. *Manuel's list of equivalent fractions*

The idea that any fraction has an infinite number of equivalent forms is essential to the concept of equivalence. Lola's repeated splitting of a piece of cake and imagining it continuing forever is typical of children's first expression of this idea. Many children can easily make equivalent fractions by repeated doubling of the numerator and denominators.

In contrast, Lola's classmate Manuel created the list in Figure 6–11. Here, there is no obvious way to go from one fraction to the next by operating on the numerator and denominator the way Lola did. Instead, Manuel said that he noticed the denominator was 3 times bigger than the numerator in the fraction $\frac{1}{3}$. To make each equivalent fraction, he chose a new numerator and then calculated the denominator as 3 times bigger.

The concept of equivalent fractions is fundamentally about what remains the same when one fraction is transformed into another. In a pictorial model, the area remains the same. In a list of fractions such as Lola's or Manuel's, the relationship between the numerator and the denominator remains the same. If the fractions represented sharing situations—such as 3 children sharing 1 cake, 6 children sharing 2 cakes, and so on—then the size of each child's share and the ratio between the number of children and the number of cakes remain the same. Understanding equivalence requires that children see beyond the changes to grasp the relationship between two quantities that is *invariant* across these situations.

Many children do not realize that the fractions in lists such as Lola's and Manuel's all represent the same number. To mathematicians, however, these fractions are different representations of the *same rational number*, whose value is determined by the multiplicative relationship—that is, the *ratio*—between the numerator and the denominator. If we look at each number in Lola's and Manuel's lists, we see that the denominator is always 3 times the numerator. All fractional representations of $\frac{1}{3}$ will fit into the equation, $\frac{x}{y} = \frac{1}{3}$, which is equivalent to the equation $y = 3x$. This relationship is the same one that Manuel recognized and used to generate his list of equivalent fractions.

$y = 3x$ is a simple linear equation. Equations such as this are usually introduced early in high school algebra. Understanding $y = 3x$ involves understanding that this equation represents all ordered pairs (x, y) that have the relationships $\frac{x}{y} = \frac{1}{3}$. When we graph $y = 3x$, we are representing all ordered pairs (x, y) that have this relationship (Figure 6–12).

All points on the line in Figure 6–11 have a y-coordinate that is 3 times bigger than the x-coordinate; and every point in the coordinate plane for which $y = 3x$ is true is on the line. The ordered pair $(1, 3)$ is on the line as are $(2, 6)$ and $(12, 36)$. And pairs such as ($\frac{1}{15}$, $\frac{3}{15}$) and $(.43, 1.29)$ are also on this line. A relational understanding of equivalent fractions is essential for students to understand linear equations.

Ordering Fractions

A typical ordering task looks like this: *Which fraction is larger, $\frac{1}{4}$ or $\frac{2}{7}$?* One never-fail strategy for solving such a task is to find a common denominator and convert the

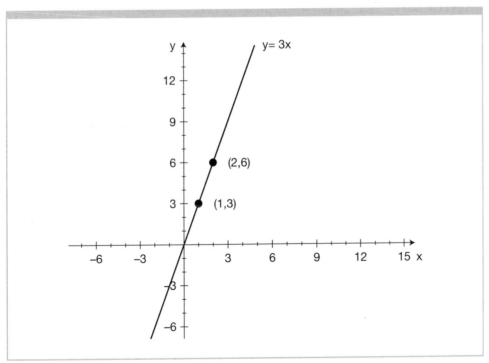

Figure 6–12. *Graph of $y = 3x$ with specific points identified*

fractions to this denominator. This strategy reduces the problem to a straightforward comparison between two numbers expressed in terms of the same unit. Like all strategies involving a fixed set of rules, however, it can be and often is executed without understanding, and there are many times when it can be tedious.

There are a number of alternative strategies for comparing fractions that children create and use that are based on their growing understanding of fraction relationships (Post et al. 1985). These strategies reflect a deeper understanding of fractions, and in many cases they are more efficient than finding a common denominator.

The most basic type of comparison is between two unit fractions, such as ⅕ and ⅙. Children who do not understand fractions as relational often mistakenly conclude that ⅙ is bigger than ⅕ because 6 is bigger than 5. They may be thinking in terms of the number of total parts that is created when a whole is partitioned, or they may simply be looking only at the denominators. However, if the comparison is couched in terms of the size of an individual share when 5 or 6 people share the same thing, these same children are often able to successfully order the two fractions:

 WHO WILL GET MORE PIZZA (if the children share equally at each table): a child sitting at a table where 5 children are sharing a medium pizza or a child sitting at a table where 6 children are sharing a medium pizza?

In a study of first graders, eleven out of seventeen answered this question correctly *before* any instruction in fractions; after instruction, all but one answered a similar question correctly (Empson 1999). Children in this study did not draw to solve this problem because they were able to make sense of the question by reasoning about relationships. In fact, drawing makes the comparison harder, because precise partitions are difficult to make. Instead, these children based their reasoning on an informal principle of order:

The more people sharing, the smaller each share will be.

This informal principle of order generalizes to other fractions besides unit fractions:

When numerators are equal, the bigger the denominator, the smaller the value of the fraction.

For example:

$$\tfrac{3}{7} < \tfrac{3}{6} < \tfrac{3}{5}$$

Other strategies are usable only with certain fractions. For example, to order $\tfrac{7}{8}$, $\tfrac{6}{7}$, and $\tfrac{1}{2}$, children might notice that each fraction can be imagined as a whole with one part missing. Because $\tfrac{1}{7}$ is a bigger part than $\tfrac{1}{8}$, $\tfrac{6}{7}$ is smaller than $\tfrac{7}{8}$. The fraction $\tfrac{1}{2}$ is smaller than both for the same reason: It has the largest part missing.

$$\tfrac{1}{2} < \tfrac{6}{7} < \tfrac{7}{8}$$

This strategy generalizes to any situation in which the fractions each lack the same number of parts to make a whole. For example, these fractions are each 2 parts away from 1:

$$\tfrac{3}{5} < \tfrac{5}{7}$$

Because sevenths are smaller than fifths, $\tfrac{5}{7}$ is closer to 1 and larger than $\tfrac{3}{5}$.

Another informal but efficient strategy that children use to order fractions involves the use of a benchmark fraction as reference point. Benchmark fractions are those fractions that are well known to children, such as $\tfrac{1}{2}$ and $\tfrac{1}{4}$. To make these comparisons, students need to understand that the value of a fraction is determined by the multiplicative relationship between the numerator and the denominator. For example, to decide whether $\tfrac{3}{5}$ is larger or smaller than $\tfrac{1}{2}$, a student might examine the relationship between 3 and 5 and see that it is close to the relationship between

Decide which fraction is greater		
$2/7$	or	$2/11$
$3/5$	or	$9/11$
$9/20$	or	$6/10$
$1/4$	or	$5/12$
$3/8$	or	$1/5$
$9/10$	or	$6/7$
$95/100$	or	$70/75$
$2/5$	or	$1/3$
$3/16$	or	$4/15$

Figure 6-13. *Fractions pairs that can be ordered using an informal strategy*

3 and 6. Because 3 is half of 6, it means 3 is a larger part of 5 and the value of $3/5$ is therefore greater than the value of $3/6 = 1/2$. Similarly, to compare $3/4$ and $4/9$, a student might see that $4/9$ is less than $1/2$ while $3/4$ is greater than $1/2$, and so conclude that $3/4$ is greater than $4/9$.

The fractions in Figure 6–13 can all be ordered using one or more of these informal strategies. We invite you to try your hand at solving these problems using one of these informal strategies, without finding common denominators.

Not all comparisons lend themselves to the use of informal strategies such as these. In those cases, finding a common denominator is the most efficient strategy. It is nonetheless beneficial to children to be encouraged to develop and use these more informal strategies. In the long run, the use of these strategies reinforces students' understanding of relationships and develops flexibility in reasoning.

Reflecting Back and Looking Ahead

In this chapter, we described the development of children's understanding of equivalence and order by introducing several new problem types and discussing children's solution strategies. In particular, we discussed how to use students' solutions to Equal Sharing problems as a platform to introduce equivalent fractions and how to use Open Number Sentences to extend students' understanding of equivalence relationships. We examined how the set of all fractions equivalent to a given fraction represented the same rational number and could be represented by a linear equation passing through the origin of an xy-coordinate plane.

Throughout the chapter, we emphasized the need for children to learn to reason about equivalent fractions on the basis of relationships between fractions. We saw how children use relationships to compare nonequivalent fractions, too. In the next chapter, we examine the role of children's Relational Thinking in the development of decimals, and describe how instruction can help children build on what they understand about fractions and base ten.

Problems for Fraction Equivalence and Order

Here are some problems to use with your students to develop their understanding of fraction equivalence and order. The problems are arranged by problem type and include a variety of number choices. Number choices significantly affect the difficulty of equivalence and order problems. Children may look at the relationship *within* a situation (e.g., how much popcorn per person) or *between* two situations (e.g., how do the number of bags of popcorn at one table compare to the number of bags at the other table?). Listen for which relationships students are using and how they use these relationships to solve problems. You can change the numbers in these problems to meet the needs of your students. Refer to the instructional guide on page 144 for suggestions.

Equal Sharing Problems and Variations

See Figure 6–6 for more information on how number choice makes these problems more or less difficult.

    A. ___ children want to share ___ tins of fudge so that everyone gets the same amount. How much fudge can each child have?

        (8, 6)   (12, 9)   (15, 5)   (20, 12)   (36, 12)   (100, 60)

    The vignettes of Ms. Keller and Mr. Li in Chapter 6 show how discussing solutions to these problems can lead to a discussion of equivalent fractions.

B. Some girls were sharing some bananas so that each person got the same amount. Each girl got ___ of a banana. How many bananas and how many girls could there have been? (Find more than one solution.)

$\frac{1}{2}$ $\frac{1}{4}$ $\frac{3}{4}$ $\frac{5}{8}$ $\frac{9}{10}$

C. 24 gators wanted to share 6 key lime pies. One of the gators was just about to split each pie into 24 equal pieces and give every gator 1 piece from each of the pies, when another gator complained. He said these pieces would be way too small, and he wanted the pies to be split into bigger pieces. How can the gators share the pies equally without splitting each pie into 24 pieces? (Inspired by the book *Gator Pie*, by Louise Matthews.)

Equivalencing Problems

The problems below progress in difficulty. Both the context and number combination affect the difficulty of the problems. Further number combinations are provided following these problems. Before posing any of these problems to students, decide which number combination to insert, keeping in mind your instructional goals and what you know about your students' thinking.

A. A group of 3 children are sharing 2 burritos so that each person gets the same amount. How many burritos should a group of 6 children get so that each child gets as much burrito as a child in the first group?

B. At one table, 4 children are sharing 3 liters of juice. How many liters of juice should a table of 12 children get so that each child has as much juice as a child at the first table?

C. David used exactly 8 cups of flour to make 6 loaves of bread. How many loaves of bread can he make with 12 cups of flour?

Easier number combinations:

(3, 2, and 6)   (6, 4, and 12)   (5, 3, and 10)   (12, 7, and 6)

Next easier number combinations:

(2, 1, and 6)   (4, 3, and 12)   (6, 4, and 24)   (5, 2, and 20)
(7, 8, and 56)   (24, 8, and 6)   (20, 8, and 5)

More difficult number combinations:

(8, 6, and 12)   (6, 5, and 9)   (10, 7, and 25)

Most difficult number combinations:

(6, 4, and 16) (15, 18, and 25)

Equivalencing Problems—Price and Rate Contexts

A. Notebooks are 2 for $3. Sanita needs to buy 6 notebooks for school. How much will they cost, before tax?

B. Socks are selling for $5 for 4 pairs. How much will 9 pairs of socks cost?

C. A small airplane can fly 12 miles in 3 minutes. At this rate, how far can it fly in 7 minutes? In an hour?

D. A hiking club is planning a hike in the mountains. They estimate that it will take ___ hours to walk ___ km. How long will it take the group to walk ___ km?

(3, 6, 12) (4, 7, 21) (5, 8, 20) (9, 12, 32)

Open Number Sentences

Find the value for the variable that makes the equation true:

Simpler

A. $2 \times d = \frac{1}{2}$

B. $\frac{3}{4} = \frac{1}{4} + m$

C. $2 \times \frac{1}{3} = j \times \frac{1}{6}$

D. $\frac{1}{3} = 2 \times h$

More Complex

A. $\frac{3}{4} = k \times \frac{1}{8}$

B. $3 \times \frac{1}{4} = 9 \times a$

C. $\frac{10}{6} = n \times \frac{1}{3}$

D. $c \times \frac{1}{6} = \frac{1}{3} + \frac{1}{6}$

E. $\frac{1}{3} = 4 \times b$

F. $\frac{2}{6} + \frac{2}{6} + \frac{2}{6} + \frac{2}{6} = c \times \frac{1}{12}$

G. $\frac{2}{3} = \frac{1}{2} + j$

Find at least two sets of values for *a* and *b* that make the equation true.

A. $a \times \frac{1}{4} = b \times \frac{1}{2}$

B. $a \times \frac{1}{5} = b \times \frac{1}{10}$

C. $^a/_{12} = ^b/_6$

D. $^7/_9 = a \times \frac{1}{3} + b \times \frac{1}{9}$

Comparison Problems

The problems below progress in difficulty. Both the context and number combination affect the difficulty of the problems. Further number combinations are provided following these problems. Before posing any of these problems to students, decide which number combination to insert, keeping in mind your instructional goals and what you know about your students' thinking.

A. Who gets more clay: a child at a table where 4 children are sharing 1 box of modeling clay equally or a child at a table where 3 children are sharing 1 box of modeling clay equally?

B. Who gets more popcorn? A person in a group where 3 people are sharing 2 small bags of popcorn or a person in a group where 6 people are sharing 4 small bags of popcorn?

C. Which is a better deal? 8 pairs of socks for 6 dollars or 12 pairs of socks for 9 dollars?

D. Which plant grows faster? A plant that can grow 5 cm in 3 days or a plant that can grow 7 cm in 2 days?

Easier comparisons:

(3, 1 versus 4, 1)   (5, 3 versus 7, 3)   (10, 4 versus 20, 4)

Equivalent comparisons:

(4, 2 versus 2, 1)   (3, 2 versus 6, 4)   (3, 5 versus 9, 15)
(8, 6 versus 12, 9) (15, 10 versus 12, 8)

More difficult comparisons:

(4, 2 versus 12, 5) (6, 2 versus 9, 6)   (3, 2 versus 4, 3)
(5, 3 versus 7, 2)   (7, 6 versus 6, 5)   (10, 6 versus 8, 4)

Comparison problems without a story

A. Which is bigger, $^2/_5$ or $^1/_3$?

B. Which is smaller, $^8/_7$ or $^9/_8$?

C. Which is bigger, $^2/_3$ or $^4/_5$?

Find three fractions between:

   A. 0 and ½

   B. ½ and 1

   C. ¼ and ¾

   D. ¼ and ½

   E. ⅔ and 1

   F. ⅔ and ¾

Instructional Guidelines for Fraction Order and Equivalence

In this section, we provide guidelines for posing problems to develop children's understanding of fraction equivalence and order. Students without prior experience in earlier grades are likely to need to begin with problems and concepts aimed at lower grades. We recommend that you read the suggestions for all of the grade levels rather than only for the grade level you teach.

In these problems, number choices affect the difficulty of the problem more than any other factor. Listen to your students as they solve problems and discuss solutions to find out what fraction relationships they understand and then choose numbers for problems in this section that build on those relationships.

FIRST AND SECOND GRADES

✔ **Comparison word problems in which one thing is being shared in each group.**
- *Who gets more: A child in a group where 4 children are sharing a cake or a child in a group where 5 children are sharing a cake of the same size?*
- Encourage children to reason qualitatively about the relationship rather than draw pictures.

✔ **Equal Sharing problems in which children get two fractional amounts for answers. Focus on fractions ½ and ²⁄₄ and possibly ⅓ and ²⁄₆—for example:**
- *4 children share 10 brownies so that each child gets the same amount. How much would each child get?* Leads to possible answers of 2½ or 2²⁄₄ for each person. Ask students, *"Are these the same amount of brownie?"*

✔ **Equal Sharing** problems in which children get two fractional amounts for answers. Focus on fractions ½ and ²⁄₄, ⅓ and ²⁄₆, ¼ and ²⁄₈, ⅕ and ²⁄₁₀, and other equivalent fractions with the these denominators, such as ⅔ and ⁴⁄₆—for example:

- *There are 6 cookies for 8 children to share. If they share the cookies equally, how much cookie would each child get?* Leads to possible answers of ⁶⁄₈ and ¾. Ask students, *"Would ⁶⁄₈ of a cookie be the same amount as ¾ of a cookie?"*

✔ **Equivalencing** word problems in which children deal with the same fractions as above—for example:

- *At one table, 3 children had 1 bag of popcorn to share. At another table, there were 6 children. How many bags of popcorn should they get so that each child gets the same size share of popcorn as a child at the first table?*

✔ **Equal Sharing** problems and variations in which children get two fractional amounts for answers. Focus on equivalent fractions involving halves, fourths, thirds, eighths, sixths, fifths, tenths, ninths, and twelfths. See examples of possible problems and questions to prompt discussions in first, second, and third grades.

✔ **Equivalencing** word problems that involve the fractional amounts above—for example:

- *At the big table 12 kids shared 8 bottles of juice so that everyone got the same amount of juice. There are 3 kids sitting at the little table. How much juice should we put on the little table if we want each kid at the little table to have as much juice as each kid at the big table?*

✔ **Open Number Sentences.** Focus on relationships involving halves and relationships where one denominator is twice the size of another—for example:

- $½ = a + ¼$
- $⅚ = t \times ¹⁄₁₂$
- $⅓ = 2 \times b$

✔ **Comparison** word problems:

- *Who gets more popcorn: a child at a table where 6 children are sharing 3 small bags of popcorn or a child at a table where 5 children are sharing 3 small bags of popcorn?*
- *Who gets more brownie: a child at a table where 4 children are sharing 3 brownies or a child at a table where 8 children are sharing 6 brownies?*

✔ Equal Sharing problems and variations in which children get two fractional amounts for answers. Focus on equivalent fractions involving sixths, tenths, fifths, sevenths, ninths, twelfths, fifteenths, twentieths, and others. See examples of possible problems and questions to prompt discussions in first, second, and third grades.

✔ Equivalencing word problems, with a focus on price and rate contexts. Most problems will involve a quantity that is a multiple of another quantity—for example:

- *The photocopier can copy 3 pages in 4 seconds. How long would it take this machine to copy 27 pages?* (27 is a multiple of 3.)

✔ Open Number Sentences—focus on number sentences with fractions where one denominator is a factor of the other—for example:

- $\frac{1}{10} = 2 \times a$
- $\frac{8}{5} = b \times \frac{1}{10}$
- $2 \times \frac{1}{3} = n \times \frac{1}{6}$
- $\frac{3}{12} = \frac{j}{4}$

✔ Comparison word problems, with a focus on price and rate contexts. Most problems should involve a quantity that is a multiple of another quantity—for example:

- *Which toy car is faster? The blue car, which can go 10 meters in 6 seconds, or the red car, which can go 5 meters in 2 seconds?* (10 is a multiple of 5.)
- *Which is a better deal? 3 pairs of socks for 5 dollars or 9 pairs of socks for 14 dollars?*

✔ Ordering problems, involving three or more fractions. Have students either list the fractions in order or place them on a number line.

- Ordering fractions where one fraction's denominator is a factor of the others'—for example:
  - $\frac{5}{6}, \frac{2}{3}, \frac{7}{9}$
  - $\frac{3}{4}, \frac{5}{8}, \frac{7}{12}$
- Ordering fractions where students can use $\frac{1}{2}$ or 1 as a benchmark—for example:
  - $\frac{7}{8}, \frac{11}{12}, \frac{10}{11}$
  - $\frac{3}{8}, \frac{5}{7}, \frac{1}{2}$

✔ Equal Sharing problems and variations in which children get two fractional amounts for answers. Focus on equivalent fractions involving sixths, tenths, fifths, sevenths, ninths, twelfths, fifteenths, twentieths, and others. See examples of possible problems and questions to prompt discussions in first, second, and third grades.

✔ Equivalencing word problems, with a focus on price and rate contexts. Start with problems where one quantity is a multiple of another quantity (see grade 5). Include problems where no quantity is a multiple of another, but where two of the quantities have a common factor—for example:

- *The photocopier can copy 18 pages in 4 seconds. How long would it take this machine to copy 27 pages?* (18 and 27 are both multiples of 9, but neither is a multiple of the other.)

✔ Open Number Sentences. Start with number sentences containing fractions where one denominator is a factor of the other (see grade 5). Include number sentences with fractions where one denominator is not a factor of the other—for example:

- $\frac{6}{10} = j \times \frac{1}{15}$
- $2 \times \frac{1}{6} = n \times \frac{1}{9}$
- $\frac{6}{8} = b \times \frac{1}{12}$

✔ Comparison word problems, with a focus on price and rate contexts, using number choices similar to those for Equivalencing problems for this grade—for example:

- *Which toy car is faster? The blue car, which can go 10 meters in 6 seconds, or the red car, which can go 15 meters in 8 seconds?*
- *Which is a better deal? 6 pairs of socks for 5 dollars or 9 pairs of socks for 7 dollars?*

✔ Ordering problems, involving three or more fractions. Have students either list the fractions in order or place them on a number line.

- Start with ordering fractions where one fraction's denominator is a factor of the others'—see grade 5.
- Include ordering fractions where one fraction's denominator is not a factor of the others'.
  - $\frac{5}{6}, \frac{8}{12}, \frac{7}{9}$
  - $\frac{11}{16}, \frac{5}{8}, \frac{7}{12}$
- Ordering fractions where students can use ¼, ½, ¾ or 1 as a benchmark—for example:
  - $\frac{7}{8}, \frac{2}{3}, \frac{3}{4}$
  - $\frac{1}{4}, \frac{3}{8}, \frac{1}{3}$

chapter 7

Understanding Decimals

in this chapter, we describe how students can learn decimals as a natural extension of what they understand about base ten and fractions. We start by discussing some of the concepts involved in understanding base ten. These concepts are the same for groups of 10, 100, 1,000, and so on as they are for groups of .1, .01, .001, and so on. We then present a classroom unit on decimals, focusing on the problems the teacher used, how the students solved these problems, and how the teacher used information about what her students understood to make decisions about what to teach. We highlight how different students' understanding of decimals progressed and the teacher's work in differentiating instruction, with an emphasis on the development of Relational Thinking.

A New Notation for a Familiar Type of Number

Decimal notation is useful when writing numbers whose partitions are powers of 10 such as ⅒, ¹⁄₁₀₀, ¹⁄₁₀₀₀, and so on. We usually represent these numbers using a decimal point rather than a fraction bar, but either notation is correct. For example, 34.57 and 34⁵⁷⁄₁₀₀ are the same number, as are ⅝ and 0.625. If children have a basic understanding of fractions, then introducing decimals essentially involves introducing a new notation for familiar numbers.

Base-Ten Number Concepts

Our positional base-ten number system is the most widely used number system in modern civilization. It holds amazing power—with only 10 different digit symbols (0, 1, 2, 3, 4, 5, 6, 7, 8, 9) and a decimal point, we can represent an infinite number of quantities from very large ones in the trillions or more, to very small ones in the trillionths or less. Consider the following numbers:

$$3{,}104 \quad 4.013 \quad 4{,}103 \quad 31.40 \quad .4301$$

Although they are all composed of the digits 0, 1, 3, and 4, these numbers represent different quantities, because the value of a digit is determined by the digit itself and by its position in the number.

When we represent numbers with decimal notation, we highlight how numbers are grouped into multiples of powers of ten (tens, hundreds, thousands, tenths, hundredths, thousandths, and so on). Just as the places to the left of the decimal points are powers of ten:

$$1 = 10^0$$
$$10 = 10^1$$
$$100 = 10^2$$

The place values to the right of the decimal place are also powers of ten:

$$.1 = 10^{-1}$$
$$.01 = 10^{-2}$$
$$.001 = 10^{-3}$$

When numbers are written with decimal notation, the relationship between the places to the right of the decimal point is the same as the relationship between the places to the left of the decimal point—each place has a value that is 10 times that of the place to its right.

One of the most important goals in early base-ten instruction is for children to understand that numbers can be composed of groups of 10. Word problems with groups of 10 are effective vehicles for teaching this concept.[1]

 MULTIPLICATION WITH 10 IN A GROUP: Susan has 8 bags with 10 marbles in each bag. How many marbles does Susan have?

 MEASUREMENT DIVISION WITH 10 IN A GROUP: Linda has 47 tomatoes. If it takes 10 tomatoes to make a jar of tomato sauce, how many jars of tomato sauce can Linda make?

These problems have the same structure as Multiple Groups problems but instead of a fractional amount in each group, they have 10 in each group. Note that Partitive Division problems with divisors of 10, such as, "If 10 children share 70 gumdrops equally, how many gumdrops does each child get?" are less useful for developing an understanding of base ten because children tend to work with 10 groups rather than groups of 10 when they solve these problems.[2]

There are a variety of strategies children use to solve Multiplication and Measurement Division problems with groups of 10. Consider how two third-graders solved the following problem:

---

[1] See Chapter 6: Multidigit Number Concepts in *Children's Mathematics: Cognitively Guided Instruction* (Carpenter et al. 1999).

[2] If you are unsure of how the Partitive Division problem differs from the other problems, ask some first or second graders to solve these three problems. It will probably be easy to see how children's strategies for Partitive Division differ from their strategies for the other two problem types.

MR. JONES HAS 237 DOLLARS. He wants to use this money to buy books to donate to the children's hospital. If each book costs 10 dollars, how many books could he buy?

Lei solved this problem by first counting out 237 individual blocks and then pulling out groups of 10 blocks from the 237 blocks until she could not pull out any more groups of 10. Lei counted how many groups of 10 she made and found that Mr. Jones could buy 23 books. Ayesha solved the problem by saying, "I know that 100 is 10 tens, so 200 is 20 tens; 37 has 3 more tens so he could buy 23 books." Ayesha has a relational understanding of 237. She understands how 237 can be decomposed into groups of tens and ones and how she could use a grouping she knew (10 tens is 100) to figure out a different grouping (20 tens is 200). In contrast, Lei's strategy indicates that she may see 237 only as 237 ones.

Multiplication and Measurement Division problems with larger numbers can engage students in the upper grades in thinking about base-ten number concepts beyond two-digit numbers. Rather than 10 in each group, these problems have other positive powers of 10 (e.g. 100, 1,000, 10,000…) in each group. Here are some examples:

THE CRYSTAL CLEAR COMPANY sells water in 10-gallon bottles for water coolers. If they pump 57,000 gallons of water, how many bottles can they fill?

PHOTOSPOT CAN STORE 1 million photos on each of its mega-servers. If they want to store 3.2 billion photos, how many mega-servers would they need?

IF 52,348 PEOPLE EACH DONATED 100 dollars to Habitat for Humanity, how much money would Habitat for Humanity receive?

THE NATIONAL DEBT IS ABOUT 12 trillion dollars. How many people would have to pay $100,000 in order to clear the debt?

A full discussion of solutions for problems like these is beyond the scope of this book, but it is worth noting that students solve these problems using Relational Thinking strategies that are similar to the strategies used for Multiple Groups problems. For example Kari, a sixth grader, solved the problem about bottled water by reasoning, "There are 10 tens in 100, so there are 100 tens in 1,000. If there are 100 tens in 1,000 there are 57 hundred tens in 57,000. 57 hundred is the same as 5,700 so they can fill 5,700 bottles." In Chapter 3, we described how Kylie figured out how many three-eighths there were in 10½. She figured out that 8 groups of ⅜ was 3 and used this grouping to find how many ⅜ were in 10½. Kari's reasoning is similar in that she used the grouping 100 tens in 1,000 to find out how many tens there were in 57,000.

From the Classroom: Teaching Decimals

Ms. Andrews taught a multiage class of fourth and fifth graders at a school where about 40 percent of the students came from low-income families. Her approach to teaching decimals encouraged students to integrate their understanding of base ten with their understanding of fractions. Our account of her teaching provides two perspectives. The first is on the students and their thinking. The students in Ms. Andrews' class were operating from a variety of levels of understanding, which we describe in detail. The second perspective is on the teacher and her thinking. Ms. Andrews listened to her students as they solved problems and discussed their solutions. She gained information about each student's understanding that she used to make decisions about what to do next, moment to moment and when she planned problems for the next day.

Even though there was a range of understanding in her class, Ms. Andrews did not group students by grade or achievement level to teach them. Instead, she differentiated for individuals in the context of whole-group instruction.

Ms. Andrews' students had a variety of mathematical experiences in prior grades. Some students came from classrooms where they worked with word problems involving groups of 10 to develop their understanding of base-ten concepts and Equal Sharing problems to develop a relational understanding of fractions. Other students came from classrooms where base-ten instruction focused on naming place values and writing numbers in expanded notation and fraction instruction focused on identifying a fraction represented by a shape with shaded and unshaded parts. Ten of Ms. Andrews' twelve fifth graders had been in her class as fourth graders. At the beginning of the year, she concentrated on establishing routines so that students new to her class could become accustomed to solving problems using their own strategies.

Getting Started: Students' Understanding of Tenths

Ms. Andrews started her decimal unit with this problem:

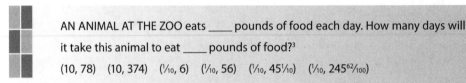

AN ANIMAL AT THE ZOO eats _____ pounds of food each day. How many days will it take this animal to eat _____ pounds of food?[3]

(10, 78) (10, 374) ($\frac{1}{10}$, 6) ($\frac{1}{10}$, 56) ($\frac{1}{10}$, 45$\frac{1}{10}$) ($\frac{1}{10}$, 245$\frac{62}{100}$)

Before reading on:

1) Decide what problem type this is.

2) Think about how you could use Relational Thinking to solve this problem with $\frac{1}{10}$ and 245$\frac{62}{100}$. Although you may find the answer without much thought for the easiest sets of numbers, the type of thinking you might use to solve this problem with $\frac{1}{10}$ and 245$\frac{62}{100}$ could be similar to the type of thinking children use to solve problems with groups of 10.

Ms. Andrews wrote the numbers using fraction notation because she knew it would prompt students to use what they knew about fractions to solve the problem and because the fourth graders in the class had not yet been introduced to decimal notation.

---

[3] See the Problem Set at the end of Chapter 1 for information on presenting problems in this format, with differentiated number choices. The number choices progress in difficulty from left to right.

Because this was the first day of the decimal unit, Ms. Andrews was especially focused on getting information about her students' understanding. Although Ms. Andrews had a general idea about how decimal instruction would progress, decisions about pacing, sequencing problems, what numbers to put into the problems, and what concepts to focus on were to be based on the information she gathered about what her students understood.

Not surprisingly, the strategies her students used indicated a great deal of variety in their understanding. She loosely categorized her students into four different groups based on their solutions. She used these groups as a way to think about instructional goals, but not to physically separate the students. These groups were flexible in that students often moved from one group to another. (To help you keep track of the students, the names of students in each group start with the letter of the group.)

Group A

These students showed no evidence of being able to use base-ten relationships to solve the problem about food for the animals in the zoo. They all chose the numbers 10 and 78 and were not immediately able to say that there were 7 tens in 78. For example, Adam got the base-ten blocks and constructed 78 with 7 tens and 8 ones (see Figure 7–1). He then counted the sticks of ten to find that there were 7 tens in 78.

Ms. Andrews' first goal for these students was to understand how whole numbers are composed of groups of 10 so that they would have a foundation to understand decimals less than 1. Because they did not immediately know how many tens there were in 78, she did not expect them to understand how many one-tenths there were in 6 or how tenths related to hundredths. To help them meet this goal, she provided them with many opportunities to solve and reflect on

Figure 7–1. *Adam finds how many tens are in 78 using base-ten blocks*

Multiplication and Measurement Division problems with groups of 10. Her second goal was for these students to develop an understanding of $\frac{1}{10}$ as a quantity. Equal Sharing problems with 10 sharers would help them develop this understanding. None of the students in this group had had much, if any, experience working with these kinds of problems in earlier grades. The two fifth graders who were new to her class this year both fell into this group.

Group B

Students in this group used what they knew about fractions to solve this problem. They relied on pictures rather than relationships. For example, Brie chose the numbers $\frac{1}{10}$ and 6. She said, "First I drew the 6 pounds of food. I had to see how many tenths I had so I split each pound into tenths. There are 10 tenths in each 1 pound. They are supposed to be equal but they don't look that way; I did my best. So then I just counted, 10, 20, 30, 40, 50, 60, and found there's enough food for 60 days." (See Figure 7–2.)

Students who used this strategy usually chose the numbers $\frac{1}{10}$ and 6. These numbers did not allow Ms. Andrews to assess whether these students could relate whole numbers to groups of 10, so over the next few days, she asked each of these students questions such as, "How many tens are in 345?" All students in group B used Relational Thinking (e.g., "There are 10 tens in 100, so 30 tens in 300, and 4 in 40, so it's 34 tens altogether") to solve these problems.

Ms. Andrews' goal for these students was to help them connect what they understood about base ten with what they understood about fractions so that they could use relationships rather than pictures to solve problems with tenths. More experiences solving Multiple Groups problems with groups of $\frac{1}{10}$ and opportunities to reflect on how other students used relationships to solve these types of problems would help

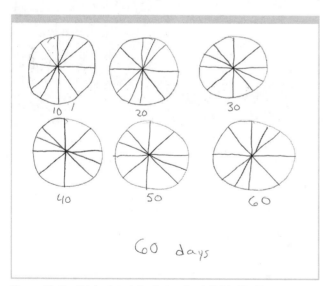

Figure 7–2. *Brie's pictorial solution for 6 divided by $\frac{1}{10}$*

these students meet this goal. Urging some of them to work with larger numbers could also help them meet this goal because drawing pictures gets tedious when the numbers are large.

Group C

Students in this group used Relational Thinking to solve this problem. They drew on base-ten and fraction

10 days would be 1 pound of food
60 days would be 6 pounds of food
100 days would be 10 pounds of food
500 days would be 50 pounds of food

So 500 + 60 = 560

560 days

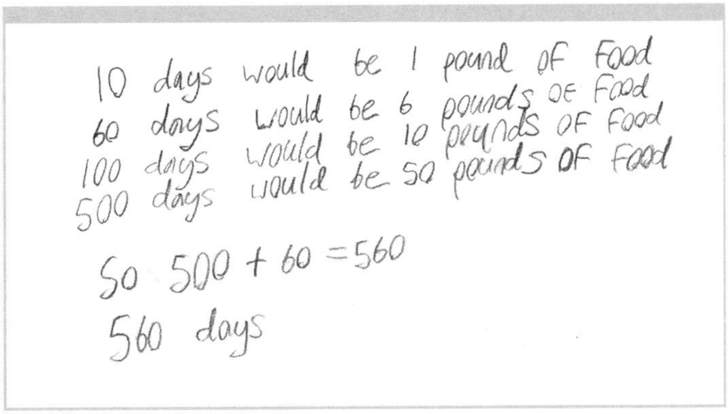

Figure 7–3. Clayton's Relational Thinking strategy for 56 divided by ¹⁄₁₀

relationships to combine groupings of fractions. For example, Figure 7–3 shows how Clayton solved the problem with the numbers ¹⁄₁₀ and 56. Clayton explained to Ms. Andrews, "I knew that 10, tenths is 1; so 60 tenths would be 6. Then since 10 tenths is 1, 100 tenths is 10, I just kept going like that. 50 pounds would last 500 days and then 6 pounds would last 60 days, so 56 pounds would last 560 days."

Ms. Andrews' goal for students in group C was for them to develop more sophisticated and efficient uses of Relational Thinking to solve problems. As was the case for group B, more experience solving problems like these coupled with discussions of other students' various strategies would help them meet this goal.

Group D

Like students in group C, students in group D used Relational Thinking to solve this problem. However, their strategies were significantly more sophisticated than those used by students in group C. There were only two students in this group—Doug and Dominique. They were also the only students who chose to solve the problem with the numbers ¹⁄₁₀ and 245⁶²⁄₁₀₀. Dominique's strategy is shown in Figure 7–4.

To explain her strategy, she said, "I know that 10 tenths is 1, so there will be 2,450 tenths in 245. I then had to figure out how many tenths there were in 62 hundredths. 60 hundredths is the same as 6 tenths; that's 6 more days. Two hundredths is a fifth of a tenth, so that's another fifth of a day." She then added, "This problem's a little weird because I don't think they would keep over 2,000 days worth of food for an animal at the zoo. It would probably get rotten!" Ms. Andrews agreed with

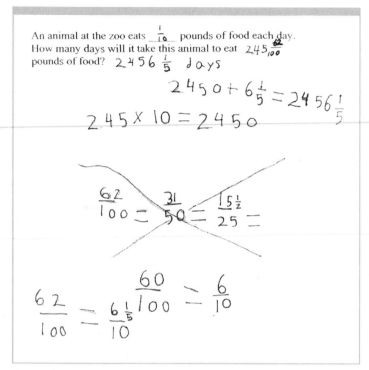

An animal at the zoo eats $\frac{1}{10}$ pounds of food each day. How many days will it take this animal to eat $245\frac{62}{100}$ pounds of food? $2456\frac{1}{5}$ days

$$2450 + 6\frac{1}{5} = 2456\frac{1}{5}$$

$$245 \times 10 = 2450$$

$$\frac{62}{100} = \frac{31}{50} = \frac{15\frac{1}{2}}{25} =$$

$$\frac{62}{100} = \frac{6\frac{1}{5}}{10} \quad \frac{60}{100} \sim \frac{6}{10}$$

Figure 7–4. *Dominque's strategy for 245⁶²⁄₁₀₀ divided by ⅒*

her; sometimes to challenge her more sophisticated thinkers she sacrifices realism in her story problems.

There are two ways in which the group D strategies were more sophisticated than the group C strategies. First, Dominique and Doug's answer—the number of days—was not a whole number. Second, they showed that they understood that 245 ones was the same as 2,450 tenths without breaking 245 into ones, tens, and hundreds.

Because these students had already met grade-level expectations for working with groups of ¹⁄₁₀, Ms. Andrews' goal was to help them use Relational Thinking strategies when they worked with groups of nonunit decimals such as ³⁄₁₀ or ³²⁄₁₀₀. She provided them with problems with these numbers to help them reach this goal. Listening to and reflecting on each other's strategies, explaining their strategies to students in other groups, and listening to the strategies of students in group C would also help them meet this goal.

Reflections on Group C and D's Relational Thinking Strategies

Clayton and Dominique used multiplicative strategies similar to Trenton's and Kylie's strategies described in Chapters 3 and 4. Like Trenton and Kylie, they used a convenient grouping, 10 groups of ¹⁄₁₀ is 1, and then applied the associative property to generate new groupings. Clayton's and Dominique's strategies may seem simpler than the Relational Thinking strategies used for nondecimal fractions because the computation is simpler. However, the mathematical relationships that underlie these strategies are the same. For adults, relationships such as $10 \times \frac{1}{10} = 1$ can seem obvious, which leads us to underestimate the difficulty of working with decimals. For students, these relationships can be complex.

Dominique's and Doug's ability to provide an answer that included a fractional number of days is notable. When we ask students how many tens are in a whole number such as 87 or 345, for example, we expect a whole-number answer of 8 or 34, even though there really are 8.7 tens in 87 and 34½ tens in 345. When it comes to decimals, we expect students to be able to tell us how many whole units and how many fractional units are in a given number. For example, when we ask students how many tenths are in .87, we expect an answer of 8.7, not 8. The ability to express a remainder as a fractional unit of a whole unit is an important goal in the development of both decimal and fraction understanding.

Ms. Andrews does not always follow the textbook to teach mathematics, but she consults it to make sure that her students can solve problems that are at least as difficult as those in the text. After this lesson, she looked at the fourth-grade textbook. One of the first decimal lessons was about moving the decimal point to show the relationships between a whole number and tenths. After being taught how to move the decimal point, students were asked questions like, "35 is equal to how many tenths?" In Ms. Andrews' class, only Dominique and Doug were able to relate whole numbers to tenths without breaking the whole number into tens and ones. Ms. Andrews believed that if she had taught the procedure where students move the decimal to divide, only Dominique and Doug would have been ready to understand it—and they did not need the procedure because they already had an efficient and accurate strategy to find how many tenths were in 245.

A Broad Range of Understanding

Ms. Andrews' students exhibited a range of conceptual development with respect to decimals. This spectrum of understanding may seem broad, but we were not surprised to see it. When teachers have students solve problems that reveal what they understand, they usually discover a broad range of understanding. A task in which students are expected to use a specific procedure (such as move the decimal point to divide) tends to differentiate students into two groups: those who can successfully execute the procedure and those who cannot. In contrast, tasks that require students to use their conceptual understanding reveal students' developing thinking in ways that allow teachers to differentiate students based on a variety of levels of understanding.

Open Number Sentences as Tools for Developing Decimals

After building students' understanding of decimals by solving and discussing Multiple Groups problems, Ms. Andrews began posing Open Number Sentences. She started with some simple Open Number Sentences that the group solved together so that students could see how Open Number Sentences worked. She wrote $50 + b = 75$ on the board and asked the students to find a value for b that made the equation true. They talked about how when a letter was written into an equation, it meant that the letter was representing some value; many of the students knew that these letters were called *variables*.

Next she wrote $y + y = 10$ and asked students to find a value of y that would make this number sentence true. The students wondered whether or not y could stand for more than one value. Ms. Andrews explained that if the same variable appears more than once in an equation, it represents the same value each time. The students concluded that the only value that would make this number sentence true was $y = 5$.

Then Ms. Andrews moved to equations with two variables. She wrote: $a \times 5 + b = 30$ on the board. At first the students were surprised to find that there was more than one pair of values that made this equation true. They were also surprised to learn that a and b did not necessarily need to be different values in that $a = 5$, $b = 5$ was a valid solution.

When Ms. Andrews was confident that students understood how Open Number Sentences worked, she gave all of the students the following problem:

FIND THREE SOLUTIONS that will make this number sentence true:

$a \times 10 + b = 87$

The word problems that the class had been working on had only one answer, which did not allow Ms. Andrews to assess how flexible students were in decomposing a number such as 87 into groups of tens and ones. This number sentence allowed her to assess that flexibility because it required students to think of 87 in ways other than 8 tens (*a* = 8) and 7 ones (*b* = 7).

Adam (who used base-ten blocks to solve the problem about how many days 78 pounds of food would last if 10 pounds were eaten each day) took out base-ten blocks to solve this problem and produced the work in Figure 7–5. Ms. Andrews was pleased to see Adam thinking of different ways that 87 could be made of tens and ones. This flexibility indicated clear growth since the beginning of the unit. Most of the students in group A were able to think flexibly about the number of tens in a number like 87, as Adam had.

However, a few students in group A struggled. Aaron pulled out base-ten blocks and made 87 with 8 tens and 7 ones. He rearranged the values in the equation, but he did not think of

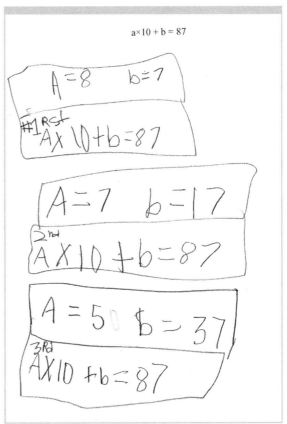

Figure 7–5. Adam's solutions to $a \times 10 + b = 87$

any other ways that 87 could be made from tens and ones (see Figure 7–6). Ms. Andrews made sure to draw him into the discussion when other students were sharing their thinking. After a few more lessons like this one, he became more flexible in how he decomposed numbers into base-ten units.

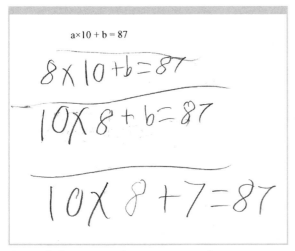

Figure 7–6. Aaron's solutions to $a \times 10 + b = 87$

All of the students in the groups B, C, and D were able to use the relationship between tens and ones to find many solutions to this problem. Clara produced the paper in Figure 7–7. She generated the different pairs of values in a systematic fashion. When Ms. Andrews asked her how she solved this problem, she said, "each time I took away a 10, I added 10 more ones."

This problem provided an appropriate challenge for even the most sophisticated students. Figure 7–8 shows how Dominique solved this problem and Figure 7–9 shows how Doug solved the problem.

Once again, Dominique and Doug provided solutions that showed they could conceptualize a fraction of a group of 10: Dominique saw 87 as 8.7 tens and Doug saw 7 as .7 tens. After a week of working with decimals, they were still the only students working with fractional groups these ways. When they shared their solutions with the rest of the class, some students asked questions that indicated that they were starting to understand the idea of fractional groups. For example, Clara asked Doug, "How did you figure out what $\frac{7}{10}$ of 10 was?"

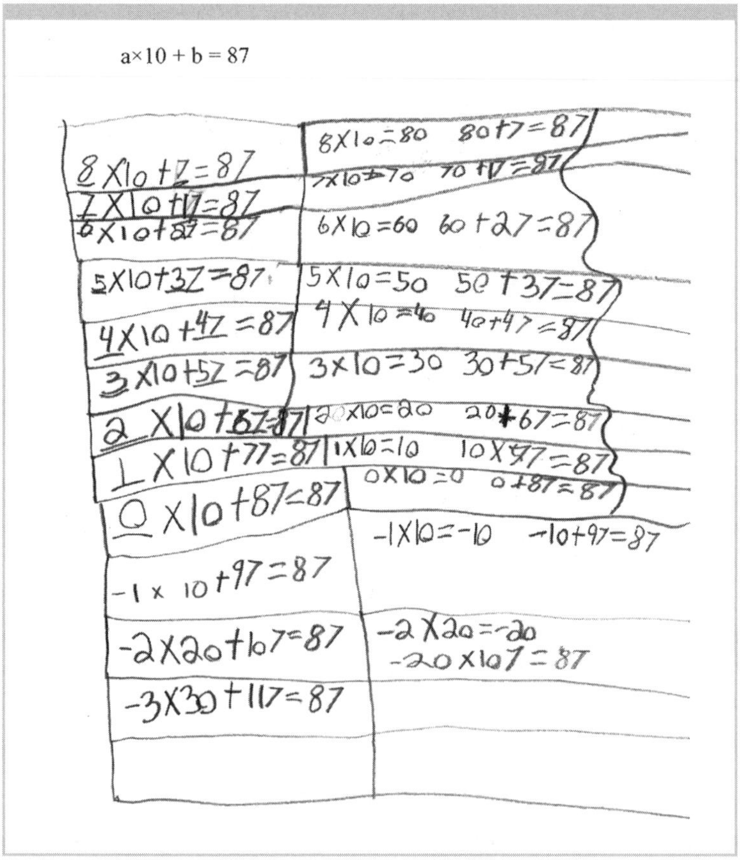

Figure 7–7. *Clara's solutions to* $a \times 10 + b = 87$

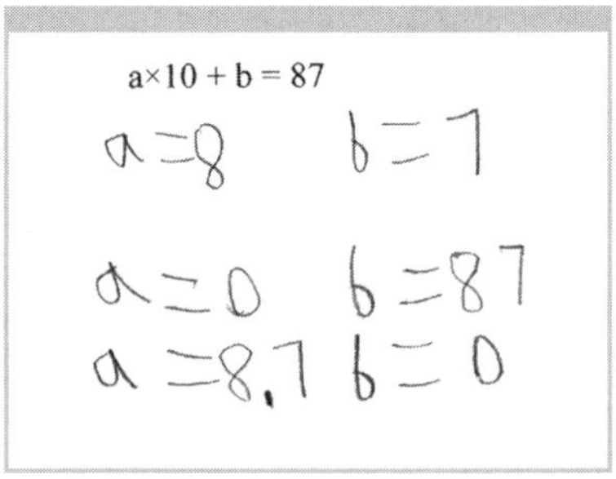

Figure 7–8. *Dominique's solutions to* $a \times 10 + b = 87$

Instruction Progresses

Decimal Notation. Once most students showed some relational understanding of tens, ones, and tenths, Ms. Andrews introduced decimal notation by pointing out that fractions with a denominator of 10 could also be written with a decimal point. She showed examples such as:

$$\frac{7}{10} = .7$$
$$4\frac{2}{10} = 4.2$$
$$54\frac{1}{10} = 54.1$$

Her fifth graders had seen this notation before and several were already using it, but it was new to her fourth graders. As students started using and discussing decimal notation, they realized that the relationship between the place values to the right of the decimal point is the same as the relationships between the place values to the left of the decimal point. Ms. Andrews saw evidence of this understanding when students said things such as, "There are 10 hundreds in a thousand, then you go 1 [place] over and there are 10 tens in a hundred, then you go 1 more over and there are 10 ones in 10, and you can even go 1 more over still and there are 10 tenths in 1. It keeps going and going and going."

$$a \times 10 + b = 87$$

$$a = 8 \qquad b = 7 \qquad 8 \times 10 = 80$$
$$80 + 7 = 87$$

$$a = 4 \qquad b = 47 \qquad 4 \times 10 = 40$$
$$40 + 47 = 87$$

$$a = 0 \qquad b = 87 \qquad 0 + 87 = 87$$

$$a = 10 \qquad b = -13 \qquad 10 \times 10 = 100$$
$$100 - 13 = 87$$

$$a = .7 \qquad b = 80 \qquad 10 \times .7 = 7$$
$$7 + 80 = 87$$

Figure 7–9. *Doug's solutions to $a \times 10 + b = 87$*

Problems Posed. Multiplication and Measurement Division problems and Open Number Sentences were the core of Ms. Andrews' decimal instruction. As students' understanding grew, she used increasingly complex numbers in these problems. At first, she wrote problems with only .1 or .01 in each group, because she wanted students to understand the relationship among unit decimals before they started working with nonunit decimals. She gradually began to introduce nonunit decimals into problems. For example, here is a problem she posed toward the end of the unit:

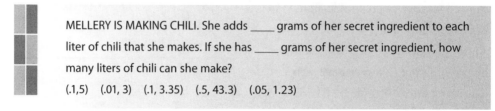

MELLERY IS MAKING CHILI. She adds _____ grams of her secret ingredient to each liter of chili that she makes. If she has _____ grams of her secret ingredient, how many liters of chili can she make?

(.1, 5)   (.01, 3)   (.1, 3.35)   (.5, 43.3)   (.05, 1.23)

Although the first three number choices involve groups of unit fractions (either .1 or .01), the last two number choices include groups of nonunit decimals (.5 or .05).

Throughout instruction, Ms. Andrews chose numbers based on her goals for students. She explained to us that for the problem above, she included the first number choice (.1 and 5) because many of the students in group A still needed to make pictures to solve these problems and these numbers allowed this kind of strategy. The second number choice is tedious to solve with a picture (because it involves 300 groups) and supports working with a relatively basic relationship between hundredths and 1 ($100 \times \frac{1}{100} = 1$). The last three number choices allow students to work with more complex relationships and fractional groups. The context of this problem supports students to think about groups that are not whole numbers. For example, with 3.35 grams of secret ingredient, Mellery can actually make 33.5 or 33½ liters of chili. The numbers .5 and 43.3 provide the dual challenge of working with a nonunit decimal amount in each group (.5) and a remainder that is expressed as a fractional group, since Mellery could use her secret ingredient to make 86.6 or 86⅗ liters of chili here. The final numbers provide a similar dual challenge but with hundredths rather than tenths.

Ms. Andrews often wrote carefully sequenced Open Number Sentences to help students build on a relationship they used for one number sentence to solve the next one. Open Number Sentences sequenced in this way are especially useful for extending students' use of relationships. Figure 7–10 is an example of one such sequence of number sentences and how Cerise solved each of these problems. Notice how Cerise extended the use of relationships from one problem to the next.

When Ms. Andrews gave students a sequence of Open Number Sentences such as the one in Figure 7–10, she asked students to work through the problems in order.

Open Number Sentence	Cerise's Strategy
A. $k \times .1 = 1$	"I know that 10 tenths is 1, so $k = 10$."
B. $m \times .1 = 3$	"Since 10 tenths is 1, 30 tenths is 3, so $m = 30$."
C. $j \times .1 = 30$	"Since 30 tenths is 3, I need 10 times as many tenths to make 30, so $j = 10 \times 30 = 300$."
D. $y \times .1 = 300$	"Since 300 tenths is 30, I need 10 times as many tenths to make 300, so I need 10 times 300 tenths, so $y = 10 \times 300 = 3,000$."
E. $r \times .01 = 3$	"I am going back to B here. 30 tenths is 3, but hundredths are 10 times smaller than tenths so I need 10 times more of them to still make 3, so $r = 10 \times 30 = 300$."
F. $j \times .01 = 30$	"Since 300 hundredths is 3, I need 10 times as many to make 30, so $j = 10 \times 300 = 3,000$."
G. $s \times .01 = 300$	"Since 3,000 hundredths is 30, I need 10 times as many to make 300, so $s = 10 \times 3000 = 30,000$."
H. $r \times .1 = 43$	"10 tenths are 1, I need 43 times as many tenths to make 43, so $r = 43 \times 10 = 430$."
I. $r \times .01 = 43$	"430 tenths is 43. Since hundredths are 10 times smaller than tenths, I need 10 times as many of them to make 43, so $r = 430 \times 10 = 4,300$."

Figure 7–10. *A progression of Open Number Sentences and one student's Relational Thinking strategies*

She noticed that many students used more sophisticated Relational Thinking when she sequenced the problems this way than when she presented challenging Open Number Sentences in isolation. Not all of her students were able to solve all the number sentences in Figure 7–10.

Classroom Interactions. Ms. Andrews regularly devoted time for students to share and discuss their strategies with the rest of the class even though there was a broad range of understanding. At the beginning of the year, she worked with students to help them understand what it meant to explain their strategy to someone else and to listen to another person's strategy. When students presented their strategies, Ms. Andrews helped them verbalize the relationships they used, and she used mathematical notation to represent the relationships for all to see.

Ms. Andrews also put students into pairs to share strategies with each other. She often arranged it so that one student in the pair heard a strategy that was just a little more sophisticated than what they were currently using. This pairing helped the student who was explaining as much as it helped the student who was listening. As students explained their strategies and answered clarifying questions, they reflected on their strategy and solidified their understanding.

Moving to Addition and Subtraction. Once students could reason relationally about decimals, addition and subtraction were not challenging. A few weeks into instruction, Ms. Andrews posed the problem $8 + .3 + 1.02 = m$ in a horizontal number sentence; she said nothing about lining up decimals to add. Almost all students quickly gave the correct answer of 9.32, which they said as "9 and 32 hundredths" rather than "9 point 32." The fact that students readily solved this problem and said the number this way shows that they understood decimals in terms of relationships between the different place values. Ms. Andrews moved on to more challenging addition and subtraction problems and even tested the strength of their understanding by providing problems where the decimal points were not lined up. For example:

$$
\begin{array}{r}
89.2 \\
35.89 \\
+.09 \\
\hline
\end{array}
$$

Most of her students correctly solved these problems.

Progression of Students' Understanding

Ms. Andrews' followed her school district's pacing guide and spent about six weeks focusing on decimals. However, after the unit was over, she continued to include decimals in the problems she gave to students. Students' strategies continued to grow. She noted a dramatic increase in particular after they had done some focused work on fractions. Ms. Andrews was not surprised by this increase because students' reasoning about fractions and decimals is governed by the same kinds of mathematical relationships.

During the six concentrated weeks they spent on decimals, Ms. Andrews saw a great deal of growth for all students. Although each student was unique, she tended to think of them in terms of the four groups that she had observed on the first day of instruction. Not all students within a group progressed at the same rate, and many students moved from one group to another.

Group A. These students started the unit with little understanding of the relationships underlying our base-ten number system for groups of 10. Recall that Adam used base-ten blocks to solve the problems about how many tens were in 78. Ms. Andrews spent a lot of time with these children and made special efforts to help them understand how other students solved problems. She knew that simple statements like, "Adam, make sure you listen," usually did not help much, so instead she asked questions to help them focus on particular aspects of a strategy such as, "Brian just said that since 10 tens are 100, and 20 tens would be 200. Adam, how do you think Brian figured that out?"

By the end of the decimal unit, these students were able to use relationships to solve problems with groups of 10 and 100. They were also able to solve problems that involved groups of ⅒ using pictures. Although they tended to use pictures to solve Equal Sharing problems with 10 sharers, sometimes they drew how the first item could be shared and then deduced the answer without drawing the rest of the items. For example, Figure 7–11 shows what Anna drew to solve a problem about 10 people are sharing 3 pizzas.

Group B. These students started the unit with an understanding of the relationships between hundreds, tens, and ones but did not use relationships to solve problems involving tenths. Recall that Brie solved the zoo problem by drawing out each pound and dividing it into tenths and then counting the tenths to see how many days the food would last.

Ms. Andrews spent a lot of time having these students explain how they used relationships to solve problems

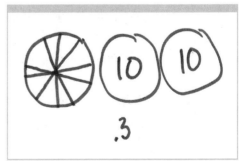

Figure 7–11.
Anna's solution to 10 people sharing 3 pizzas

with groups of 10 and how they might use a similar type of thinking when they solved problems with tenths. She made special efforts to draw these students into the discussion when other students were sharing strategies that used relationships involving tenths. For example, she would direct specific questions to them such as, "Brandon, Clayton just said that since there were 10 tenths in 1, there had to be 20 tenths in 2. Why do you think that might be true?" Even though most of the students in this group could solve problems involving nonunit decimals if they drew a picture, Ms. Andrews made sure they spent some time working with problems that involved groups of $\frac{1}{10}$ until she saw that they could use relationships rather than drawings to solve those problems.

By the end of the unit, the students in this group used relationships to solve problems with groups of .1. They tended to rely on pictures to solve problems with nonunit decimals and were inconsistent in their use of relationships to solve problems with groups of .01.

Group C. These students started the unit able to use Relational Thinking to solve problems with groups of .1. Recall that Clayton solved the problem about how many tenths were in 56 by breaking 56 into 50 and 6 and then figuring out how many tenths were in each. Ms. Andrews' goal for this group was for them to become more efficient in their use of relationships.

Sharing strategies with other students—either from group B or group D—really helped these students reflect on how their strategies could become more efficient. When they verbalized their strategy or answered questions about it, they often saw how steps could be combined. Ms. Andrews also made a concerted effort to support these students to use mathematical notation to record their strategies, which also helped them reflect on their strategies and become more efficient. Open Number Sentences, especially those with multiple solutions, helped these students increase their understanding of the relationships between the base-ten units. The students in this group especially benefitted from sequenced number sentences designed to increase Relational Thinking.

All of the students in this group became more efficient in their use of Relational Thinking. By the end of the unit, they could say how many tenths or hundredths were in a whole number without breaking the number apart. They were sometimes able to use relationships for problems with groups of nonunit decimals. Some of these students were able to find solutions that involved fractional groups, but not all of them were.

Group D. These students already understood a great deal about decimals and used some fairly sophisticated Relational Thinking at the beginning of the unit. Ms. Andrews' goal for these students was that their Relational Thinking continued to grow. Early in the unit, Ms. Andrews moved these students from problems with unit decimals to problems with nonunit decimals, such as this:

> A PATIENT AT THE HOSPITAL is connected to an intravenous drip. The medicine drips into her body at the rate of .07 grams per hour. The drip has .8 grams of medicine in it now. How long will it take for the medicine to run out?

The number relationships that these students were ready to think about were not always well suited to word problems. Rather than struggle to write appropriate word problems, Ms. Andrews often wrote Open Number Sentences for these students such as:

$.04 \times m = .91$ or $.38 = .03 \times r + m$.

These students learned a great deal from sharing their strategies with each other and listening to the strategies of their classmates. Some students with sophisticated strategies have difficulty explaining their strategies to others. Dominique had difficulty explaining her strategies to the whole group and tended to not include enough detail when she wrote them down. Ms. Andrews found that Dominique had more opportunities to reflect when she explained her strategies to students from other groups because these students needed to ask a lot of questions to understand her strategies. Ms. Andrews also introduced these students to mathematical equations to record their strategies. These equations became another tool for reflection and communication. Their use of relationships grew more sophisticated throughout the unit. By the end of the unit, they were able to use Relational Thinking to solve problems with nonunit decimals.

Reflecting Back and Looking Ahead

In this chapter, we described how decimal instruction can lead students to integrate their understanding of base ten with their understanding of fractions. Students who understand fractions and base-ten numbers as relational can use that understanding to learn decimals and apply their understanding of whole-number computation to generate procedures for decimal computation without direct instruction.

Unfortunately, many students begin the study of decimals without a strong understanding of fractions, base ten, or both. Too often base-ten instruction focuses on naming places and writing numerals with little attention to understanding groups of powers of 10 and the relationships among these groups. Similarly, fraction instruction too often focuses on counting parts of the whole without attention to developing a relational understanding of fractions as amounts and relationships among fraction amounts. Few students can develop a strong understanding of base-ten or fractions from such instruction. Added to the problem of lack of background understanding is the fact that students are often introduced to fractions, place value for numbers larger than ten thousand, and decimals all in the fourth grade. Even with instruction that focuses on building understanding, many students simply will not have enough experiences to develop a strong relational understanding of base ten and fractions by the time they study decimals.

The earlier children are supported to build understanding for base-ten and fraction concepts, the more likely they are to develop a relational understanding of these topics that can serve as a foundation for learning decimals. However, you might be a fourth-, fifth-, or sixth-grade teacher who has to teach decimals to students who lack a relational understanding of base ten and/or fractions. In this case, you can take the approach that Ms. Andrews did and integrate the study of decimals with the study of base ten and fractions. Some students may not proceed as far as you wish they would, but the important thing is that you are helping them build a strong foundation for understanding base ten, fractions, and decimals.

In the next chapter, we extend our discussion of learning with understanding to more complex fraction and decimal computation. Students who have engaged in solving and reflecting on the problems described in Chapters 1 through 7 are likely to be well prepared to learn more complex fraction computation with understanding.

Problems for Decimals

Here are some problems to use with your students to develop their understanding of decimals. The problems are roughly arranged from least to most sophisticated with the exception that the word problems K through N have number choices that influence their difficulty. Refer to the instructional guide on page 174 for suggestions for choosing problems for your grade level.

Word Problems—Multiplication and Measurement Division

A. Selena has 6 bags of books with 10 books in each bag. How many books does Selena have?

B. I have 84 potatoes. 10 potatoes fit in each bag. How many bags would it take to hold all of my potatoes?

C. Jose has 24 boxes with 10 rocks in each box. How many rocks does Jose have?

D. Ms. Gomez has 359 dollars. She wants to use this money to buy teddy bears for the children's hospital. If each teddy bear costs 10 dollars, how many teddy bears could she buy?

E. The pencil factory makes 3,875 pencils a day. They put the pencils into boxes with 10 pencils in each box. How many boxes of pencils do they make in 1 day?

F. The pencil factory makes 3,875 pencils a day. They put the pencils into cartons with 100 pencils in each carton. How many cartons of pencils do they make in one day?

G. Julie has 6 huge candy bars. If she eats $\frac{1}{10}$ candy bar each day, how long will these 6 huge candy bars last?

H. The bakery has 58 pounds of frosting. It takes ¹⁄₁₀ pound of frosting to frost a cupcake. How many cupcakes could the bakery frost with the frosting they have?

I. Henry uses ¹⁄₁₀ package of cinnamon in each batch of cinnamon cookies he makes. If Henry has 3⁷⁄₁₀ packages of cinnamon, how many batches of cookies can he make?

J. Juan uses .1 pound of flour to make a batch of cookies. How many batches of cookies can he make with 3.75 pounds of flour?

K. Hayley has ___ boxes of candy with ___ pounds of candy in each box. How many pounds of candy does Hayley have?

(4, 10)   (57, 10)   (4, .1)   (57, .1)   (364, .1)

L. Cameron has ___ pounds of clay. It takes ___ pounds of clay to make an art project. How many art projects could Cameron make with his clay?

(80, 10)   (630, 10)   (5, .1)   (12, .1)

M. There are ___ students in Mr. Jones' art class. Mr. Jones is planning a project where each student will need ___ jars of paint. How much paint will Mr. Jones need all together?

(15, 10)   (15, .1)   (25, .3)

N. My pet eats ___ jars of applesauce each day. How many days would it take my pet to eat ___ jars of applesauce?

(10, 56)   (.1, 8)   (.1, 23.4)

Equations

When posing these number sentences, ask your students, "Can you find at least 3 different solutions that will make this number sentence true?" (Sometimes you may want to ask for more than 3 solutions.)

A. $a \times 10 + b = 53$

B. $832 = a \times 100 + b \times 10 + g$

C. $874 = b \times 10 + c$

D. $874 = c \times 100 + b \times 10$

E. $h \times .1 + j = 4.5$

F. $y \times .1 = 4.5$ (There is only one solution that will make this number sentence true.)

G. $p \times 10 = 546$ (There is only one solution that will make this number sentence true.)

H. $52 = a \times 10 + b \times .1$

I. $a \times .1 + b \times .01 = .45$

J. $g + h \times .1 = 3.47$

K. $a \times .1 = .56$ (There is only one solution that will make this number sentence true.)

Instructional Guidelines for Teaching Decimal Numbers

In this section, we provide guidelines for teaching decimals. Students should have some understanding of base ten and fractions before they embark on concentrated study of decimals. (See Chapter 6 in *Children's Mathematics* [Carpenter et al. 1999] for base ten and Chapters 1 and 3 in this book for fractions. We have included some problems here for base ten instruction in the early grades.) Grade levels are provided as suggestions—older students who have not had experience solving these types of problems are likely to need to start with problems designated for earlier grades. We recommend that you read the suggestions for all of the grade levels rather than only for the grade level you teach.

KINDERGARTEN

✔ Multiplication and Measurement Division problems: focus on problems with 2, 3, 4, 5, or 10 in each group but include other amounts as well—for example:

- Multiplication: *I have 4 buckets with 3 marbles in each bucket. How many marbles do I have?*
- Measurement Division: *3 goldfish can fit in each bowl. How many bowls would I need for 15 goldfish?*

FIRST GRADE

✔ Multiplication and Measurement Division problems: focus on problems with 10 in each group for teaching base ten. (Include problems with other amounts in each group to develop other grouping ideas.) For example:

- Multiplication: *I have 4 buckets with 10 marbles in each bucket. How many marbles do I have?*
- Measurement Division: *10 goldfish can fit in each bowl. How many bowls would I need for 56 goldfish?*

SECOND GRADE

✔ Multiplication and Measurement Division problems: focus on problems with 10 or 100 in each group, including problems with totals over 100—for example:
- Multiplication:
  - *I have 4 buckets with 100 marbles in each bucket. How many marbles do I have?*
  - *I have 24 buckets with 10 marbles in each bucket. How many marbles do I have?*
- Measurement Division:
  - *100 goldfish can fit in each tank. How many tanks does the pet store need for 324 goldfish?*
  - *10 goldfish can fit in each bowl. How many bowls does the pet store need for 564 goldfish?*

THIRD GRADE

✔ Multiplication and Measurement Division problems: focus on problems with 10 or 100 in each group. Include problems with totals over 100. (See examples for second grade.)
- Look for students who use relationships to solve these problems. For example, a student might say *10 buckets with 10 in each bucket would be 100, so 20 buckets with 10 in each bucket would be 200*; highlight these strategies for other students to hear.

✔ Equal Sharing problems with 10 sharers—for example:
- *10 children had 2 small cakes to share. How much cake would each child get?*

✔ Children can express their answers with fraction notation (e.g., $^2/_{10}$) or natural language (e.g., 2-tenths).

FOURTH GRADE

✔ Multiplication and Measurement Division problems with 10, 100, 1,000, and .1 in each group—for example:
- Multiplication:
  - *A flat screen TV costs $1,000. If a hotel wanted to buy 24 of these TVs, how much would they cost?*

- *The bookstore was selling all of their children's books for $10 each. How much would 35 books cost?*
- *My lizard eats .1 pound of food a day. How much food does it eat in 6 days? 12 days? 24 days?*

- **Measurement Division:**
  - *The goldfish nursery had 2,400 goldfish. They send their fish to pet stores in bags of 10. How many bags of fish could they make?*
  - *I have 3 pounds of lizard food. If my lizard eats .1 pound of food a day, how many days can I feed my lizard before the food runs out?*

✔ **Open Number Sentences with groups of 10, 100, 1,000, and .1.**
- **With one unknown—for example:**
  - $a \times 10 = 240$
  - $b \times .1 = 10$
- **With two or more unknowns (ask students to find multiple solutions to these problems)—for example:**
  - $g \times 10 + h = 58$
  - $245 = r \times 100 + g \times 10 + p$
  - $y + b \times .1 = 34.7$

✔ **With all of these problems, look for students who use relationships in their solutions and have them share their solutions with other students. (For example, a student may say, "I know that 10 tenths is 1, so 20 tenths would be 2.")**

FIFTH GRADE

✔ **Multiplication and Measurement Division problems with 10, 100, 1,000, 10,000, 100,000, .1, and .01 in each group, including problems where the number of groups is not a whole number—for example:**
- **Measurement Division:** *Eric drinks 10 ounces of water for every kilometer he rides his bike. If his water bottle holds 34 ounces of water, how many kilometers could he ride before he runs out of water?*
- **Multiplication:** *Nick uses .1 gram of chili powder to make a pot of chili. How much chili powder would he need to make 4½ pots of chili?*

(Examples of problems with a whole number of groups are listed in the fourth-grade examples.)

✔ Open Number Sentences with groups of 10, 100, 1,000, 10,000, 100,000, .1, and .01. Include problems where the number of groups in not a whole number, such as:

- $m \times 10 = 35$
- $j \times .1 = 2.46$
- $346 = p \times 10 + y \times 100$

✔ Encourage students to find solutions that are not whole numbers for problems, such as:

- $346 = b \times 100 + j \times 10$ (some examples of non–whole-number solutions include: $b = 3.46$ and $j = 0$; $b = 0$ and $j = 34.6$; $b = 3$ and $j = 4.6$)

✔ With all of these problems, look for students who use relationships in their solutions and have them share their solutions with other students.

SIXTH GRADE

✔ Multiplication and Measurement Division problems with 10, 100, 1,000, 10,000, 100,000, one million, one billion, .1, .01, and .001 in each group, as well as other powers of 10 such as 10 million and 10 billion, including problems where the number of groups is not a whole number (see fourth and fifth grades for examples), including problems where the number in each group is not a power of 10, such as:

- Multiplication: *A patient in the hospital receives .34 ounces of medicine each hour. How much medicine would she receive in 24 hours?*
- Measurement Division: *I have 10 pounds of chili powder. I want to make jars of chili powder with .24 pounds in each jar. How many jars can I fill?*

✔ Open Number Sentences with groups of 10, 100, 1,000, 10,000, 100,000, .1, and .01, including problems where the number of groups in not a whole number. Include problems where the number in each group is not a power of 10, such as:

- $34 \times r = 68,000$
- $.02 = h \times .2$
- $.32 = y \times .2$
- $2.4 \times m = 48$

✔ With all of these problems, look for students who use relationships in their solutions and have them share their solutions with other students

chapter 8

Understanding Operations on Fractions and Decimals

in this chapter, we describe the development of children's strategies for adding, subtracting, multiplying, and dividing fractions and decimals. Multiplication and division, in particular, involve new conceptual challenges. We show how children are able to extend what they have learned solving and discussing the problems presented in earlier chapters to these operations involving more difficult fractions and decimals and how you can sequence problems to encourage children to draw on increasingly sophisticated relationships. We also address the role of standard algorithms in the development of children's thinking and how to decide when to introduce them.

The evolution of children's strategies for these operations is marked by increasingly efficient uses of Relational Thinking. Thinking relationally drives children's ability to understand and reason with insight, flexibility, and confidence about operations involving fractions and decimals and develops students' understanding of the fundamental properties of operations.

Addition and Subtraction

Adding and subtracting numbers of any sort involve combining like units. A *unit* is an amount that is counted as a whole or one. It can refer to realistic quantities, such as an orange, a package of cookies, or a grouping of minutes or it can simply be a number, such as 1, 10, 100, ½, or ¼. Any amount can be conceptualized as a unit. When children solve story problems that involve adding and subtracting whole numbers, they implicitly understand the need for like units. Consider this problem: *Aisha has 25 pennies. Imani has 2 dimes. How much money do they have altogether?* Children who understand coin equivalencies will naturally choose a common unit—probably pennies, but dimes would work too—to combine the two amounts. This principle governs all addition and subtraction. For example, a common Relational Thinking strategy children use to add numbers such as 47 and 58 is to add the tens (40 plus 50 is 90), then add the ones (7 plus 8 is 15), and then combine the partial sums (90 plus 15 is 105). Children who use this strategy understand that they cannot add 4 tens with 8 ones and get 12. Understanding the need for like units is essential to this strategy.

When children solve Equal Sharing and other Multiple Groups problems, they encounter frequent opportunities to combine like fractional units in their solutions. (See for example, James' and Breelyn's strategies in Chapter 1 and Kay's, Grace's, Luke's, and Shawn's strategies in Chapter 3.) If your students have spent time solving these problems and discussing their solutions, then many of them will have a well-developed understanding of combining like units from which to reason through problems such as ¾ + ¼ on their own. Similarly, adding and subtracting decimals can be treated as an extension of adding multidigit numbers because children are working with fractional units that are common to all decimals—tenths, hundredths, and so on. For example, the children in Ms. Andrews' class in Chapter 7 solved 8 + .3 + 1.02 = m by combining like units rather than by lining up the decimal points.

As children's understanding of equivalent fractions grows, they extend their strategies for combining like units to add and subtract fractions involving *unlike* fractional units, such as ⅚ + ⅔. Children who understand fractions know that they cannot just add ⅚ and ⅔ and get 7 of something. Before quantities expressed in unlike units can be combined, each quantity needs to be related to a common unit.

Addition and Subtraction with Unlike Denominators: A Sequence of Problems to Extend Students' Thinking

The question of how to add fractions with unlike denominators often emerges in children's solutions to Equal Sharing problems. You can take advantage of these opportunities by following up with problems that directly involve adding and subtracting.

Emily and Katy were third graders who had been solving and discussing Multiple Groups problems for a couple of weeks when their teacher, Ms. Lewis, gave them the following problem:

TWO PEOPLE WANT TO SHARE 1¾ submarine sandwiches so that each gets the same amount. How much should each person get?

Emily drew the picture in Figure 8–1 and said "Each person gets ½, ¼, and ⅛," and after a pause, "There is probably another way to say it."

Ms. Lewis saw an opportunity to investigate adding fractions with unlike denominators. She knew that Emily understood relationships between halves, fourths, and eighths and believed she could use that understanding to think about combining fractions. She sat down and wrote "½ ¼ ⅛" on Emily's paper, and asked "What are we doing with these numbers? Are we adding, subtracting, multiplying, or dividing?" Katy, who was sitting next to Emily, was drawn into the conversation and

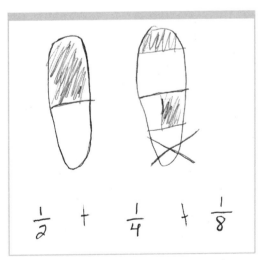

Figure 8–1. *Emily's initial solution to 2 people share 1¾ sandwiches*

immediately said, "Adding." Emily agreed and wrote "+" between each of the fractions (see Figure 8–1).

Katy, reflecting on the problem of how to add unlike fractional units said, "It's confusing. But I think I have an idea." She drew a large circle and split it in half, then another large circle, which she split into fourths, and finally another circle, which she split into eighths. She shaded in ½, ¼, and ⅛, respectively, in each of the circles (Figure 8–2). She studied the pictures and then said, "Um, I think we should use *eighths* to say that. The fourth is ²⁄₈. And the half is ⁴⁄₈. That makes ⁷⁄₈."

Emily said, "I have a different idea." She drew a single circle, split it in half, and explained that it showed 2 halves of a submarine sandwich. Then she split 1 of the halves in half and said "and we've also got a fourth and," splitting 1 of the fourths in half, "an eighth, which would be half of this [fourth]." She shaded in each part as she spoke (Figure 8–3).

When she was done, Ms. Lewis asked her how much it made altogether. At first Emily was not sure but she continued to think, saying, "When the circle is shaded in, it leaves ⅛ out. So … 1 minus ⅛." "Oh, write that down," Ms. Lewis encouraged, "that's how you would talk about your answer." Emily wrote 1 – ⅛. Ms. Lewis then said, "I want you girls to look at each other's work. Your answers look different and I am wondering if you found that these people would get different amounts of sandwiches."

Emily saw how the two answers were related and said, "Katy got ⁷⁄₈. That is basically like 1 minus ⅛ because ⁸⁄₈ is 1, and take away ⅛ would be ⁷⁄₈."

Emily and Katy approached the problem of combining fractions with unlike denominators in two different ways. Katy looked at all of the fractions at once and saw that she needed a common fractional unit to combine them. Her strategy was guided by the goal of finding this common unit. In contrast, Emily worked more informally with the idea of combining. Her strategy was guided by her understanding

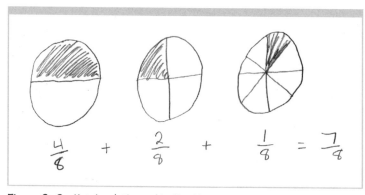

Figure 8–2. *Katy's solution to ½ + ¼ + ⅛*

of how to relate one fraction to the next—halves to fourths, fourths to eighths, and then finally, eighths to one whole.

To help the girls work on developing their insights, Ms. Lewis wrote this problem for them:

$$1 - \tfrac{1}{6} = \square$$

This problem focused the students' attention on the relationship between 1 whole and sixths. After several seconds of thinking, Emily said, "⅚!" Katy quickly agreed. Ms. Lewis asked why, and Emily explained, "Because ⁶⁄₆ is 1 and so then minus 1 of those, you would get ⅚." Ms. Lewis then gave the girls the problem

$$2 - \tfrac{1}{9} = \square$$

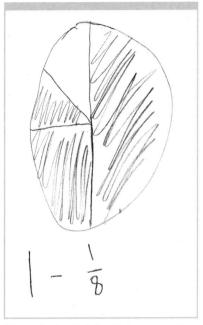

Figure 8–3. *Emily's solution to ½ + ¼ + ⅛*

and asked Katy to answer first, to give her a chance to verbalize the relationship. "That would be … 1 and ⁸⁄₉. The answer has to be 1 and something. And then ⁹⁄₉ is the whole and so ⁸⁄₉ has to be ⅑ less."

Satisfied that Emily and Katy understood how to relate unit fractions to wholes, Ms. Lewis posed this problem for them to solve. She chose two fractions that were familiar to the girls:

$$\tfrac{3}{4} + 1\tfrac{1}{2} = n$$

Both girls used the relationship that ¾ = ½ + ¼ to solve the problem. Emily drew pictures (Figure 8–4). Katy reasoned without pictures. She said, "I knew that ¾ was ½ and ¼, so I put the halves together and then with the 1 that makes 2 (wholes). And then there's ¼ left, so 2 and 1 fourth."

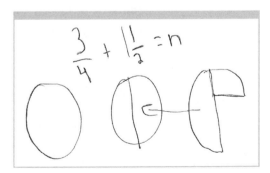

Figure 8–4. *Emily's solution to ¾ + 1½ = n*

Ms. Lewis made the next problem a little harder:

$$\tfrac{1}{2} + \tfrac{3}{8} = p$$

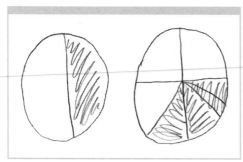

Figure 8–5. *Katy's solution to ½ + ⅜*

Both girls again related the fractions to a common fractional unit and both used pictures to facilitate reasoning about the relationships (Figure 8–5). Katy said, "I did a half and I knew that that was ⁴⁄₈. And then this is ⅜ and I added them together and I got ⅞." Emily drew a single circled partitioned into eighths. She shaded in ⁴⁄₈ of it and said that was equal to ½. And then she shaded in ⅜ more. She said that it was ⅞ because "it only took 1 more to make the whole."

Finally, Ms. Lewis gave a problem that involved two fractions where neither could be easily expressed in terms of the other:

$$\tfrac{1}{2} + \tfrac{2}{3} = m$$

After some thinking and drawing models, Katy exclaimed, "This one's hard! How many thirds is a half?" Emily said, "Well, ⅔ is the same as ⁴⁄₆." Ms. Lewis asked her how she knew and she said, "1 third is the same as ²⁄₆, so ⅔ would have to be ⁴⁄₆." But she was not sure how this insight could help her add the fraction to ½.

> **Emily:** Well a half is ²⁄₄, but that doesn't help.
> **Ms. Lewis:** What would help?
> **Emily:** Oh, Some sort of sixths, that would help. Wait, a half is ³⁄₆!
> **Katy:** Yes, it is.
> **Emily:** Oh, ³⁄₆ plus ⁴⁄₆, that's ⁷⁄₆.

Ms. Lewis had Emily elaborate her strategy for Katy, and Katy agreed, "Yes, ⁷⁄₆." Emily said, "It's ⅙ more than 1. ⁷⁄₆ is 1 and ⅙."

Ms. Lewis regularly reviews students' strategies so that she can design problems to help specific students extend what they know. Sometimes, like today, she designs these problems on the spot and spends some extra time with the students. Other times, she writes the problems beforehand for the entire class. Sometimes, she poses carefully sequenced problems in a single lesson; others times, they are spread out over a few days.

The addition and subtraction problems that Ms. Lewis posed were sequenced to involve increasingly challenging equivalent fraction relationships. Emily and Katy used pictures as tools to help them reason about these relationships. Problems with familiar fractions such as halves, fourths, and eighths or thirds and sixths are easiest for children to solve, because children's early understanding of equivalent fractions is strongest for those fractions. Next easiest are problems where one denominator is twice the size of another, such as $\frac{3}{10} + \frac{2}{20}$. Finally, problems whose denominators have a common factor (other than 2), such as $\frac{4}{5} + \frac{9}{20}$ and $\frac{1}{9} + \frac{1}{3}$ tend to be easier than problems involving fractions whose denominators have no common factor, such as $\frac{2}{3} + \frac{1}{4}$ and $\frac{5}{9} + \frac{4}{7}$.

Word problems can provide a context for adding or subtracting that support children to identify the units that can be counted as wholes, such as inches or cups, and relate them to fractional units. For example:

GABRIEL USED A RAIN GAUGE to measure the rainfall for 1 week. One day, it rained 2.85 inches. Another day, it rained .4 of an inch. There was no rain the rest of the week. How much rain fell that week?

RORY IS MAKING BROWNIES from a boxed mix. She wants to combine 2 boxes. 1 box calls for ½ of a cup of water. The other calls for ⅓ of a cup of water. How much water will Rory need to make brownies?

Solving and discussing word problems before equations helps children verbalize the need for a common unit and avoid mistaken strategies such as $\frac{1}{2} + \frac{1}{3} = \frac{2}{5}$.

Ms. Lewis' problems represent one possible way to sequence problems for children who are just beginning to add and subtract fractions with unlike denominators. Here is a similar sequence for more experienced students, which could be put into word problems or given as number problems:

$3/4 + 1/2$

$4/6 + 1/3$

$11/12 - 2/3$

$1/6 + 2/15$

Addition and subtraction of decimals is easier (as long as children understand decimals) because the possible common units are given—tenths, hundredths, thousandths, and so on. Students do not need to find them. Problems involving mixed numbers and fractions, such as the following, help students relate whole numbers and fractions:

$1 - 1/3$	$4 - 1.5$
$60 - 5/8$	$2 - .1$
$12 7/8 + 10 1/2$	$10 - .28$
$7 1/8 - 3 3/4$	$3.2 - 1.01$

If you give students a mix of addition and subtraction problems that include problems involving mixed numbers and those involving only proper fractions, it will help develop students' ability to look at a problem in its entirety to decide what relationships could be used to simplify the problem.

Standard Algorithms for Adding and Subtracting Fractions

The most difficult part of adding or subtracting fractions with unlike denominators is finding a common fractional unit to use to express both fractions. Many teachers show students how to find a common denominator by finding the least common multiple (LCM) between the two denominators as the first step in adding fractions with unlike denominators. Other teachers teach fraction addition by teaching students to use this algorithm:

$$\frac{a}{b} + \frac{c}{d} = \frac{(ad + cb)}{bd}$$

Both of these procedures can be cumbersome and, if introduced too early, students' attention is focused on following steps without understanding how they relate to finding common units or combining fractions. For example, a fourth grader who used the second procedure to correctly compute ⅞ + ⁸⁄₁₉ told us, "I have no idea why this works. I don't even know why this is adding." When we asked her to solve ½ + ⅚ in a way that made sense to her, she said, "½ is the same as ³⁄₆. ³⁄₆ and ⅚ is ⁸⁄₆, which is 1 and ²⁄₆ or 1 and ⅓."

If students are given time to grapple with the problem of finding common fractional units—as Katy and Emily were, above—they learn how to find common units to add and subtract at the same time as they develop their understanding of equivalent fractions and the fundamental properties of operations and equality. In the long run, students who do not have an integrated understanding of these things will be hard-pressed to understand how to simplify algebraic expressions such as these:

$$\frac{3}{2x} + \frac{6}{x}$$

$$\frac{4}{x^2 - 1} + \frac{6}{x + 1}$$

It takes a lot of practice for most students to remember standard procedures for adding or subtracting fractions by finding a common denominator. This practice does not necessarily lead to understanding, and so it's important that students have some conceptual understanding in place before you introduce them to such procedures. As a rule of thumb, if students do not have intuitive strategies for solving the problems on page 186, then they are not ready to learn standardized procedures for adding and subtraction fractions.

Multiplication and Division

The multiplication and division problems that we introduced in Chapters 1 and 3 involved a whole number of groups with a fractional amount in each group. In this chapter, we introduce Partial Groups problems. These are multiplication and

It is my role to support students to help them develop an understanding of fraction relationships. I want to teach my kids to navigate the world—not just solve the school math problems. My goal is to help kids develop a real understanding of the ideas rather than just learn procedures to follow. When I teach for understanding, I need to think about what the kid knows and build on that. If we limit our curriculum to procedures to follow, then students learn that this math is only used in math class. Teachers say they will need the procedures for next year's math. This is not acceptable to me. We need to teach children things that are inherently worthwhile, not just things that they need for next year.

Kids are at different levels of understanding, and I need to build on their understanding, but this doesn't mean that we are all solving different problems during math class. All of my students work on the same problem, but different students use different numbers and different students use different strategies. All of my students learn and are challenged. They share their ideas with each other, and they all learn from each other.

I know that many kids get to middle school without knowing procedures for fraction computation. If we show them what to do, they can get the right answer. But this doesn't mean that they learned. My goal isn't to get them to be able to get the right answer for twenty problems. My goal is for them to learn mathematics. If the problems are simple enough that they can solve twenty of them in an hour, then they are just practicing. Sometimes that is OK, but we can't tell ourselves that kids are learning important mathematics when they are doing this.

Kathy Oker,
sixth- to eighth-grade teacher
Wingra School
Madison, WI

division word problems in which the number of groups is not a whole number, such as:

I HAVE 2½ BAGS OF CANDY. A bag of candy weighs ½ pound. How many pounds of candy do I have?

I HAVE ¾ BAG OF CANDY. A full bag of candy weighs ½ pound. How many pounds of candy do I have?

In these problems, each bag represents a group. They are multiplication problems, because we know the number of groups and the amount per group (½ pound). Partial Groups problems may have a mixed number of groups (2½ bags) or less than 1 group (¾ bag). These problems pose new conceptual challenges, because they involve working with parts of parts and relating a part to two different units. For example, the second problem involves ¾ of ½ of 1 pound and the same amount of candy is both ¾ of a bag and ⅜ of a pound.

We distinguish as before between Multiplication, Measurement Division, and Partitive Division. It can be challenging to think of Partial Groups problems in terms of the number of groups and the number in each group, especially when the number of groups is less than 1. Many teachers find it helpful to substitute whole numbers for the fractions in these problems to decide whether a quantity represents the number of groups, the amount per group, or the total amount. For example, if we substitute whole numbers for the fractions in the candy problem above, you may find it easier to identify the problem type:

I HAVE 3 BAGS OF CANDY. A bag of candy weighs 4 pounds. How many pounds of candy do I have?

As you study the problems in Figure 8–6 and later in the chapter, you may want to try substituting whole numbers to see if it helps you clarify what type of problem it is.

When we write number sentences for these problems in the form of $a \times b = c$, we adopt the convention that a (the multiplier) stands for the number of groups and b (the multiplicand) stands for the amount per group. Because students distinguish between the number of groups and the amount per group,[1] this convention helps students understand each other's number sentences.

Children with prior experience solving Multiple Groups problems are quite capable of solving these problems without direct instruction in standard algorithms. At first, many children draw to solve these problems and use pictures to identify critical relationships. Later, they use Relational Thinking in increasingly sophisticated ways.

You can support children to use and extend their understanding of basic relationships by sequencing problems to reflect increasingly complex relationships. In the following sections, we present a variety of number choices from simple to complex for multiplication and division word problems and discuss some of the most significant aspects of children's evolving thinking about these operations, including their relationship to algebraic thinking.

Multiplication: Operating on Units

Multiplication problems in which the multiplier (number of groups) is a whole number are easier than problems where the multiplier is a fraction or a decimal:

Problem A. JOSIE HAD 20 CANS OF PAINT with ⅞ liter of paint in each can. How many liters of paint does Josie have?

---

[1] Some teachers find it helpful to think of the amount per group as a *unit rate*. In Measurement Division, a unit rate is *given*. For example, for the problems in Figure 8–6, ¾ *pound of candy per box* is a unit rate, because it represents the amount per group, in this case, a box. In Partitive Division, the unit rate is *unknown*. In Figure 8–6, ⅔ box of candy weighs ½ pound and the *amount of candy in a full box* is unknown. The idea of unit rate generalizes to other contexts such as rate and change over time (miles per hour, for example) and proportional reasoning problems.

Problem Type	Number of Groups (is not a whole number)	Amount per Group	Total Amount	Possible Equation
Partial Groups: Multiplication *I have 2/3 box of candy. A full box of candy weighs 3/4 pound. How many pounds of candy do I have?*	$\frac{2}{3}$	$\frac{3}{4}$	Unknown	$\frac{2}{3} \times \frac{3}{4} = b$
Partial Groups: Measurement Division *A full box of candy weighs 3/4 pound. I have 1/2 pound of candy. How much of a box do I have?*	Unknown	$\frac{3}{4}$	$\frac{1}{2}$	$c \times \frac{3}{4} = \frac{1}{2}$
Partial Groups: Partitive Division *I have 2/3 box of candy. It weighs 1/2 pound. How many pounds does a full box of candy weigh?*	$\frac{2}{3}$	Unknown	$\frac{1}{2}$	$\frac{2}{3} \times a = \frac{1}{2}$

Figure 8–6. *Partial Groups problems*

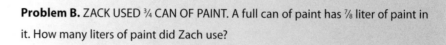

Problem B. ZACK USED ¾ CAN OF PAINT. A full can of paint has ⅞ liter of paint in it. How many liters of paint did Zach use?

Problem A is a Multiple Groups problem since the multiplier (number of groups) is 20. Problem B is a Partial Groups problem since the multiplier (number of groups) is ¾. Children can solve problem A by combining groups of ⅞. Even the most sophisticated strategies for solving problem A do not require finding a part of ⅞. To solve problem B, however, children need to find a part of ⅞. Specifically, they need to find ¾ of ⅞. That is, they need to find a part of a part.

Posing a Sequence of Problems to Develop Multiplication Strategies

Bella was a fourth grader whose class had been solving and discussing Multiple Groups problems. Her teacher, Ms. Reinhardt, decided that students were ready for some simple Partial Groups problems. She provided three choices for the multiplier:

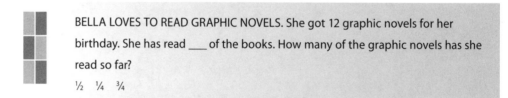

BELLA LOVES TO READ GRAPHIC NOVELS. She got 12 graphic novels for her birthday. She has read ___ of the books. How many of the graphic novels has she read so far?

½   ¼   ¾

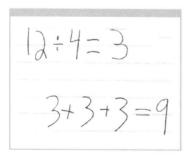

Figure 8–7. Bella's strategy for ¾ × 12

Like Ms. Andrews in Chapter 7, Ms. Reinhardt provided number choices that increased in difficulty and encouraged her students to solve the problem using the numbers that they felt were a "just-right" challenge.

Bella solved the problem using ¾. Showing her work to Ms. Reinhardt (Figure 8–7) she explained, "First I found a fourth of 12.

12 divided by 4 is 3. And then I needed to find ¾ of 12. So it needed to be 3 groups of 3, that is 9."

Bella used an intuitive understanding of the associative property to break the problem down into two easier computations. Her thinking followed this logic:

$$¾ \times 12 = (3 \times ¼) \times 12 \quad \textit{Relational understanding of ¾}$$
$$= 3 \times (¼ \times 12) \quad \textit{Associative property of multiplication}$$

She began by decomposing ¾ into $3 \times ¼$ so that she could find ¼ of 12, because that was easier to figure than ¾ of 12. She then knew that she could multiply that result by 3 to find ¾ of 12.

Ms. Reinhardt decided to pose another problem just for Bella, to see if she could extend her thinking. Ms. Reinhardt observed that Bella did not rely on the structure of the story to help her solve the previous problem, so she posed the next problem as a number sentence rather than a word problem. She chose a whole number, 22, that was not evenly divisible by 4:

$$¾ \times 22 = j$$

Bella went off to solve the problem while Ms. Reinhardt worked with other students. She returned a few minutes later and showed Ms. Reinhardt her work (Figure 8–8).

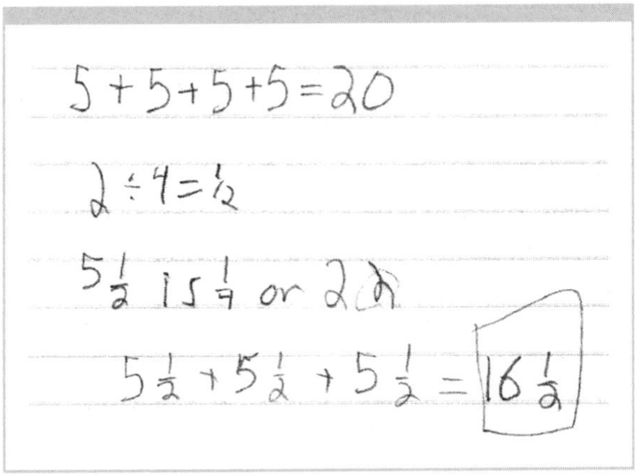

Figure 8–8. *Bella's strategy for ¾ × 22*

Bella's strategy followed the same logic as her first one. First, she told Ms. Reinhardt that she found ¼ of 22 by breaking the computation down into two simpler computations. She said, "I did ¼ of 20 because it's easy. It's 5 since 5 + 5 + 5 + 5 = 20. Then I needed to do ¼ of 2. 2 divided by 4 is ½, so ¼ of 2 is a half.

So ¼ of 22 is 5 and a half. Then, like before, I was finding ¾, so I just added 5 and a half plus 5 and a half plus 5 and a half, which is 16 and a half."

Now Ms. Reinhardt was wondering if Bella could apply her strategy to multiply two fractions less than 1. She was not planning to give these problems to the rest of the class, but saw that Bella's strategy could be extended in this way. She posed this problem to Bella:

$$¾ \times ½ = p$$

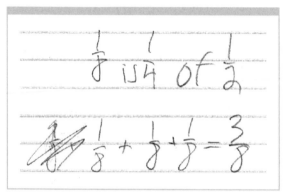

Figure 8–9. *Bella's strategy for ¾ × ½*

Again Bella went off to solve the problem while Ms. Reinhardt worked with other children. (We encourage you to pause here and think about how to apply Bella's strategy to this problem.) A few minutes later, Bella showed Ms. Reinhardt her work (Figure 8–9).

She reported that she solved it just the same as the problem before. Ms. Reinhardt asked her how she knew that ¼ of ½ was ⅛. Bella said that "half of a half is ¼ and half of a fourth is ⅛ so ⅛ is ¼ of ½." Once she had found ¼ of ½ was ⅛, she multiplied ⅛ by 3, as before. Bella was continuing to apply the associative property of multiplication to simplify each problem:

$$(3 \times ¼) \times ½ = 3 \times (¼ \times ½)$$

Finally, Ms. Reinhardt posed this problem for Bella:

$$¾ \times ⅞ = y$$

and asked her if she could use her strategy for that one. It is considerably harder than the other problems because finding ¼ of ⅞ is challenging. Bella said, "First I would need to find ¼ of ⅛. I don't know if I could do that. Half of an eighth is ¹⁄₁₆. This one is hard." It was time for lunch and so they stopped. Bella may have reached the limit of what she could do then and Ms. Reinhardt did not feel the need to press her to solve the problem.

Problem Difficulty. In this sequence, Ms. Reinhardt gradually increased the difficulty of the problems to extend Bella's thinking. She kept the multiplier, $\frac{3}{4}$, the same in all of the problems. The difficulty of a multiplication problem depends whether the multiplier is a unit fraction such as $\frac{1}{4}$ or a nonunit fraction such as $\frac{3}{4}$. It also depends on the relationship between the multiplier and the fraction that is multiplied. Each sequence of problems in Figure 8–10 increases in difficulty from top to bottom and from left to right. These problems are written so that as students move down a column they can extend their reasoning on one problem to solve the next, more challenging problem.

$\frac{1}{3} \times 15 = m$	$.1 \times 35 = n$	$\frac{2}{3} \times 12 = z$
$\frac{1}{3} \times 10 = x$	$.1 \times 4 = y$	$\frac{2}{3} \times 10 = k$
$\frac{1}{3} \times \frac{3}{4} = a$	$.3 \times 4 = b$	$\frac{2}{3} \times \frac{1}{4} = d$
$\frac{1}{3} \times \frac{7}{10} = c$	$.3 \times .4 = d$	$\frac{2}{3} \times \frac{5}{6} = f$
$\frac{1}{3} \times 6\frac{3}{4} = h$	$.3 \times 20.4 = t$	$\frac{2}{3} \times 3\frac{5}{6} = h$
$\frac{1}{3} \times 8\frac{7}{10} = g$	$.3 \times 22.4 = y$	$\frac{2}{3} \times 4\frac{5}{6} = k$

Figure 8–10. Multiplication equations arranged in order of difficultly

Standard Algorithm for Multiplying Fractions

Deon, a sixth grader, solved $\frac{3}{4} \times \frac{7}{8}$ using a Relational Thinking strategy (Figure 8–11). He explained, "With these problems you can first find $\frac{1}{8}$ of $\frac{3}{4}$ and then multiply by 7. That will give you $\frac{7}{8}$ of $\frac{3}{4}$."

Deon's strategy is efficient and draws on his integrated understanding of fractions as relational, multiplication properties, and parts of parts. An additional benefit of this Relational Thinking approach is that it can be more efficient than the standard algorithm for multiplying mixed numbers. Figure 8–12 shows how Deon solved $63\frac{3}{4} \times \frac{2}{3}$.

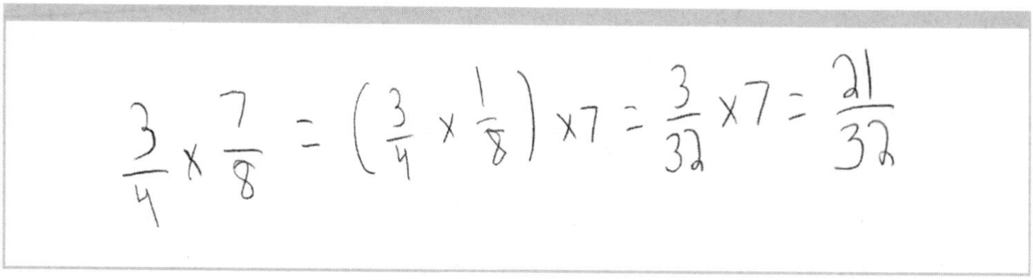

$$\frac{3}{4} \times \frac{7}{8} = \left(\frac{3}{4} \times \frac{1}{8}\right) \times 7 = \frac{3}{32} \times 7 = \frac{21}{32}$$

Figure 8–11. *Deon's strategy for ¾ × ⅞*

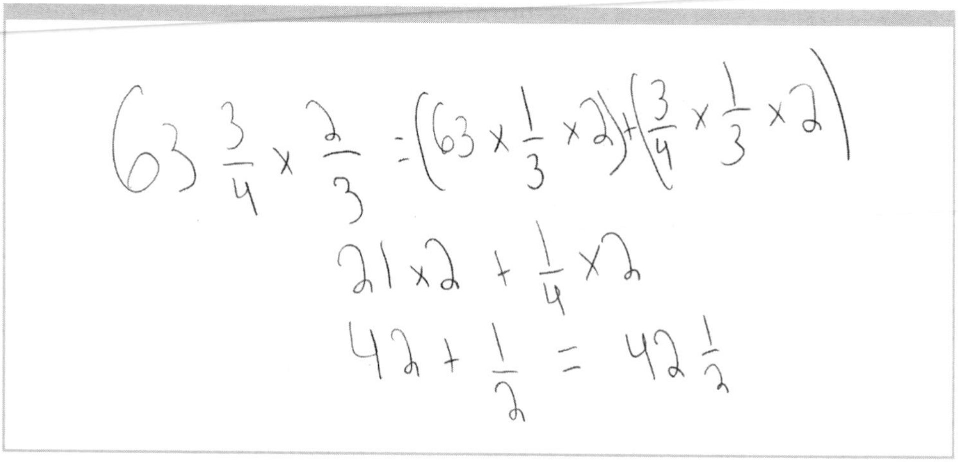

$$63\frac{3}{4} \times \frac{2}{3} = \left(63 \times \frac{1}{3} \times 2\right) + \left(\frac{3}{4} \times \frac{1}{3} \times 2\right)$$

$$21 \times 2 + \frac{1}{4} \times 2$$

$$42 + \frac{1}{2} = 42\frac{1}{2}$$

Figure 8–12. *A Relational Thinking strategy for 63¾ × ⅔*

Deon's classmate Gus solved 63¾ × ⅔ using a standard algorithm (Figure 8–13). His work is correct, but required more writing and more calculating than Deon's strategy.

Students like Bella and Deon who are supported to develop Relational Thinking strategies for multiplying fractions understand how to use the associative and distributive properties to multiply fractions. Although the standard algorithm for multiplying fractions is easy for students to remember, it is hard to understand why it works.

$$\frac{3}{4} \times \frac{7}{8} = \frac{3 \times 7}{4 \times 8} = \frac{21}{32}$$

Deon's strategy is almost identical to the standard algorithm for multiplying fractions, except the explicit use of the associative property makes his strategy easier to understand and it does not require conversion from a mixed number to an improper

$$63\frac{3}{4} \times \frac{2}{3} = \frac{255}{4} \times \frac{2\,'}{3} = \frac{255}{6} = 42\frac{3}{6} = 42\frac{1}{2}$$

$$\begin{array}{r} 63 \\ \times\ 4 \\ \hline 25\,2 \end{array} \qquad \begin{array}{r} 42\ R\,3 \\ 6\overline{)255} \\ \underline{24} \\ 15 \\ \underline{12} \\ 3 \end{array}$$

Figure 8–13. *Standard algorithm for 63¾ × ⅔ can be less efficient*

fraction. Students with experience using strategies like Deon's are ready to be introduced to a standard algorithm such as the one above for multiplying fractions. When students understand relationships between multiplication and the fundamental properties, they are prepared to examine why this standard algorithm works and to consider when using it is a more efficient strategy and when it is not.

Division: Dealing with Partial Groups

Partial Groups Measurement and Partitive Division involve a number of groups (the multiplier) that is not a whole number. Each type of division poses different challenges for students.

Measurement Division. A fifth-grade teacher gave her class the following Measurement Division problem:

SHEILA DRINKS ¾ OF A CUP of water for every mile that she hikes. Her water bottle holds 5 cups of water. How far can she hike before her water runs out?

It's Measurement Division because the amount per group (¾ cup per mile) is known and the number of groups (how many miles she can hike) is unknown. The context of this problem admits a non–whole number of groups as the answer because it is possible to hike a non–whole number of miles.

Figure 8-14. *Solving a division problem*

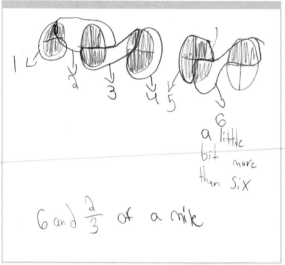

Figure 8-15. *Lyla's strategy for how many groups of ¾ are in 5*

Lyla solved the problem by drawing each of the cups of water and partitioning them into fourths. She counted every group of 3 fourths as 1 mile of hiking (Figure 8–15). After counting 6 groups, she saw that she had ²⁄₄ cup left and wrote, "a little bit more than 6," because she knew it could not count for another mile. Her teacher asked her how much of a mile the last ²⁄₄ cup of water would last. Lyla studied the relationship between the leftover amount of water and the amount of water she needed for a whole mile and reasoned that because it took ¾ cup for a whole mile, ²⁄₄ cup would last for ²⁄₃ mile. Her final answer was that the water would last for 6²⁄₃ miles. Lyla understood that the leftover water was both ²⁄₄ of a cup of water *and* ²⁄₃ of the water needed for 1 mile.

Tanner, a sixth grader, used similar reasoning for a similar type of problem but represented the fractional quantities with numbers rather than pictures (see Figure 8–16). The problem was:

 A BATCH OF PEANUT BUTTER COOKIES calls for ⅝ cup of peanut butter. A baker has 2⅝ cups of peanut butter. How many batches of cookies can she make, using up all of the peanut butter?

As above, the number of groups (batches) that can be made is not a whole number. The student needed to relate the leftover quantity, ⅛ cup of peanut butter, to the amount per group, ⅝ cup of peanut butter per batch. Because a whole batch calls for a total of ⅝ cup, ⅛ cup can make ⅕ of a batch.

These strategies illustrate the challenge posed by Measurement Division problems. Both strategies involved finding as many whole groups as possible and then relating the leftover amount to the amount per group. In particular, children had to find a multiplicative relationship between two fractions. For the first problem, the amount per group was ¾ cup of water for every mile and the leftover amount was ½ cup of water. For the

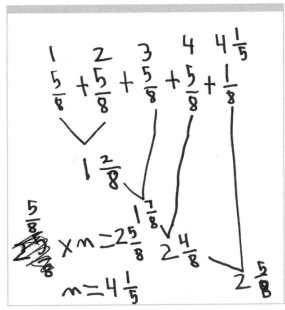

Figure 8–16 *Tanner finds how many five-eighths are in 2⅝*

second problem, the amount per group was ⅝ cup per batch and the leftover amount was ⅛ cup of peanut butter (see Figure 8–17).

It's easy for children to confuse the unit of measure for a group with other units of measure in the problem. For example, sometimes children will say that because ½ cup of water is leftover, it can last for ½ mile. If this happens, you can try reminding

	Water Problem	Cookie Problem
Amount per group	¾ cup per mile	⅝ cup per batch
How much is left over?	½ cup	⅛ cup
How much of a group is the leftover amount?	⅔ mile	⅕ batch
Relationship	½ is ⅔ of ¾	⅛ is ⅕ of ⅝

Figure 8–17. *The relationship between the leftover amount and the amount per group*

students to think about how much water is needed for a whole mile and ask how $\frac{1}{2}$ cup is related to this amount.

As children's strategies for these kinds of Measurement Division problems evolve, they use Relational Thinking in increasingly efficient ways. This development parallels the development of children's strategies for Multiple Groups problems. Eventually, students use multiplicative strategies similar to those described in Chapters 4 and 5.

For example, David, a sixth grader, used a multiplicative strategy to solve this Measurement Division problem (see Figure 8–18).

IT TAKES $\frac{4}{9}$ JAR of blue pigment to mix a gallon of paint that is just the right shade of sky blue. How many gallons of paint can I make with 13 jars of pigment?

When we asked David to explain how he solved this problem, he said, "I needed to find out how many $\frac{4}{9}$ there were in 13. I knew it would be easier if I could work with a whole number. 9 times $\frac{4}{9}$ is 4, which is a whole number. Then I had to figure out how many fours there were in 13. 3 times 4 is 12 and then I needed 1 more to make 13, so it's 3 groups of 4 plus some part of a group. 1 is $\frac{1}{4}$ of 4 so $3\frac{1}{4}$ times 4 is 13. If I did $3\frac{1}{4}$ times 9, I would figure out how many four-ninths are in 13. $3\frac{1}{4}$ times 9 is 3 times 9, which is 27, plus $\frac{1}{4}$ times 9, which is $2\frac{1}{4}$, and so altogether it is $29\frac{1}{4}$."

$$\_ \times \frac{4}{9} = 13$$

$$9 \times \frac{4}{9} = 4$$

$$\_ \times 4 = 13$$

$$3\frac{1}{4} \times 4 = 13$$

$$3\frac{1}{4} \times 9 \times \frac{4}{9} = 13$$

$$\boxed{29\frac{1}{4}} \times \frac{4}{9} = 13$$

Figure 8–18. *David finds how many four-ninths are in 13*

David used multiplication to work efficiently to solve this problem. He relied on relationships that were well known to him, including in particular $\frac{n}{m} \times m = n$. He related smaller groupings (9 groups of ⁴⁄₉ is 4) to larger groupings (how many groups of 4 is 13) by applying the associative property of multiplication:

$$3\tfrac{1}{4} \times (9 \times \tfrac{4}{9}) = (3\tfrac{1}{4} \times 9) \times \tfrac{4}{9}$$

Students such as David are well-equipped to learn and understand a standard algorithm for dividing fractions.

Partitive Division. Equal Sharing problems are Partitive Division problems that involve a whole number of groups. For example:

> 8 BAGS OF COFFEE WEIGH 6 POUNDS. How much does 1 bag of coffee weigh?

In this problem, pounds of coffee are "shared" among 8 bags of coffee. The amount per group, or bag, is unknown. This problem may help you see how the following Partial Groups problems is also Partitive Division:

> ⅗ BAG OF COFFEE WEIGHS ⁶⁄₇ POUND. How much does a whole bag of coffee weigh?

The question is still, what is the amount of coffee per group, or bag? We know the total amount of coffee (⁶⁄₇ pound) and the number of groups (⅗ bag). What differs is that there is only a fraction of a group (⅗ bag) instead of multiple groups (8 bags). To illustrate some issues in solving these problems, we describe how two sixth graders solved this second problem.

Denzel drew a picture to represent 1 bag and show how much ⅗ bag weighs (see Figure 8–19). He said, "When I looked at this I saw that each fifth of a bag had to be ²⁄₇ pounds. For the whole bag, I needed to add ²⁄₇ 5 times to make 5 fifths. So I added ²⁄₇ plus ²⁄₇ plus ²⁄₇ plus ²⁄₇ plus ²⁄₇. That's ¹⁰⁄₇, so that's what the whole bag weighs."

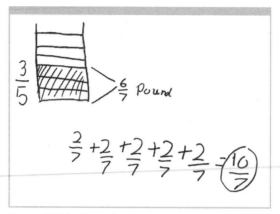

Figure 8–19. *Denzel's solution to a Partitive Division problem*

Figure 8–20 shows how Keesha solved the same problem. She said, "I first figured out that ⅕ of the bag would be ²⁄₇ of a pound. Then I found that ⅖ of the bag would be ⁴⁄₇ of a pound. I knew if I added what ⅗ of the bag weighed to what ⅖ of the bag weighed, I would have the whole bag. That is 1³⁄₇." Like Denzel, Keesha first found how much ⅕ bag would weigh and then built up to what a whole bag (⁵⁄₅ bag) would weigh. She found the weight of ⅕ bag by dividing ⁶⁄₇ by 3, because ⁶⁄₇ bag weighed 3 × ⅕ = ⅗ pound.

It is especially difficult for students to identify word problems like this one as division before they attempt a solution. Students who are taught to solve problems by first writing an equation and then solving the equation often struggle with Partitive Division. We posed the problem above to Jan, a fifth-grade student who had been accelerated into a ninth-grade mathematics curriculum. She read the problem and wrote the equation:

$$\tfrac{3}{5} \times \tfrac{6}{7} = n$$

and then quickly solved it using the standard algorithm:

$$n = {}^{18}\!/_{35}$$

We asked her to estimate the value of $^{18}/_{35}$ and she said ½. We next asked her if it made sense that a full bag of coffee would weigh about half a pound when

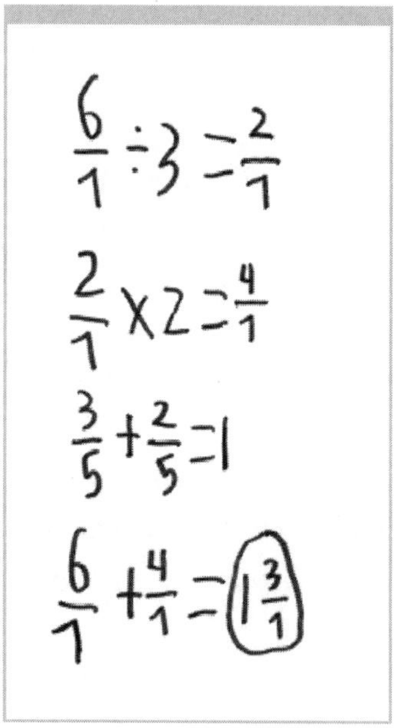

Figure 8–20. *Keesha's solution to the same Partitive Division problem that Denzel solved*

⅗ of the bag weighed ⁶⁄₇ of a pound. Jan checked her computation and said that it did. We asked her to look at Denzel's work and pointed out that he had gotten a different answer. She replied that she was in an advanced mathematics class and did not draw pictures anymore. She checked her computation again and maintained that her answer was right. Jan's conviction that writing an equation and solving it with a standard algorithm was the correct way to solve this problem interfered with her ability to make sense of her work in light of the context of the word problem. Although she knew how to multiply fractions, it did not help her to solve this problem.

Equations as Tools for Learning Division of Fractions

Using word problems to teach division of fractions helps students develop conceptual models for division that they can use later to solve equations. Figure 8–21 shows some examples of equations that can further develop students' understanding of fraction division. Students who understand division of fractions will use the same strategies to solve these problems as they do to solve word problems. Each sequence of equations increases in difficulty from top to bottom. These problems are written so that as students move down a column, they can extend their reasoning on one problem to solve the next, more challenging problem.

   Students can draw on two different conceptual models to solve these problems, which follow the structure of the word problems we have presented. An equation such as $3\frac{1}{2} \div \frac{3}{4} = n$ can be thought of as either (a) how many three-fourths are in

$6 \div \frac{1}{2} = n$	$8 \div .1 = p$	$6 \div \frac{3}{4} = n$
$3\frac{1}{2} \div \frac{1}{2} = j$	$8.4 \div .1 = y$	$7\frac{1}{2} \div \frac{3}{4} = h$
$\frac{3}{4} \div \frac{1}{2} = m$	$.45 \div .1 = h$	$8 \div \frac{3}{4} = t$
$6\frac{3}{4} \div \frac{1}{2} = y$	$8.42 \div .2 = j$	$5\frac{5}{8} \div 2\frac{3}{4} = q$
$6\frac{3}{4} \div 1\frac{1}{2} = y$	$8.45 \div 2.2 = t$	$3\frac{2}{3} \div \frac{3}{4} = t$
$6\frac{1}{5} \div 1\frac{1}{2} = h$	$8.04 \div 2.2 = w$	$\frac{2}{3} \div \frac{3}{4} = j$

Figure 8–21. *Division equations arranged in order of difficultly*

If $\frac{3}{5}$ of a bag of candy weighs $6\frac{3}{4}$ pounds how much does 1 bag of candy weigh?

$11\frac{1}{4}$ pounds

$$6\frac{3}{4} \div 3 = 2\frac{1}{4}$$

$$6 \div 3 = 2$$

$$\frac{3}{4} \div 3 = \frac{1}{4}$$

$$2\frac{1}{4} \times 5 = 11\frac{1}{4}$$

Figure 8-22. *Keesha's solution closely resembles the standard algorithm for division*

$3\frac{1}{2}$? (Measurement Division or $a \times \frac{3}{4} = 3\frac{1}{2}$), or (b) if $3\frac{1}{2}$ is $\frac{3}{4}$ of 1 group, how much is the whole group? (Partitive Division or $\frac{3}{4} \times b = 3\frac{1}{2}$). Depending on the numbers in the problem, sometimes one way of thinking about the division is more productive than the other. For $1\frac{7}{8} \div \frac{1}{2}$, it is easier to think, "If $1\frac{7}{8}$ is half of the group, how much is the whole group?" than, "How many one-halves fit in $1\frac{7}{8}$?" For $6\frac{1}{4} \div 2\frac{1}{2}$, it is probably easier to think, "How many 2 and one-halves are in $6\frac{1}{4}$?" than it is to think, "If $2\frac{1}{2}$ groups are $6\frac{1}{4}$, how much is 1 group?" Students who have a well-developed understanding of division are able to decide which conceptual model is best suited for the numbers in a given problem.

Standard Division Algorithm. The common "invert-and-multiply" algorithm for division of fractions is surprisingly similar to a common Relational Thinking strategy that students use for Partitive Division problems. For example, Keesha's reasoning for the following Partitive Division problem can be easily mapped onto the standard algorithm (see Figure 8–22).

IF ⅗ OF A BAG OF CANDY weighs 6¾ pounds, how much does 1 bag of candy weigh?

When we her asked to explain her thinking, she said, "When you divide by $\frac{3}{5}$, you can first divide by 3, and then you will know what $\frac{1}{5}$ of a bag weighs. Then you multiply by 5 and that tells you how much a whole bag weighs." We then asked, "How would you divide a number by $\frac{11}{9}$?", she said, "First you would divide by 9 and then multiply by 11." This is essentially inverting and multiplying.

$$\frac{a}{b} \div \frac{c}{d} = \frac{a}{b} \times \frac{d}{c} = \frac{(a \times d)}{(b \times c)}$$

$$6\tfrac{3}{4} \div \tfrac{3}{5} = 6\tfrac{3}{4} \div 3 \times 5 = 6\tfrac{3}{4} \times \tfrac{5}{3}$$

Similarly, students also use a strategy for Measurement Division that is close to the standard invert-and-multiply algorithm. For example, to solve

SHEILA DRINKS ¾ CUP of water for every mile that she hikes. Her water bottle holds 5 cups of water. How far can she hike before her water runs out?

Caroline said, "First I will find out how many one-fourths are in 5. Since there are 4 one-fourths in 1, there are 5 times 4 or 20 one-fourths in 5. But I really need to find out how many three-fourths are in 5. There will be $\frac{1}{3}$ as many three-fourths in 5 as there are one-fourths in 5. 20 divided by 3 is $6\frac{2}{3}$." Again, the strategy essentially involves invert and multiply[2]:

$$5 \div \tfrac{3}{4} = 5 \div \tfrac{1}{4} \div 3 = 5 \times 4 \div 3 = 5 \times \tfrac{4}{3}$$

As with the other operations, if students are encouraged to develop Relational Thinking strategies to solve division of fractions problems before they learn the standard algorithm, they are better prepared to understand how it works and when to use

---

[2] Another, less common way to solve this problem that is directly related to invert and multiply involves counting the number of *miles per cup*. Each cup of water is good for $1\frac{1}{4}$ or $\frac{4}{3}$ mile. There are 5 cups of water. So the number of miles for which the water can last is $5 \times \frac{4}{3} = \frac{20}{3} = 6\frac{2}{3}$.

It is important to me that students first think about the problem before they even begin solving it. They need to read the problem and understand what it is saying. It doesn't matter if it is a story problem or an equation. They need to start with questions like, "Do I understand this? How can I visualize this in my head? If I don't understand this or can't visualize this, what do I need to do so that I can get it?" When students start this way, they don't just think, "This is an addition of fractions problem, and this is the way to do those problems," but they think about what is happening in the problem, what the numbers are, and what relationships they can use to solve the problem. It is similar to making connections in reading, but students are making connections to other problems they have solved and what they know about number and operations.

I didn't show my students how to add fractions. When I gave them the problem $3/4$ plus $7/8$, they knew that they couldn't add the 3 and the 7 because they understood that adding only worked when the units were the same. They first worked to make the units the same and then they added the numbers. I also didn't show them how to solve problems like $6\,3/7 - 2\,5/7$. They took what they understood from whole numbers and connected it to this problem. The students were thinking about what they knew, how their thinking made sense, and how it helped them solve the problem more easily.

I always want my students to analyze the problems to see which relationships work best. I never want them to just jump in and start solving the problem or to rely just on one strategy for all problems of a certain type.

Annie Keith
fourth/fifth-grade teacher, John Muir School
Madison, WI

it. Further, they will be better able to extend their understanding of fraction division to help them solve algebra problems that involve dividing algebraic expressions.

Relational Thinking and Thinking Mathematically

Relational Thinking enhances students' competency and efficiency with computation, and it helps them develop and reinforce concepts that they will need when they learn algebra. Relational Thinking also engages children in thinking processes that are essential to algebra, in that it involves reflecting on a problem before solving it to decide what relationships could be used to simplify the solution.

For example, David saw that he could find a whole number that was a multiple of ⁴⁄₉, and he understood how it would help him find the number of four-ninths in 13. Bella saw that she could find ¼ of ½ and then use it to figure ¾ × ½. Making these kinds of decisions is the essence of Relational Thinking and cannot be cultivated by having students practice specific strategies, whether the strategies are relational or algorithmic. Rather, students need opportunities *to practice deciding for themselves* how to go about solving a problem.

Students who have not been encouraged to decide for themselves how to proceed often use the tools they have been provided without reflection. For example, we gave the problem 300 – 299 to all of the sixth graders in one school ($n = 94$). Just under half of these students—45 percent—used a standard algorithm to find that the answer was 1 (see Figure 8–23).

Using a standard algorithm for this problem provides a vivid example of the "do next" mind set of using a standard algorithm. If these sixth graders had taken a moment to reflect, they would have easily seen that the difference between 300 and 299 was 1. Instead, they saw a subtraction problem and using the standard algorithm was cued, even though it was an inefficient and highly error-prone strategy here.

Similarly, we want students to be flexible enough in their thinking so that they do not automatically find a common denominator to

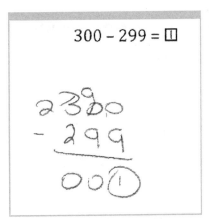

Figure 8–23. *How 45 percent of sixth graders in one school solved this problem*

Anticipatory Thinking and Its Relationship to Algebra

Framing a problem in terms of a goal and then relating that goal to simpler subgoals is a type of anticipatory thinking. As is the case for many Relational Thinking strategies, David's and Keesha's strategies involve anticipatory thinking. Anticipatory thinking is fundamental to high school algebra in which a series of properties of operations and equality are used to simplify a complex equation. Although equation solving can be taught as a series of steps to follow, the steps are justified by this interplay between the final goal and the related subgoals that lead from the problem to the solution.

For example, to solve a linear equation with one unknown (an equation that can be expressed as $ax + b = 0$ and where the goal is to find a value for x that will make the equation true), students set subgoals that involve finding successively simpler equations that take them closer to the goal of finding an equation of the form x equal to some number. For example, to solve $3x + 2 = 14$, students first simplify the problem to $3x = 12$ and then $x = 4$. Students are usually taught to do this step by step and lose the opportunity to actively set subgoals that make sense to them.

Just as in David's solution, the equation at each step is simplified by the application of fundamental properties of operations and equality. Similarly, the goal of solving a quadratic equation (an equation that can be expressed as $ax^2 + bx + c = 0$) can be transformed into subgoals of solving simpler linear equations by applying a corollary of the zero property of multiplication ($a \times b = 0$, if and only if $a = 0$ or $b = 0$).* In other words, the way David created and transformed equations to bring him closer and closer to the solution of the main problem is central to the process of solving algebra equations.

_____

* Many quadratic equations can be solved by factoring. For example, in the equation $3x^2 + 5x - 2 = 0$, the expression to the left of the equals sign can be factored: $(3x - 1)(x + 2) = 0$. The more complex quadratic expression has been transformed into the product of two simpler linear expressions. Because the product of these factors is 0, it means that one of the factors must also be 0, in order for the equation to be true.

compare $^{23}\!/_{98}$ and $^{22}\!/_{99}$ or convert to improper fractions to solve $\frac{1}{2} \times 486\frac{2}{3}$. Even a problem such as $20^8\!/_{15} \div 4$ can be easily solved without tedious calculation if students have been encouraged to work from their understanding of relationships.[3]

Reflecting Back and Looking Ahead

In this chapter, we examined children's thinking about the four operations involving fractions and decimals. Children's thinking about problems involving Partial Groups can be seen as an extension of children's strategies for Multiple Groups problems. Solving and discussing these problems provide students with further opportunities to develop their capacity for Relational Thinking. The capacity to think relationally contributes to understanding operations on fractions and decimals and prepares students to solve algebraic equations with insight. In the long run, a focus on thinking relationally about operations supports the development of mathematical proficiency more effectively than knowledge of standard algorithms alone.

_____

[3] The numbers in this problem, for example, are better suited for thinking of the division in terms of Equal Sharing rather than Measurement Division. To see this relationship requires a flexible understanding of possible interpretations of division and knowledge of divisibility by 4.

Problems for Operations on Fractions and Decimals

Here are some problems to use with your students to develop their understanding of operations on fractions and decimals. In general, it works best to use these problems with students who are able to use Relational Thinking to solve Equal Sharing problems and Multiple Groups problems. Refer to the instructional guide on page 217 for suggestions on choosing problems for your grade level.

Addition and Subtraction

A. Lupita has $2\frac{5}{6}$ packages of clay. She used $\frac{1}{3}$ package to make a model of a skull. How much clay does Lupita have left?

$(2, \frac{3}{4})$ $(1\frac{1}{2}, \frac{3}{4})$ $(2\frac{1}{6}, \frac{1}{2})$ $(3\frac{1}{8}, \frac{1}{2})$ $(2\frac{2}{3}, \frac{5}{6})$

B. Lisa is going on a $3\frac{1}{2}$ mile hike. She has already hiked $2\frac{3}{4}$ miles. How many more miles does she have left to hike?

C. Eric is $69\frac{1}{2}$ inches tall. Nick is $67\frac{3}{4}$ inches tall. How much taller is Eric than Nick?

D. A fence post needs to be set about $1\frac{1}{2}$ feet into the ground. How long should the entire post be if it is to stand 4 feet above ground?

E. Colton's mom made a big burrito for lunch. Colton ate $\frac{1}{3}$ burrito and his little brother Aidan ate $\frac{1}{4}$ burrito. How much of the burrito did the 2 boys eat at lunch? How much of the burrito was left?

F. Maggie made 3 pounds of fudge. She and her friends ate some of the fudge and now there are $1\frac{3}{4}$ pounds of fudge left. How many pounds of fudge did Maggie and her friends eat?

G. Jessie and Jocelyn were eating pancakes. Jessie poured ⅓ cup syrup on his pancakes. Jocelyn poured ⅛ cup syrup on hers. How much syrup did they use? If the bottle of syrup holds 1 cup, is there enough syrup for them to eat pancakes the next day if they each want to use the same amount?

H. Valeria planted a rectangular vegetable garden that is 2.4 meters long and 1.75 meters wide. She wants to put a fence around it. How many meters of fencing should she buy to completely enclose the garden?

I. Two boys were competing in a long jump. The first boy jumped 5.9 meters. The second boy jumped 7.22 meters. How much longer did the second boy jump than the first?

J. Two girls were competing in a 100-meter dash. The first girl ran it in 14.47 seconds. The second girl ran it in 13.88 seconds. How much faster was the second girl than the first?

Addition and Subtraction Equations

These equations involve combining fractions with common denominators and developing an understanding of how to group fractions to make whole units. If students struggle with these equations, it may mean they need more work with word problems.

A. $1 + \frac{5}{4} = a$

B. $10\frac{5}{8} - c = 10$

C. $1\frac{1}{4} - \frac{3}{4} = b$

D. $h = 2\frac{3}{4} + 5\frac{1}{4}$

E. $j = 3 - \frac{3}{8}$

F. $2\frac{5}{8} + \frac{7}{8} = k$

G. $8\frac{2}{3} + m = 9$

H. $n = \frac{4}{6} + 2\frac{5}{6}$

I. $5\frac{6}{10} - \frac{9}{10} = p$

These equations involve combining fractions with unlike denominators and solidify an understanding of equivalent fractions. In all of these examples, one denominator is a multiple of the other.

A. $y = \frac{3}{4} + \frac{1}{2}$

B. $\frac{3}{4} + \frac{3}{8} = w$

C. $\frac{3}{8} + x = \frac{3}{4}$

D. $\frac{1}{2} + \frac{5}{6} = v$

E. $\frac{1}{2} + \frac{1}{6} = r$

F. $\frac{1}{2} + t = \frac{7}{8}$

G. $a = \frac{1}{2} - \frac{1}{4}$

H. $\frac{5}{6} - \frac{1}{2} = b$

I. $\frac{5}{12} + \frac{1}{6} = d$

J. $\frac{8}{12} + \frac{5}{6} = m$

K. $p = \frac{3}{2} - \frac{3}{4}$

L. $\frac{3}{8} = \frac{1}{2} - k$

M. $c = \frac{1}{3} + \frac{1}{15}$

N. $f = \frac{1}{2} + \frac{1}{4} + \frac{1}{8}$

O. $\frac{1}{2} + \frac{1}{3} + \frac{1}{6} = h$

P. $k = \frac{9}{20} + \frac{3}{5}$

Q. $g = \frac{2}{9} + \frac{1}{3}$

R. $\frac{5}{16} - \frac{1}{4} = j$

S. $\frac{5}{16} + t = \frac{3}{4}$

T. $\frac{5}{16} + \frac{3}{4} = r$

U. $\frac{1}{3} = \frac{7}{15} - m$

V. $1\frac{8}{15} - \frac{2}{3} = p$

These equations involve combining fractions with unlike denominators where one denominator is not a multiple of the other.

A. $\frac{2}{3} + \frac{1}{2} = w$

B. $t = \frac{3}{4} + \frac{2}{3}$

C. $v = \frac{2}{3} + \frac{3}{5}$

D. $\frac{1}{3} + u = \frac{1}{2}$

E. $8\frac{1}{2} = 9\frac{1}{3} - x$

F. $7\frac{1}{4} - \frac{2}{3} = g$

G. $1\frac{3}{4} - 1\frac{2}{3} = d$

H. $3\frac{3}{5} + 2\frac{3}{4} = c$

I. $7\frac{1}{5} = 6\frac{1}{2} + b$

Is it more or less than 1?

A. $\frac{2}{3} + \frac{1}{4}$

B. $\frac{2}{8} + \frac{6}{7}$

C. $\frac{2}{3} + \frac{4}{9}$

D. $\frac{1}{12} + \frac{5}{6}$

Partial Groups Problems—Multiplication

   A. Jose has 2½ bags of candy. A bag of candy weighs 5 pounds. How many pounds of candy does Jose have?

   B. I drink 3½ cups of water for every mile that I hike. If I only hike ½ mile, how much water would I drink? If I hike 3½ miles, how much water would I drink?

   C. A homemade recipe for macaroni and cheese takes ⁸⁄₁₀ of a pound of cheese for each pan. Mom wants to make 2¼ pans of macaroni and cheese for a family gathering. How many pounds of cheese will she need to use?

   D. Dora had ____ quart of yellow paint to paint a bookcase. She used ____ of this paint. How much paint did Dora use for the bookcase?

   (⅓, ½)   (⅔, ½)   (⅘, ¼)   (⅘, ¾)

   E. Nick had 4 ice cream sandwiches. He ate ⅔ of them. How many ice cream sandwiches did he eat?

   F. Myra was watching a video online that was 6½ minutes long. The progress bar showed that she had watched ⅔ of the video. How many minutes had she watched?

   G. Autumn had ⅜ birthday cake left over from her party. She ate ¾ of the leftover cake for breakfast. How much of the whole cake did Autumn have at breakfast?

   H. It was ¾ mile from Lesley's house to the grocery store. She ran ⅔ of the way and walked the rest. How far did she run?

Partial Groups Problems—Measurement Division

Some of these problems include number choices that result in an answer that is a whole number of groups. The number choices that result in a whole number of groups are in **bold**; these problems are Multiple Groups rather than Partial Groups problems.

   A. The cross country track is 3 miles. If Samuel wanted to run for 8 miles, how many times around the track would he need to run?

   B. It takes ¾ cup of seeds to fill a bird feeder. How many birdfeeders can you fill with ____ cups of seeds?

   4½ **6** **18** 1 3¼ 5½

   C. It takes ____ cup of sugar to make a batch of cookies. I have 5½ cups of sugar. How many batches of cookies can I make?

   ½ ¼ ¾ ⅜

D. Andy makes $8 an hour raking leaves. He made $45 last weekend raking leaves. How many hours did he work?

E. Mom has ____ pounds of cheese. It takes ____ pound to make a pan of homemade macaroni and cheese. How many pans of macaroni and cheese can Mom make?

   (4½, 1¼)   (1⅘, ⁸⁄₁₀)

F. It takes ___ pint of paint to paint a whole bookcase. Lora has ___ pint of paint. How much of the bookcase can Lora cover before she runs out of paint?

   (¾, ½)   (⅚, ⅓)   (⅞, ³⁄₁₆)

G. A stretch of road 8½ miles long was damaged by freezing weather. Each day, workers repair ⅘ mile of road. At that rate, how long will it take them to repair the entire stretch?

Partial Groups Problems—Partitive Division (These problems tend to be most difficult when they involve a nonunit fraction such as ⅔ as the divisor)

A. Mom used 1⅘ pounds of cheese to make 3 pans of her homemade macaroni and cheese. How much cheese did she need for each pan?

B. The bakery had ___ chocolate chip cookies left over at the end of the day. They took up ___ tray. How many cookies fit on a whole tray?

   (14, ½)   (15, ¾)   (12, ⅔)

C. Mike can run ⅝ mile in ⅙ hour. How far can he run in an hour, if he runs at the same rate?

D. It takes me ___ hour to eat ___ pizza. At that rate, how long will it take me to eat a whole pizza?

   (¼, ½)   (¼, ⅓)   (¾, ⅓)   (¾, ⅔)

E. This weekend it took me ⅔ hour to clean ¼ of my house. At that rate, how long will it take me to clean the whole house?

F. Jason bought ⁴⁄₁₀ pound of jellybeans for $5. How much would a whole pound cost?

G. Lora used ½ can of paint to cover ⅔ of a bookcase. How much paint does she need to cover the whole bookcase?

H. 2½ bags of beads weigh 4 pounds. How much does one bag of beads weigh?

Area/Array Multiplication and Division

1) A rectangular plot of land has an area of $\frac{3}{5}$ square km. The plot is $\frac{3}{4}$ km long on one side. How long is the other side?

2) The bricklayer charges \$10 for each square foot of brick that she lays. If she laid bricks on a patio that was $6\frac{3}{4}$ feet long and $12\frac{1}{2}$ feet wide, how much money would she make?

Multiplication Equations

Equations can be particularly useful for developing Relational Thinking. These problems build off each other either down the column or across the row.

A. $\frac{1}{5} \times 10 = k$ $\frac{3}{5} \times 10 = j$

B. $\frac{1}{5} \times 12 = j$ $\frac{3}{5} \times 12 = p$

C. $\frac{1}{5} \times \frac{5}{8} = y$ $\frac{3}{5} \times \frac{5}{8} = t$

D. $\frac{1}{5} \times 10\frac{5}{8} = p$ $\frac{3}{5} \times 10\frac{5}{8} = y$

E. $\frac{1}{5} \times \frac{6}{10} = r$ $\frac{3}{5} \times \frac{6}{10} = k$

F. $\frac{1}{5} \times 8 = g$ $\frac{3}{5} \times 8 = y$

G. $\frac{1}{5} \times 8\frac{6}{10} = w$ $\frac{3}{5} \times 8\frac{6}{10} = k$

Division Equations

Students may interpret problems in terms of Measurement or Partitive Division or they may relate division to its inverse operation, multiplication. If students have difficulty solving these problems, they probably need more experience solving and discussing word problems involving division, including Multiple and Fractional Groups problems.

A. $a = \frac{3}{4} \div \frac{1}{4}$

B. $\frac{2}{3} \div 2 = b$

C. $\frac{5}{6} \div 5 = c$

D. $\frac{3}{4} \div \frac{3}{8} = d$

More Multiplication and Division Open Number Sentences

A. $\frac{1}{2} \times k = 5$

B. $\frac{1}{3} \times p = 2$

C. $\frac{2}{3} \times m = 3$

D. $\frac{2}{3} \times n = 6$

E. $\frac{3}{7} \times r = 3$

F. $m = \frac{5}{8} \div 5$

G. $\frac{3}{2} \div 3 = n$

H. $\frac{3}{2} \div 6 = q$

I. $h = 3\frac{3}{5} \div \frac{1}{5}$

J. $3\frac{3}{5} \div \frac{2}{5} = a$

K. $k \times 3 = \frac{1}{2}$

L. $\frac{5}{8} \times j = 5$

M. $\frac{1}{3} = y \times 4$

N. $4 = k \times \frac{4}{7}$

O. $6 \div c = 12$

P. $4 \div d = 12$

Q. $m \div \frac{1}{8} = 7$

R. $12 \times 2\frac{3}{4} = 24 + m$

S. $13\frac{1}{2} \times \frac{4}{5} = 27 \times k$

T. $48\frac{4}{5} \div 4 = 12 + j$

Variations

A. A pair of jeans was on sale for $\frac{1}{3}$ off the regular price. The regular price was $24. What was the sale price of the jeans?

B. Sean has a lawn-mowing business. The gas tank on his lawn mower holds $2\frac{1}{2}$ gallons. It takes about $\frac{5}{8}$ gallon to mow each yard. If his tank is full, does he have enough gas to mow 3 yards?

C. Gil and Harry ate a whole pizza. Harry ate $\frac{1}{2}$ as much as Gil. How much of the pizza did each boy eat?

D. Gil, Harry, and Isaac ate a whole pizza. Isaac ate $\frac{1}{3}$ as much as Gil and he ate $\frac{1}{2}$ as much as Harry. How much of the pizza did each boy eat? If the pizza cost $12, how much money should each boy contribute to paying for the pizza?

E. Selena used 28 meters of ribbon to makes bows and streamers. She used ¾ as much ribbon for bows and she did for streamers. How many meters of ribbon did she use for bows and how many for streamers?

F. Cassie and Samantha shared a foot-long submarine sandwich. Samantha ate ⅘ as much as Cassie. How much of the submarine sandwich did each girl eat?

Instructional Guidelines for Teaching Fraction Computation

In this section, we provide guidelines for teaching children to think relationally about operations involving fractions. Suggested problems include the operations of addition, subtraction, multiplication, and division. Students need experience with Equal Sharing problems (see Chapter 1) and Multiple Groups problems (see Chapter 3) before solving and discussing problem types from this chapter. We recommend that you read the suggestions for all of the grade levels rather than only for the grade level you teach. If students have a strong relational understanding of fraction computation before they learn standard algorithms, they will be more proficient, fluent, and confident in their reasoning about fractions and decimals and be able to apply these ideas to the study of algebra.

FIRST GRADE

✔ Most first grade children will not be ready for the problems in this chapter.

SECOND GRADE

✔ Addition and subtraction word problems involving like denominators or a whole number and a fraction, after students have experience with Equal Sharing problems. Focus on ½ and ¼ and decide whether to write the fractions in the problems as words ("a half") or symbols (½)—for example:

- *Jim had one-fourth of a quesadilla. His brother gave him another one-fourth of a quesadilla. How much quesadilla did Jim have then?*

- *Jo had 3 cupcakes. She ate ½ of a cupcake. How many cupcakes did she have left?*
- *Joey has 6½ dollars. How much more money does he need to have 7 dollars to buy a game that he wants?*
- *Pete had 2¾ pizzas. José had 1¼ pizzas. How much more pizza does Pete have than José?*

✔ **Partial Groups problems: Multiplication.** Choose problems where the multiplier (number of groups) is ½ or ¼—for example:

- *Emma had 12 cookies. She gave ½ of them to her brother. How many cookies did Emma's brother get?*
- *Emma had 12 cookies. She gave ¼ of them to her sister. How many cookies did Emma's sister get?*

THIRD GRADE

✔ **Addition and Subtraction word problems involving like denominators,** after students have experience with Equal Sharing problems. Focus on ½, ¼, ⅓, ⅛, ⅙, including some problems with nonunit fractions, such as ⅔ and ⅚—for example:

- *Claudia had ¾ sandwich for lunch and ¾ sandwich for dinner. How many sandwiches did Claudia eat in all?*
- *Nate ate 1⅔ burritos for breakfast. David ate 2⅓ burrito. How much more burrito did David eat than Nate?*

✔ **Partial Groups problems: Multiplication.** Choose problems where multiplier (number of groups) is a unit fraction: focus on ½, ¼, and ⅓—for example:

- *Ernie had 6 problems to solve for homework. He solved ⅓ of the problems before dinner. How many problems did he solve before dinner?*

FOURTH GRADE

✔ **Addition and Subtraction word problems involving like denominators,** including unit and nonunit fractions. Focus on ½, ¼, ⅓, ⅛, ⅙, ¹⁄₁₂, ¹⁄₁₀, and ¹⁄₁₀₀ as well as nonunit fractions with these denominators, including whole-number amounts.

- *Tim has 3⅓ pounds of clay. He wants to make an animal figure that uses 4 pounds of clay. How much more clay does he need?*

✔ **Addition and Subtraction word problems with unlike denominators involving halves and fourths**—for example:

- *Sara likes to eat $\frac{1}{2}$ sandwich for snack and $\frac{3}{4}$ sandwich for lunch. If Sara is going to eat her snack and lunch at school, how many sandwiches does she need to bring with her?*
- *Yvette had $3\frac{1}{4}$ jars of jam. After she made sandwiches for her friends, she had $2\frac{1}{2}$ jars of jam left. How much jam did she use making sandwiches for her friends?*
- *Anna ate $\frac{1}{2}$ of a peanut butter and jelly sandwich. Li ate $\frac{1}{4}$ of a peanut butter and jelly sandwich. Together did they eat more or less than 1 sandwich? How much did they eat?*

✔ Addition and subtraction equations with fractions described above—for example:

- $1\frac{1}{4} - \frac{3}{4} = t$
- $2\frac{5}{8} + \frac{7}{8} = f$
- $3\frac{1}{3} + g = 4$
- $h = 2\frac{3}{4} + 5\frac{1}{4}$
- $12 = 12\frac{3}{4} - s$

✔ Addition and subtraction estimation problems involving unlike denominators and familiar fractions—for example:

- *Is it more or less than 1?*

  $\frac{2}{3} + \frac{1}{4}$

  $\frac{6}{8} + \frac{1}{3}$

✔ Partial Groups Problems—Multiplication. Choose problems where multiplier (number of groups) is a unit fraction: focus on $\frac{1}{2}$, $\frac{1}{4}$, $\frac{1}{3}$, $\frac{1}{8}$, $\frac{1}{6}$, and $\frac{1}{10}$. For some students, include nonunit fractions, such as $\frac{2}{3}$ and $\frac{3}{4}$. Try giving sequences of problems—for example,

- *I have $\frac{1}{3}$ bag a candy. A whole bag of candy weighs 6 pounds. How much candy do I have?*
- *I have $\frac{2}{3}$ bag of candy. A whole bag of candy weighs 6 pounds. How much candy do I have?*
- *I have $2\frac{2}{3}$ bags of candy. A whole bag of candy weighs 6 pounds. How much candy do I have?*
- *I have $\frac{1}{3}$ bag of candy. A whole bag of candy weighs $6\frac{1}{2}$ pounds. How much candy do I have?*

✔ Partial Groups Problems—Measurement Division. Choose problems with a simple relationship (such as $\frac{1}{2}$) between the leftover amount and the amount per group—for example:

- *The dog sled team eats 10 pounds of dog food a day. How many days would it take the dog sled team to eat 35 pounds of dog food?* (Children may express the answer in two ways: 3½ days or 3 days with 5 pounds left over. Either is acceptable depending on your goals.)

- *I use ½ cup of peanut butter in each batch of peanut butter cookies I bake. If I have 2¼ cups of peanut butter, how many batches of cookies can I bake?* (Children may express the answer in two ways: 4½ batches or 4 batches with ¼ cup left over. Either is acceptable depending on your goals.)

FIFTH GRADE

✔ Once your students have some understanding of equivalent fraction relationships (see Chapter 6), give addition and subtraction word problems with unlike denominators, focusing on fractions whose denominators have a common factor—for example:

- *Paula ate ¾ burrito. Manuel ate ⅜ burrito. How much more burrito did Paula eat than Manuel?*
- *Linda ate ⅔ tub of popcorn. Susan ate ⅚ tub of popcorn. How much popcorn did Linda and Susan eat together?* (Also: *Who ate more popcorn? How much more?*)

✔ Addition and subtraction equations with the fractions described above—for example:

- $¾ + w = ⅞$
- $3½ = 3⅞ - q$
- $⅔ + ½ = a$
- $8⅓ - 7½ = k$
- $9^1/_{12} - v = 7½$
- $⅙ + b = ½$

✔ Partial Groups Problems—Multiplication. Choose problems where multiplier (number of groups) is either a unit or nonunit fraction. Also include some fractions as multiplicand (e.g., $⅓ × ¾ = a$). Pay attention to the difficulty of the relationship between the multiplier and multiplicand (e.g., finding one-third of ¾ is easier than finding one-third of ½; finding one-fourth of ⅘ is easier than finding one-fourth of ¾; finding half of ⁴/₇ is easier than finding half of ¾; include sequences of problems—for example:

- *Nestor was going on a 10-mile hike. He walked ¼ of the way before lunch. How did he walk before lunch?*
- *Nestor was going on a 20-mile hike. He walked ¾ of the way and decided to stop for the night and camp. How far had he walked?*
- *Nestor was going on a backpacking trip that was 22 miles long. He walked ¾ of the way and decided to stop for the night. How far had he walked?*

- *Nestor's snail was in a race that was ¾ feet long. The snail has finished ⅔ of the race. How far has the snail gone so far?*

✔ Multiplication equations, using number combinations similar to what students can solve in multiplication word problems—for example:
  - $⅓ × ⁶⁄₇ = y$
  - $j = ⅔ × ⁶⁄₁₀$

✔ Area multiplication word problems, such as:
  - *If flooring costs $1 per square foot, how much money will a new floor cost?*

✔ Partial Groups Problems—Measurement Division. Pay attention to the difficulty of the relationship between the leftover amount and the amount per group. Choose problems with a simple relationship between the leftover amount and the amount per group.
  - *It takes ⅝ can of paint to paint a wall. How many walls can I paint with 4½ cans of paint?* (⅛ can is left over. ⅛ is ⅕ of ⅝.)
  - *It takes ¾ can of paint to paint a wall. How many walls can I paint with 10 cans of paint?* (¼ is left over. ¼ is ⅓ of ¾.)

SIXTH GRADE

✔ Addition and subtraction word problems and equations involving unlike denominators. Include problems where one denominator is not a factor of the other. (Problems where one denominator is a factor of the other are easier to solve. For example, the first problem below is easier than the second.)
  - *Olivia had 2⅜ pounds of clay. She used ¾ pound of clay. How much clay does Olivia have left?*
  - *Anita had 2⅔ pounds of clay. She used ¾ pound of clay. How much clay does Anita have left?*

✔ Partial Groups Problems—Multiplication. Focus on problems where both multiplier (number of groups) and multiplicand (amount in a group) are fractions—for example:
  - *Sal has 2¾ bags of coffee. If a full bag of coffee weighs 3⁶⁄₇ pounds. How much coffee does Sal have?*
  - *A bracelet uses ⅜ as many beads as a necklace. Eve just used 2⅓ bags of beads to make a necklace. How many bags of beads would it take Eve to make a matching bracelet?*

✔ Partial Groups Problems—Measurement Division. Focus on helping students learn to reason about the relationship between the leftover amount and the amount per group as it increases in complexity. The following sequence of problems illustrates the increasing complexity of this relationship.

- *It takes ⅝ can of paint to paint a wall. How many walls can I paint with 5⅝ cans of paint?* (9 walls can be painted. There is no leftover paint.)

- *It takes ⅝ can of paint to paint a wall. How many walls can I paint with 4½ cans of paint?* (7⅕ walls can be painted. After 7 walls have been painted, ⅛ can is left over. ⅛ is ⅕ of ⅝.)

- *It takes ⅝ can of paint to paint a wall. How many walls can I paint with 10⅜ cans of paint?* (16⅗ walls can be painted. After 16 walls have been painted, ⅜ can is left over. ⅜ is ⅗ of ⅝.)

- *It takes ⅝ can of paint to paint a wall. How many walls can I paint with 5½ cans of paint?* (8⅘ walls can be painted. After 8 walls have been painted, ½ can is left over. ½ is ⅘ of ⅝.)

- *It takes ⅝ can of paint to paint a wall. How many walls can I paint with 10¹¹⁄₁₆ cans of paint?* (17¹⁄₁₀ walls can be painted. After 17 walls have been painted, there is ¹⁄₁₆ can of paint left over. ¹⁄₁₆ is ¹⁄₁₀ of ⅝.)

✔ Equations with addition, subtraction, multiplication, and division of fractions. See Problems for Operations on Fractions and Decimals for examples.

chapter **9**

The Long View

Learning to Use Children's Thinking to Guide Instruction

Belinda: *[In this class] I could express different ways in math. In [my regular math] class sometimes Ms. A has us do her ways and I don't like to do that. But in [this class] we got to do it our ways.... It felt good that I was able to find a different way.*

Interviewer: *What helped you to learn different ways?*

Belinda: *The problems. Mostly the problems. And the kids ... Like when I saw their ways about how they could do it, it just went in my mind, "Oh, so now I get it!"*

Javier: *The kids used to say that I wasn't understanding ... [and the teacher in my regular math class] would send one [kid] to help me.... I didn't want them to help me, because I wanted to learn. But they would help me. And then as I started learning [in this class] ... one time I was the only one in the whole class that got them all right. And the other [students] had gotten it wrong.... I also learned how to do some hard problems.* [translation from Spanish]
— *(Turner, Dominguez, Maldonado, and Empson, in press)*

Learning to Listen to Students

Belinda and Javier were fourth graders who participated in a ten-week after-school class where students engaged in problem solving and discussing their solutions with their peers. Belinda was successful in her regular mathematics class and confident in her abilities. In contrast, Javier sometimes struggled and was not nearly as confident. Their reflections on what they learned in the after-school class reveal that they both benefitted in notable ways from instruction that was different from business as usual.

The teacher in Belinda's and Javier's after-school class was skilled at listening to students' mathematical thinking. She used what she heard to design problems that encouraged students to draw on their own conceptual understanding in their solutions. She questioned children about the details of their strategies and prompted them to justify their ideas to their peers. Her role was critical to their learning and their feelings of pride and enjoyment.

We believe that at the heart of learning with understanding is a teacher who is listening closely to students' ideas. "Listening" is a teaching practice that can profoundly influence what students learn and how they see themselves as mathematical thinkers. In the words of kindergarten teacher and writer Vivian Gussin Paley, when teachers "demonstrate the acts of observing, listening, questioning, and wondering," children think, "'What are these ideas I have that are so interesting to the teacher?'" and "'I must be somebody with good ideas'" (1986, 127). The teacher's listening teaches students to pay attention to and value their own ideas and the ideas of others. Students such as Belinda and Javier learn to rely on themselves to make sense of the mathematics they are learning.

This image of teaching is different from the one that many teachers of mathematics hold. As young teachers, we believed our job was to carefully explain what we knew about mathematics to our students. We asked questions and listened to our students' answers but our listening was aimed at assessing whether our students got what we had explained rather than uncovering their understanding of the content. We now see that we missed valuable opportunities to develop students' understanding because we did not elicit their ideas or relate their ideas to the content we were teaching.

Listening with the intention to hear what a student has to say without imposing your own way of thinking is a significant challenge. A lot of teachers are surprised by how difficult it is when they first try it. We were. It can be hard for a teacher to listen without correcting or providing hints to a child who is hesitating or struggling and to know what question to ask next when a child uses an unfamiliar strategy. However, the more you interact with students about their thinking, the more you will learn and the more curious you will likely become. It can lead you to want to have longer mathematical conversations with them or to pose open-ended problems to find out more about what they really understand. The way you listen and what you do with what you hear are likely to change.

Developing the ability to listen to children's thinking and use it to guide instruction takes time.[1] There are several interrelated teaching skills that make up this ability, which cannot be learned all at once or in a short professional development session. The teaching vignettes that we have shared with you throughout the book illustrate these skills. Some of the most important of them include:

- posing problems for children to solve using their own strategies
- choosing or writing problems that elicit a variety of valid strategies and insights
- adjusting problem difficulty so that children can use what they understand to solve problems
- sequencing problems and number choices in developmentally appropriate ways
- asking probing questions to clarify and extend children's thinking
- conducting discussions of students' strategies so that students can make new mathematical connections
- identifying the important mathematics in children's thinking

---

[1] See Empson and Jacobs (2008) for an overview of what is involved in learning to listen and recommendations for organizing professional development. See Fennema et al. (1996) and Jacobs, Lamb, and Philipp (2010) for longitudinal analyses of how teachers learn to understand student thinking and make it the basis for instructional decisions.

Teachers find that a focus on posing problems and asking students how they solved them is a natural place to start. These two skills alone can help you find out a great deal about what your students understand and at the same time lead to more understanding for students. In her book *"The Having of Wonderful Ideas" and Other Essays on Teaching and Learning*, Eleanor Duckworth observed that simply having a conversation with a child "as a way of trying to understand a child's understanding" can lead the child's understanding to increase "in the very process" (1996, 96).

Research suggests that teachers are most successful learning to understand students' thinking and build on it in instruction when they see themselves as engaged in a process of inquiry (Franke et al. 2001). If possible, set aside time to reflect with other teachers on what your students did and said. Although there are teachers who may read a book such as this one and try out its ideas on their own, most teachers find it useful to discuss the ideas with other teachers and share their questions, insights, concerns, and problems. It helps to schedule a regular time to get together with colleagues to plan problems, discuss student work, and reflect on what you are experiencing in your own classroom.[2] You could videotape students or you could take written notes on what a few students did and collect student work to bring to the group to examine and discuss. Whether it is once a week or once a month, regular meetings with colleagues will help you establish a habit of inquiry into both children's mathematical thinking and teaching in ways that are responsive to their thinking. If you and your colleagues can sustain this inquiry over time, it can lead to profound changes in how you see your role and how you relate to your students.

We think of the work of teaching as a kind of problem solving (Carpenter 1988; Lampert 2002). Experienced teachers realize that there is no script that can tell you how to interact with your students just as no curriculum can predict the problems that will work best for your students. We encourage you to problem solve with your teaching and try out the problems in this book in a way that makes sense to you, your teaching style, and your students, because what works for one teacher may not work in the same way or as well for another.

---

[2] For examples of how to set up teacher inquiry groups, see Jacobs and Philipp (2004), Jacobs et al. (2006), and Kazemi and Franke (2004).

Summarizing the Big Ideas of the Book

My math teachers helped me find out my own way to solve problems. They directed me in the right way but they didn't show me what to do. I would have felt like a robot if they told me exactly what to do, but I wouldn't have learned much if they didn't direct me in some ways. Now when I look at the algebra book, I know how to solve the problems. I am using some of the same ideas, like writing an equation and then writing one underneath that says the same thing but that has changed in one way.

—*Kevin, 9th grade*

Focusing on children's thinking as we have described in this book can help you teach so that children understand mathematics in a lasting, deep, and interconnected way. The big ideas of our book are directly related to the thesis that students are most likely to develop this kind of understanding in classrooms where teachers listen to students' thinking, determine what students understand, and make instructional decisions on the basis of what they have determined.[3] Although this approach to teaching can take a variety of forms, we believe that if you use the big ideas we have presented in this book to help you make instructional decisions, you will see the benefit to your students in the form of increased understanding and confidence.

These big ideas include:

- Equal Sharing problems provide a rich context for students to connect their informal understanding of sharing with division and multiplication to generate fractions and meanings for fractions. These meanings include the relationships $\frac{1}{n} = 1 \div n$ and $\frac{m}{n} = \underbrace{\frac{1}{n} + \frac{1}{n} + \ldots + \frac{1}{n}}_{m \text{ times}} = m \times \frac{1}{n}$. Eventually, Equal Sharing leads children to understand the relationship between division and fractions: $m \div n = \frac{m}{n}$.

- Multiple Groups problems, including Measurement Division and Multiplication, provide a rich context for students to refine and strengthen their relational understanding of fractions and

---

[3] We are talking essentially about a type of *formative assessment* that is tightly integrated with instruction (Wiliam 2010). In a review of research, Black and Wiliam (1998) found that when teachers used formative assessment, students gained roughly .5 standard deviation on standardized tests. That's a huge gain—larger than the gain associated with most other educational interventions.

relationships between fractions. These relationships include $n \times \frac{1}{n} = 1$, $\frac{n}{m} \times m = n$, and $\frac{n}{m} \div \frac{1}{m} = n$.

- Students' understanding of equivalent fractions should be built on their understanding of relationships between fractional quantities rather than on their manipulation of visual or concrete models that involve matching quantities. Understanding of relationships is elicited in children's solutions to Equal Sharing and Multiple Groups problems.

- Students' understanding of decimals should be built on their understanding of fractions and integrated with their understanding of base ten. A focus on place value alone does not build this integrated understanding.

- If students are allowed to develop their own strategies to solve problems, not only are they learning *strategies and facts*, they are also learning *how to decide which* strategies and *which* facts apply. In real-time mathematical thinking, these two things are integrated with each other and cannot be disentangled.
  - In addition and subtraction of fractions, this thinking includes creating and using like units to combine fractions and equivalent fractions.
  - In multiplying and dividing fractions, this thinking includes choosing and using simpler fraction relationships developed in the contexts of solving Equal Sharing and Multiple Groups problems and multiplicative relationships between two fractions.

- Students' basic strategies for word problems represent each quantity in the problem. They rely on the context to decide how to proceed in solving the problem.

- As students' strategies evolve, they incorporate Relational Thinking. Developing Relational Thinking enhances students' understanding of arithmetic and at the same time prepares students to understand algebra. Students who use Relational Thinking are:
  - using a relatively small set of fundamental properties of operations and equality and related principles to establish connections

between quantities, operations on quantities, and equalities
between quantities

- developing the ability to look at a problem as a whole and to
  decide which relationships could be used to simplify the solution

We all learn by building on what we understand. Children connect new ideas in mathematics, such as fractions, to ideas they already understand, such as splitting and sharing. We educators have tended to underestimate the power of supporting children to make these kinds of connections for themselves.

Years ago, two first-grade teachers tested out some of the initial ideas for this book (Empson 1999). At the conclusion of a five-week unit on fractions based on solving and discussing Equal Sharing problems, the teachers reflected on how much their students had learned and how it compared to older students they had taught

Figure 9-1. *Two first graders and their solutions to the first Equal Sharing problem they ever solved in school*

using different methods. Ms. Keller said that she was "blown away" by how much the first graders had learned. Ms. Green, who had taught fifth grade the year before, agreed and said that she would have done the same kinds of problems with her fifth graders:

> There's no way my fifth graders understood what they were doing when I think about it. We were just following the fractions chapter of the textbook. I mean, we had a lot of other activities that we did, but I don't think they understood as profoundly what fractions were about as these first graders do now. It just became a bunch of symbols to them at that point, and they knew how to manipulate the symbols, but I don't think they really knew what they were doing.

These teachers normally did not teach fractions at first grade and were amazed at how far they were able to take the children. Yet their success was not a fluke, and their students were not unusual. Whether your students are first graders or sixth graders or something in between, they are like the students in Ms. Keller's and Ms. Green's classes in some important ways. They have some understanding of mathematics that they can use to solve problems. It may be simple, such as how to split a sandwich in half to share it with two people, or it may be sophisticated, such as explaining why ½ is ⅔ of ¾. Regardless, using the tools in this book, you can teach in ways that encourage students to express that understanding and extend it to learn more mathematics with understanding, confidence, and enthusiasm.

REFERENCES

Baek, J. 2008. "Developing Algebraic Thinking Through Explorations in Multiplication." In *Algebra and Algebraic Thinking in School Mathematics, NCTM 70th Yearbook*, edited by C. Greenes and R. Rubenstein, 141–54. Reston, VA: National Council of Teachers of Mathematics.

Behrend, J. L. 2003. "Learning-Disabled Students Make Sense of Mathematics." *Teaching Children Mathematics,* 9 (1): 269–273.

Black, P., and D. Wiliam. 1998. "Inside the Black Box: Raising Standards Through Classroom Assessment." *Phi Delta Kappan*, 80 (2): 139–48.

Brinker, L. 1997. "Using Structured Representations to Solve Fraction Problems: A Discussion of Seven Students' Strategies." Paper presented at the annual meeting of the American Educational Research Association Annual Meeting. Chicago, IL, March, 1997.

Carey, D. 1991. "Number Sentences: Linking Addition and Subtraction Word Problems and Symbols." *Journal for Research in Mathematics Education* 22 (4): 266–80.

Carpenter, T. P. 1988. "Teaching as Problem Solving." In *The Teaching and Assessing of Mathematical Problem Solving*, edited by R. I. Charles and E. Silver, 187–202. Reston, VA: National Council of Teachers of Mathematics.

Carpenter, T. P., E. Ansell, M. L. Franke, E. Fennema, and L. Weisbeck. 1993. "Models of Problem Solving: A Study of Kindergarten Children's Problem-Solving Processes." *Journal for Research in Mathematics Education* 24 (5): 427–40.

Carpenter, T. P., E. Fennema, M. Franke, L. Levi, and S. B. Empson. 1999. *Children's Mathematics: Cognitively Guided Instruction*. Portsmouth, NH: Heinemann.

Carpenter, T. P., M. Franke, and L. Levi. 2003. *Thinking Mathematically: Integrating Arithmetic and Algebra in Elementary School*. Portsmouth, NH: Heinemann.

Common Core Standards Initiative. 2010. *Common Core Standards for Mathematics*. Washington, D.C.: National Governors Association Center for Best Practices and the Council of Chief State School Officers. Downloaded from www.corestandards.org.

Duckworth, E. 1996. *"The Having of Wonderful Ideas" and Other Essays on Teaching and Learning*, 2d ed. New York: Teachers College Press.

Empson, S. B. 1999. "Equal Sharing and Shared Meaning: The Development of Fraction Concepts in a First Grade Classroom." *Cognition and Instruction* 17 (3): 283–342.

———. 2001. "Equal Sharing and the Roots of Fraction Equivalence." *Teaching Children Mathematics* 7: 421–25.

———. 2003. "Low Performing Students and Teaching Fractions for Understanding: An Interactional Analysis." *Journal for Research in Mathematics Education* 34: 305–43.

Empson, S. B., L. Levi, and T. P. Carpenter. (in press). "The Algebraic Nature of Fractions: Developing Relational Thinking in Elementary School." In *Early Algebraization: A Global Dialogue from Multiple Perspectives*, edited by J. Cai and E. Knuth. New York: Springer.

Empson, S. B., and V. R. Jacobs. 2008. "Learning to Listen to Children's Mathematics." In *International Handbook of Mathematics Teacher Education, Vol.1: Knowledge and Beliefs in Mathematics Teaching and Teaching Development*, edited by T. Wood and P. Sullivan, 257–81. Rotterdam, The Netherlands: Sense Publishers.

Empson, S. B., D. Junk, H. Dominguez, and E. E. Turner. 2005. "Fractions as the Coordination of Multiplicatively Related Quantities: A Cross-Sectional Study of Children's Thinking." *Educational Studies in Mathematics*.

Empson, S. B., and E. Turner. 2006. "The Emergence of Multiplicative Thinking in Children's Solutions to Paper Folding Tasks." *Journal of Mathematical Behavior* 25: 46–56.

Fennema, E., T. P. Carpenter, M. Franke, L. Levi, V. Jacobs, and S. B. Empson. 1996. "Mathematics Instruction and Teachers' Beliefs: A Longitudinal Study of Using Children's Thinking." *Journal for Research in Mathematics Education* 27 (4): 403–34.

Franke, M. L., T. P. Carpenter, L. Levi, and E. Fennema, 2001. "Capturing teachers' generative change: A follow-up study of professional development in mathematics." *American Educational Research Journal*, 38: 653–89.

Hiebert, J., T. P. Carpenter, E. Fennema, K. Fuson, D. Wearne, H. Murray, A. Olivier, and P. Human. 1997. *Making Sense: Teaching and Learning Mathematics with Understanding*. Portsmouth, NH: Heinemann.

Jacobs, V., R. Ambrose, L. Clement, and D. Brown. 2006. "Using Teacher-Produced Videotapes of Student Interviews as Discussion Catalysts." *Teaching Children Mathematics* 2 (6): 276–81.

Jacobs, V. R., L. C. Lamb, and R. Philipp. 2010. "Professional Noticing of Children's Mathematical Thinking." *Journal for Research in Mathematics Education* 41 (2): 169–202.

Jacobs, V. R., and R. Philipp. 2004. "Helping Prospective and Practicing Teachers Focus on Children's Mathematical Thinking in Student-Work Examples." *Teaching Children Mathematics* 11: 194–201.

Kaput, J., and M. M. West. 1994. "Missing-Value Proportional Reasoning Problems: Factors Affecting Informal Reasoning Patterns." In *The Development of Multiplicative Reasoning in the Learning of Mathematics*, edited by G. Harel and J. Confrey, 235–87. Albany: SUNY.

Kazemi, E., and M. L. Franke. 2004. "Teacher Learning in Mathematics: Using Student Work to Promote Collective Inquiry." *Journal of Mathematics Teacher Education* 7 (3): 203–35.

Lamon, S. 1993. "Ratio and Proportion: Children's Cognitive and Metacognitive Processes." In *Rational Numbers: An Integration of Research*, edited by T. P. Carpenter, E. Fennema, and T. Romberg, 131–56. Hillsdale, NJ: Lawrence Erlbaum.

Lamon, S. J. 1999. *Teaching Fractions and Ratios for Understanding*. Mahwah, NJ: Erlbaum.

Lampert, M. 2002. *Teaching Problems and the Problems of Teaching*. New Haven, CT: Yale.

Maldonado, L., E. E. Turner, H. Dominguez, and S. B. Empson. 2009. "English Language Learners *Learning from* and *Contributing to* Discussions." In *Mathematics for All: Instructional Strategies for Diverse Classrooms*, 7–22. National Council of Teachers of Mathematics.

Moscardini, L. 2009. "Tools or Crutches? Apparatus as a Sense-Making Aid in Mathematics Teaching With Children With Moderate Learning Difficulties." *British Journal of Support for Learning,* 24 (1): 35–41.

Paley, V. G. 1986. "On Listening to What the Children Say." *Harvard Educational Review* 56 (2): 122–31.

Post, T., I. Wachsmuth, R. Lesh, and M. Behr. 1985. "Order and Equivalence of Rational Numbers: A Cognitive Analysis." *Journal for Research in Mathematics Education* 16: 18–36.

Trends in International Mathematics and Science Study. 2003. "Mathematics Concepts, Mathematics Items, Grade 8." Available at: http://nces.ed.gov/TIMSS. Accessed July 27, 2009.

Turner, E. E., H. Dominguez, L. Maldonado, and S. B. Empson. (in press). "English Learners' Participation in Mathematical Discussion: Shifting Positionings, Dynamic Identities." In *Equity, Identity, and Power*. Special issue of *Journal for Research in Mathematics Education*, edited by R. Guttiérez. Reston, VA: National Council of Teachers of Mathematics.

United States Department of Education. 2008. *The Final Report of the National Mathematics Advisory Panel*. Washington, DC.

Van de Walle, J., K. Karp, and J. M. Bay-Williams. 2009. *Elementary and Middle School Mathematics: Teaching Developmentally*, 7th ed. Boston: Allyn and Bacon.

Wiliam, D. 2010. "An Integrative Summary of the Research Literature and Implications for a New Theory of Formative Assessment." In *Handbook of Formative Assessment*, edited by H. Andrade and G. Cizek, 18–40. New York: Routledge.

INDEX